PUBLIC TRIUMPH
PRIVATE TRAGEDY

Also by Steve Paikin

The Life:
The Seductive Call of Politics

The Dark Side:
The Personal Price of a Political Life

Contents

PUBLIC TRIUMPH
PRIVATE TRAGEDY

The double life of John P. Robarts

STEVE PAIKIN

VIKING
CANADA

VIKING CANADA

Published by the Penguin Group

Penguin Group (Canada), 90 Eglinton Avenue East, Suite 700, Toronto, Ontario, Canada M4P 2Y3
(a division of Pearson Penguin Canada Inc.)

Penguin Group (USA) Inc., 375 Hudson Street, New York, New York 10014, U.S.A.
Penguin Books Ltd, 80 Strand, London WC2R 0RL, England
Penguin Ireland, 25 St Stephen's Green, Dublin 2, Ireland (a division of Penguin Books Ltd)
Penguin Group (Australia), 250 Camberwell Road, Camberwell, Victoria 3124, Australia
(a division of Pearson Australia Group Pty Ltd)
Penguin Books India Pvt Ltd, 11 Community Centre, Panchsheel Park, New Delhi – 110 017, India
Penguin Group (NZ), cnr Airborne and Rosedale Roads, Albany, Auckland 1310, New Zealand
(a division of Pearson New Zealand Ltd)
Penguin Books (South Africa) (Pty) Ltd, 24 Sturdee Avenue, Rosebank, Johannesburg 2196,
South Africa

Penguin Books Ltd, Registered Offices: 80 Strand, London WC2R 0RL, England

First published 2005

2 3 4 5 6 7 8 9 10 (FR)

Copyright © Steve Paikin, 2005

Editor: Cynthia Good

Speech by John P. Robarts, tribute to John P. Robarts by John Cronyn, and the luncheon
speech for friends of John P. Robarts by Richard M. Dillon all used with permission.

Manufactured in Canada.

LIBRARY AND ARCHIVES CANADA CATALOGUING IN PUBLICATION

Paikin, Steve, 1960–
Public triumph, private tragedy : the double life of John P. Robarts / Steve Paikin.

Includes index.

ISBN 0-670-04329-X

1. Robarts, John P., 1917–1982. 2. Prime ministers—Ontario—Biography.
3. Ontario—Politics and government—1943–1985. I. Title.

FC3076.1.R62P33 2005   971.3'04'092   C2004-906314-6

Visit the Penguin Group (Canada) website at **www.penguin.ca**

For Zachary, Henry, Teddy, Giulia
And, of course, Francesca

Introduction

IN THE SUMMER OF 2001, I found myself in my local public library perusing the shelves with my kids for something interesting to read. I happened on a book published in 1986 titled *John P. Robarts, His Life and His Government*, written by A.K. McDougall for the *Ontario Historical Studies* series. As someone who'd studied and covered politics in Canada for twenty years, I had to confess that I knew precious little about a man who had been one of the most important Canadian political figures of his, or any other, time. So I grabbed the book and started reading.

It was a solid account of how Ontario's seventeenth premier, a self-described "management man," transformed the largest provincial government in Canada into a much more modern, sophisticated operation. And he did it in his own inimitable style, earning him the nickname "Chairman of the Board."

The author was under strict instructions from Robarts not to delve into the politician's personal life, and even though Robarts was already dead by the time the book came out, MacDougall mostly abided by those wishes. But the book hinted that the full story had not been told—the story of a great man who lived hard, died hard, and accomplished so much in the process.

After I'd read the book, it occurred to me that there were millions of Canadians who had little or no memory of Robarts but who, like me, should know more about him. I noticed that the fortieth anniversary of Robarts's becoming premier (or prime minister, actually, since that's what the office was then called) was coming up in the fall of 2001. Wouldn't this be a perfect opportunity to do a documentary on Robarts's life?

My executive producer at TVO's *Studio 2*, Doug Grant, agreed, and for the next four months I interviewed former cabinet colleagues, friends, Robarts's daughter, and his widow, culminating in the hour-long documentary *Chairman of the Board: The Life and Death of John Robarts*.

Quite frankly, the reaction to the program astonished me. For those who remembered the Robarts years, the film rekindled nostalgic feelings. For younger viewers who knew nothing of the man except that his name is on a very large library in downtown Toronto and a research institute in London, it was an eye-opener. My phone had never rung more, nor had I ever received more letters about a topic. The viewership of the program was 75 percent higher than usual for *Studio 2*.

Shortly thereafter, I received an invitation to attend the annual John Robarts Luncheon, still held faithfully by his colleagues, at the historic Toronto Club. One by one, participants would rise and tell high-spirited tales from days gone by, followed by much laughter, wine, and cigars. Little did I know there was an ulterior motive for the invitation other than a desire for my charming presence. It seems some of the former prime minister's colleagues thought it was time for another book on Robarts but one that would be an account of the life he had lived, not just the government he had run. His long-time friend from London, John Cronyn, had put a copy of my documentary beside every place setting at the tables. Most had seen it already and proceeded to tell me in some detail what they liked, and in great detail what they did not.

"John was such an amazing guy," Darcy McKeough, one of Robarts's cabinet ministers, told me. "We think you showed in the documentary that you have some understanding of that. How about another book?"

Did a man dead for more than twenty years, one who had been a first minister for fewer than ten, merit a second look? I wondered. The more I researched this question, the more I thought the answer was definitely yes. John Robarts was prime minister of Ontario from 1961 to 1971, coincidentally the best years Ontario had ever enjoyed. It was a time of significant urbanization in the province. The economy was a juggernaut, providing tax revenues for enormous numbers of publicly funded projects. And there was simply a good feeling in the land as the country celebrated its Centennial in 1967. As much as any other Canadian of his time—and that includes Pierre Elliott Trudeau—John Robarts kept the country together in the face of increasing separatist tensions from Quebec. But beyond the politics, the intriguing combination of his stellar public life and an ultimately tragic personal one made for a compelling story. And now, more than two decades after his death, his friends and colleagues were willing to say so much more about the man than was possible in the past. How could a man who, according to some observers, had such unprecedented success in the political arena have made, by his own admission, such an awful mess of his personal life? Why was one of the most respected and revered figures in our history out tavern hopping till the wee small hours of the morning? Why was the most popular man in Ontario so lonely? Admittedly, it is a cliché to say the bigger they are, the harder they fall. But in the "go-go sixties," no one was bigger in Canada's largest province than John P. Robarts. And though few saw it coming, no one had a more precipitous fall.

Comparisons with John F. Kennedy are instructive. Both JPR and JFK saw action in the Second World War. Kennedy's older brother, "Tail Gunner Joe," was killed in action. Robarts's older brother, Bob, was almost killed in a London nightclub, destroyed when German bombs rained on it. Kennedy became president of the United States in January 1961. Robarts became prime minister of Ontario in November of the same year. Both men loved governing, made good decisions in the main, and had larger-than-life personalities. When they entered a room, they sucked up all the oxygen. They both had movie-star good looks, loved to run with fast crowds, drink a lot, and be in the company of women who were not necessarily their wives. And in a final, most tragic connection, they both departed this world the same way—a fatal gunshot blast to the head. Kennedy's was via assassination, Robarts's was self-inflicted.

Kennedy promised Camelot. Robarts hoped to create his own Camelot north of the forty-ninth parallel. That we are still a country, relatively united, and that Ontario is still the economic engine of our country suggests in no small measure that in spite of his private tragedies, he was successful.

1

THE EARLY YEARS

IRONICALLY, the life of a man so singularly identified with Canada's biggest province did not begin there. But his father's did. Herbert Robarts was born in Toronto in 1880, and at the age of fifteen, he began a career in banking, in which he would remain his entire working life. He started as a clerk with the Imperial Bank of Canada in Galt (part of present-day Cambridge, Ontario), then moved west as the bank expanded. His career took him to Winnipeg and Brandon in Manitoba, then Estevan, Saskatchewan, and Nelson, British Columbia, before he hit the big time as a branch manager in Banff, Alberta, in 1912.

In Banff at this time lived a woman named Florency Brett, who had a baby daughter, Catherine. Sadly for the family, Florency's husband, Earl Brett, had died of a ruptured appendix shortly after Catherine was born. However, the new arrival in town, Herbert Robarts, and the recently widowed Florency Brett met at a social occasion. It turned out to be a good match. In 1914 they were married. He was thirty-four years old. She was twenty-three. The couple's desire to expand their family must have been rather compelling, as exactly nine months after their nuptials, in June 1915, Robert George Robarts was welcomed into the world. And then, on January 11, 1917, 2,822 kilometres away from Queen's Park in Toronto, Florency gave birth to John Parmenter Robarts. (Coincidentally, he shared a birthday with two other prominent Canadians: Sir John A. Macdonald was born on that day 102 years earlier, and Jean Chrétien seventeen years later.) His unusual middle name appears to have been in the family for some time. In the mid-nineteenth century, John's great-grandfather, Thomas Parminter Robarts (who spelled *Parmenter* with an *i*), emigrated from England to Barbados. He established a plantation near the capital of Bridgetown, where he married and had seventeen children, all boys except the last one.

The following year, the Robartses moved to Winnipeg, as Herbert was promoted to manage a larger branch of the Imperial Bank. But unfortunately Florency Brett's tragic experiences were not left behind in Banff. In 1919, the year of the great influenza outbreak, Florency contracted the disease while pregnant. She died on February 7, 1920, at the age of twenty-eight. John Robarts was just three years old. Herbert Robarts decided to move back to Galt, to be closer to his sister.

By all accounts, Herbert ran a very tight ship. He frequently brandished the strap when his boys got out of hand, forbade gum chewing on Saturday afternoons at the movies, and insisted the brothers sing in the Anglican church choir. However, he also gave them their first lessons in hunting and fishing, both of which John spent endless hours in the future pursuing.

During their formative years, the Robarts brothers were raised by a succession of nannies, some of whom they successfully managed to scare away. Family members tell anecdotes suggesting John wasn't the most diligent or responsible student. If Bob could be found in the kitchen wrapping up the day's garbage in a newspaper, John could be found lying down on the floor reading it.

Happily, in 1927, wedding bells rang for Herbert Robarts again. He married Ethel McIrvine, daughter of the mayor of Galt. (Herbert's first wife had also had a political connection. Her father-in-law was lieutenant governor of Alberta.)

Three years later, the Robartses welcomed another daughter—a sister for Catherine—whom they named Marion. They also made what would turn out to be a momentous move. Herbert was promoted to bank manager at the Imperial branch in London, Ontario, succeeding his sister's husband, Alan Goodall. This move to London put young "Jack" Robarts on a path that would eventually lead him to the very top of his province's political mountain.

Little Jack started his educational career at Ryerson Public School, then both Bob and Jack attended London South Collegiate Institute (John for Grade 9 only, in 1930–31) and went on to London Central Collegiate Institute (John for Grades 10 through 13) after the Robarts family moved residences. The girls were both sent out of town to Branksome Hall in Toronto.

A childhood friend, Beverley Shrives (née Couch), remembers meeting Jack Robarts when she was fourteen years old, and he was fifteen. "He was one of the first boys who interested me," she says with a smile. "He was the best-looking youngster I'd ever seen."

It was at this time that young John established a pattern of behaviour that would be a calling card for the rest of his life: work hard and play hard. The principal of South Collegiate, as everyone called it, told John he would never amount to anything because he played hooky far too much. That same man was still the principal when Robarts became minister of education in the provincial government of Leslie Frost.

There is a story in the previous Robarts book that finds our young hero coming home at three o'clock in the morning, only to be confronted by an angry father wondering why his son would be traipsing in so late, particularly during exam week. The answer was pure John Robarts: "Come and complain to me when I fail," he said. Herbert could not because John never did. As the author put it, "All his life, John Robarts would see no reason not to enjoy himself so long as he got his work done the next day." Prime Minister John Robarts operated on the same principle as high school student Jack Robarts.

It was also at this time that Robarts would develop a teenage romance with a young woman named Norah McCormick. Norah came from what would become an upper-middle-class London family. Her father, Garfield, began his career at a corner store but worked his way up to a management job with Kellogg's, a fixture in the city's manufacturing sector since 1906. He and his wife, Lewella, had three children—Helen, born in 1910; Shirley, born in 1912; and the baby, Norah, born in 1917, the same year as her future husband. The McCormicks were not rich but well enough off to send two of their daughters to university and the other to private school.

"They were high school sweethearts," says Robin Robarts of her parents. "I think they weren't exclusive all the time. They were both very popular."

After high school, in 1935, both John and Norah ended up at the University of Western Ontario in London. In those days, Western was small—only eighteen hundred students—and almost regarded as a continuation of high school. Neither Norah nor John was what you might call academically inclined. "Norah wouldn't attend lectures at university," remembers Bev Shrives, a fellow student and friend of both of them. "She wasn't a serious student. But she was intelligent. She'd ask to borrow my notes and would ace the course."

Ironically, the future prime minister of Ontario took no political science courses at UWO. He majored in business administration and minored in football, which he enjoyed very much. Robarts was an inside lineman on offence and defence, one of those jobs "in the trenches" on a football team. Certainly nothing as glamorous as quarterback.

Was he a good player? "He was willing to mix it up," says George Willis, one of Robarts's best friends at the time. Willis played centre, was captain of those UWO Mustangs, and a fellow business student. "John's dad was very pleasant to us," Willis says.

"He would loan John the car. We double dated a lot and went to lots of parties."

They were also frat brothers in the Delta Upsilon fraternity house, which would ultimately become a source of future Team Robarts political hands. But that notion was on nobody's radar screen at the beginning of John Robarts's post-secondary educational life. "He didn't have high political office in mind," remembers Al Hurley, quarterback of the Western Mustangs. Unlike most of the rest of the 'Stangs, Hurley was a serious footballer. He was a member of the 1944 St. Hyacinthe–Donnacona Sailors team that went to Hamilton and won the Grey Cup 7–6 against the hometown Flying Wildcats, one of the original Hamilton teams that morphed into the present-day Tiger-Cats. (Hurley's navy squad was the last team made up of servicemen to win the Grey Cup).

In 1939 John Robarts graduated from UWO and enrolled at the Osgoode Hall Law School in Toronto. Once again, his academic habits were apparent. "He was a fairly good student but not great," says classmate Eddie Goodman, the legendary Tory back-room boy. But Robarts's years at Osgoode Hall would prove to be terribly significant, and not because of anything he learned in torts or contracts class. Goodman was a member of the campus Conservative Club. He was friendly with the man he refers to as "the greatest back-room politician that ever existed"—A.D. McKenzie, the right-hand man to Leslie Frost, Ontario premier from 1949 to 1961. "Alec McKenzie said to me, 'Get me some people who are young, good Conservatives,'" Goodman says, "so I invited Robarts to a meeting."

Evidently, something took. That Robarts gravitated toward Conservative politics was no great surprise. His father's, mother's, and stepmother's families were all Tory. Perhaps Robarts would inevitably have ended up in those political circles anyway, but it was Eddie Goodman who opened the door, and John Robarts walked through it. There's a story that circulated around this time among Robarts's friends. Young John Robarts, his political feet barely wet, told his future wife, Norah, that he'd be prime minister someday. He was a man going places. According to one of her best friends, Norah was not amused with the prognostication. "She didn't want to be married to a man of destiny," says Bev Shrives, who, it turns out, read her friend quite accurately.

But before long, Robarts's plans with both the law and politics would take a back seat to the biggest story in the world. Like most Canadians, John Robarts and Norah McCormick had their lives turned upside down with the outbreak of the Second World War. Nationalism hit a fever pitch as young men across Canada signed up to protect king and country, while their women were left behind to rev up the wartime manufacturing machine and keep the home fires burning.

Both the Robarts brothers enlisted. Bob joined the Royal Canadian Armed Services Corps the very day Canada declared war on Germany—one week after Great Britain did—in September 1939. John enlisted in April 1940. Before John enlisted, however, Bob had sent a letter home to his parents, jokingly trying to dissuade his younger brother, whom he always called Parm, shortening his middle name, from joining the war effort. "Tell Parm not to bother coming," Bob wrote. "Tell him to finish his education. I'll take care of business."

Bob appears to have had a long-standing interest in the military that he hadn't pursued because money was too tight. "Bob finished high school, then went straight into the bank to work with his father," says Eleanor Robarts, Bob's widow. "He wanted to go to Royal Military College, but they couldn't afford it."

Before long, Bob would see all the ugliness of war, and much more. On March 9, 1941, he and a few other young recruits were partying the night away at the Café de Paris, advertised as the safest place to dance and date in London. A German bomber flew overhead and dropped its payload. The next thing anyone knew, the café was in flames. Snake Hips Johnson, the bandleader, was killed instantly, as were many members of his band. Bob's friend Phil Seagram was dancing right beside him and he was killed too. Somehow, Bob and the girl he was dancing with survived, but both were seriously wounded. "He ended up in a hole in the floor, which was burning," says Eleanor, who still lives in London, Ontario. "I remember Bob saying the worst part was the darkness." One of his ears was badly burned. He was temporarily blinded in one eye. One foot was crushed. Shrapnel ravaged his backbone.

"He used to pull shrapnel out of his body all the time," Eleanor says. "He almost lost his sight. His uniform was destroyed. The smell of all that burning flesh reminded him of crisp bacon. He couldn't eat it thereafter." Bob Robarts spent three months in hospital. I asked Eleanor whether he made a complete recovery. Her answer: "Wow, I'll say."

John Robarts did visit his brother in hospital at this time and wrote home with a progress report. "I'm concerned about his eye," John admitted to his parents, "but I think he'll be all right." Bob did improve, and although he experienced some lingering effects, he returned to active duty.

The Robarts brothers actually had more than occasional communication during the war. John trained in Speke, just outside Liverpool, and from time to time they would meet in London and stay at the Park Lane Hotel. Neither had much money, so they shared a room, even when John had amorous intentions, which was often. It was not unusual for a manager to knock on the brothers' hotel room door in the middle of the night and shout, "I don't care which Robarts goes. But one girl and one Robarts are going!"

John's wartime travels took him to Russia, Gibraltar, New York, and Halifax. A.A. (Bill) Macdonald, a fellow sailor who served with

Robarts, says, "Despite thousands of miles steamed, none of the Canadian FDOs [fighter direction officers] fired a shot in anger and none of our ships were torpedoed." Macdonald describes a routine where Robarts's ships would travel for two months at a time, followed by a week or two of turnaround time in port.

However, Hugh Hanson, who would work for Robarts during his second term as prime minister, confirms the recruit did see action. "I had to prod him to tell war stories," Hanson says. "He didn't volunteer anything. But he did say in Italy, he was in a ship that got shelled quite a bit."

If Robarts's predilection for hard living—wine, women, and song—began at the University of Western Ontario, he honed the talent during the war years. The monotony of military service, mixed with those moments when everything could come to a sudden, violent end, certainly prompted Robarts and so many others to enjoy their carousing and the intense friendships forged in battle. It was a lifestyle Robarts would not abandon, even after the war's end.

In July 1944 Robarts returned to Canada to perform a very pleasant task on the domestic front—marrying Norah McCormick. The two made an attractive couple with seemingly limitless potential. The wedding took place at St. John's Anglican Church in London.

After the wedding, Robarts shipped out again, to Charleston, North Carolina, and Norah went with him. This was to be the first of many years when the couple was technically together but actually spent vast amounts of time apart. And in a telling comment, Robarts gave just a hint that not everything was as wonderful as first impressions indicated. "I didn't marry Norah," he told Bob. "She married me."

Meanwhile, it took until January 1946 for Bob Robarts to return to Canada after the war. Two and a half years later, he met Eleanor Thomas, who would become his wife for the next half century. As her father, Charlie Thomas, was the general manager and secretary treasurer for *The London Free Press,* Eleanor led a charmed life as a member of London high society. Her father believed in travel, so trips to the capitals of Europe and the United States had filled her childhood.

Eleanor candidly says her father was an oppressive force in her life, and she rebelled with a vengeance. He sent her to Havergal College in Toronto to straighten her out, but there is little evidence the strategy worked. After graduation, Eleanor was engaged to be married three times before she met Bob. In fact, as she and Bob drove all night to Ottawa and a friend's home to elope, the invitations to what would have been her wedding to her third fiancé were in the mail. "I was afraid of my dad," Eleanor says. "So I defied him. No one defied Charlie." The runaway marriage was followed quickly by the arrival of a daughter, Andrea.

All of which is to say that there could not have been two more different sisters-in-law than Eleanor and Norah Robarts. "Norah was jealous of me," Eleanor says today from her apartment in London. "I was [seven years] younger and had a good figure. When I told her I was going to have a baby, boy, did that hit a bad note. There were no hugs or congratulations. She was a cold potato."

There was also something sort of odd about Norah. People would discuss it behind her back, but no one would ever confront her with questions about a strange mannerism. "I'd like to ask you something about Norah," Marion Webster, a mutual friend, once asked Eleanor at a social gathering of some of London's glitterati. "Did she go to school in England?" The answer was no.

"Did she have a British nanny?" Again, no.

"Then why does she speak with that accent?"

That accent was the talk of the town. For some reason, Norah Robarts spoke with a bit more than a hint of a British accent.

"It was pure affectation," says Judith Grieve, the only child of Norah's sister Helen. "She wanted to seem more grand. She must have felt inferior in situations in which she found herself. But she was a snob of great proportion."

Eleanor Robarts, an energetic woman who has lived a full life, speaks for many when she describes the accent as annoying. "I've lived eighty years," she says, shortchanging the count by a few. "I've seen it, done it, and taught it. Most of my friends thought Norah was so *lah-di-bloody-dah*."

While Bob Robarts did return to London sporting numerous medals and the Order of the British Empire, it was still his younger brother who turned more heads. "Everybody looked at John and thought he was a god," Eleanor Robarts recalls.

It is possible John Robarts did not have politics on his agenda when he started university. But before long, his interest in public affairs was definitely piqued. In 1946 he and many of his contemporaries started a discussion group nicknamed ADSEPA—the Association for the Discussion of Social, Economic, and Political Affairs. "They decided John was the star and had better get him into politics" is how Bev Shrives remembers it.

But first things first. In 1947 Robarts graduated from Osgoode Hall, returned to London, and established a law practice, Robarts Betts McLennan and Flinn. With those fundamentals in place, he was in a position to launch his political career.

2

THE BEGINNING OF A POLITICAL LIFE

THE FIRST PUBLIC OFFICE Brian Mulroney ever ran for was right at the top: leader of the Progressive Conservative Party of Canada, first unsuccessfully in 1976, then victoriously in 1983. Same for the former auto parts magnate Belinda Stronach, who launched her bid to enter public life by running for the leadership of the newly merged Conservative Party of Canada in 2004. Not so for John P. Robarts. He would start very modestly—a run for a seat on London City Council in December 1950.

Robarts won London's second ward by just seven votes. What came next was the beginning of a familiar battle to many couples in politics. Robarts began to love political life. His wife, conversely, began to hate it. "Norah didn't want him to run for London City Council," says Judith Grieve, Norah's niece. "She thought that any of his public time was time away from her, and she was jealous of that." Ultimately, the tension would drive a wedge between them. But in the short run, Robarts liked having a wife who did not make politics the centre of her existence. In some respects, he had the best of both worlds. He could be in politics when he wanted to be, and have a refuge away from it with his wife when he needed a break.

Who knows whether Robarts's political career would have ended right there in 1950 if a handful of voters had opted to go a different way? What is known is that with the victory, Robarts began to capture the attention of the folks at Queen's Park, who were looking for a good candidate to take London back from the Liberals. Unfortunately for the Tories, the man they had their eye on showed little interest in moving into the provincial arena. A.D. McKenzie was burning up the phone lines to Eddie Goodman, asking a future quintessential back-room boy what he was doing to get Robarts to change his mind. Goodman got on the case. He sought advice from Richard Dillon, one of Robarts's best friends from his days at UWO. Dillon suggested that if Robarts's wife had her way, the Ontario Conservative Party's fortunes with the man were not promising. Goodman eventually approached Robarts directly. "Jack, do you want to run?" he asked, calling him by the more familiar first name all Robarts's friends used.

"Yeah," Robarts answered, "but my wife's against it."

So Goodman invited Norah and John Robarts out to dinner at the popular Towne Tavern in downtown Toronto and made his pitch. More than a half century after that dinner, Goodman relishes retelling the story. "I talked my head off," he says. "I did say someday he could be premier of this province." Did Goodman really believe that?

"What the hell could I tell who would be premier," he says, laughing hysterically. "I was selling!"

Norah was absolutely clear in her position. "I think this is a mistake, but if John wants to, he can," she said.

What was Goodman's reaction? "Once she said okay, that was it. I wasn't going to carry on the conversation. I'm a better lawyer than that."

So less than a year after winning a city council seat, Robarts successfully sought the Conservative nomination to contest the riding of

London in the November 22, 1951, provincial election—Leslie Frost's first as premier. The night ended well for Robarts. He bested the incumbent Liberal MPP, Cam Calder, by three thousand votes. While Robarts could take significant personal satisfaction in the win, the reality was it was really Leslie Frost's victory. Frost, who was finally emerging from the shadow of his predecessor, George Drew, captured seventy-nine of ninety seats in that election. With 88 percent of the seats in the legislature, the Conservatives had a huge majority government.

Yes, John Robarts was on his way to a bigger stage. It was also true that there were a lot more people on that stage competing for the attention of the prime minister of Ontario. And, of course, unsuccessfully competing for Robarts's attention would be his wife, Norah.

"He said more than once, 'I wasn't fair to my family,'" recalls J.J. Barnicke, the Toronto real estate developer and an old friend. Robarts told him he got engaged to Norah, then spent six years in the navy. Almost as soon as Robarts returned home, he found himself regularly driving to Toronto. "He admitted his activity in the military and in politics didn't help his marriage," Barnicke says.

Like most young couples, the Robartses tried to have children, but they could not. No one today seems to know exactly what the problem was. And certainly in those days no one discussed it. And so in 1953 Norah and John Robarts adopted a baby girl with a mop of red hair and named her Robin Hollis Robarts. Robarts appeared to be overjoyed with his introduction to parenthood. (Apparently, Robin was not named after Robarts's brother, Robert. The couple simply liked the name. They took the child's middle name from the daughter of Robin's godmother, whose first name was Hollis).

Robarts was also overjoyed to be partaking in all that Toronto's nightlife had to offer. As a young man spending a few nights a week in the provincial capital, the rookie MPP used to boast (privately) that he had visited virtually every nightspot in the city. "He was a person who needed very little sleep," says Darcy McKeough, who would become an MPP in 1963 and a minister in both Robarts's and William Davis's cabinets. "He could stay out late and show up in the morning. He enjoyed life and was able to size up a lot of people in the process of doing that."

However, rumours of Robarts's love of the nightlife got back to Leslie Frost, who was less than amused. Frost was concerned that his MPP from London was devoting too much energy to his social life and not enough to his political life. Robarts was still practising law in London as well, partly as a self-defence mechanism. It was an approach he would recommend to a young Gordon Walker a decade and a half later, when Walker replaced Robarts as the new MPP for London North. "Gordon, be sure you keep a foot in the door of the law office," Walker's mentor told him. "Don't ever give that up. You need it for your own protection. You need it to be able to say, I don't want this job any more. I can leave it."

For his first couple of years as an MPP, Robarts asked Frost not to give him any additional responsibilities, as he wanted to build his law practice. Eventually, however, Frost wanted to see just what Robarts was capable of achieving, and by 1953, Robarts was ready. The issue would be water.

"Leslie Frost had apparently been to a dinner in Ottawa, where he met [visiting U.S. president] Dwight Eisenhower," says the historian Randall White. "At some point, Eisenhower said to Frost, 'You have a nice little country here. Don't let them ruin your water the way they've ruined ours.'" Frost was apparently so moved by Eisenhower's admonition that he created the Ontario Water Resources Commission and gave Robarts the chairmanship. Two years later, Frost gave him another job—chairman of a select legislative committee studying whether to put tolls on Ontario's new superhighways. (The committee recommended against doing it, and Frost accepted the advice.)

His second provincial election on June 9, 1955, would prove to be significant for Robarts in so many ways. Leslie Frost kept the government in Tory hands, winning another massive majority government (eighty-three PCs, ten Liberals, two CCFers). The legislature added eight seats, including another in London, so John Robarts became the new member for London North. Winning London South was Ernie Jackson, a man who would serve just one term in the provincial legislature but would become Robarts's best friend and in many respects his alter ego. Completing the trio was James Auld from Leeds in eastern Ontario. The three amigos got on so well that they decided to become roommates, but not at the Royal York Hotel, where all the other out-of-town MPPs were staying. "Mrs. Frost and others would be sitting in the lobby doing their knitting, seeing who was coming and going, and at what time," says Darcy McKeough. The trio wanted no part of that scrutiny.

One postscript to that 1955 election. The Liberal candidate Robarts defeated in London North was Clarence Peterson, a signatory to the Regina Manifesto, and the father of future Ontario premier David Peterson, future Willowdale MP Jim Peterson, and future Mississauga South MPP Tim Peterson. After David Peterson entered Ontario politics in 1975, John Robarts often introduced him this way: "I ran against David's father. It was the closest election I faced in my life and the reason it was so close was that Clarence was the finest man I ever faced in my life."

David Peterson still gets visibly moved when he remembers those introductions.

"How could you not love the man," he says. "There was a generosity of spirit that swept up everybody in his wake. It's one of the reasons I'm such a fan of this generous and kind man."

No story about the rise of John Robarts would be complete without ample mention of Ernie Jackson. He became the single most important driving force in transforming Robarts from backbencher to the next prime minister of Ontario. Like Robarts, Jackson went to London South Collegiate Institute but never made it to university. He volunteered for the Canadian Army, was sent to Italy, and had such awful experiences there that he refused ever to go back, even as a tourist. (He would never travel to Germany either.) His antipathy to Italy was so intense that when his daughter Barbara brought home her fiancé, Franco Prevedello, Jackson called him Bruno for the first five years of his and Barbara's marriage. Jackson returned to Ontario in 1945, got into the insurance business, and made a very good living at it.

Strangely enough for a politician, Ernie Jackson did not like the limelight. He was a poor public speaker and had to take lessons to improve his performance. Most acknowledge that the lessons did not help. Jackson quickly realized his greatest contribution to politics would take place in the back rooms, where his favourite cause was his friend John Robarts.

"One of the things John told me was the influence the war had on him," says Hugh Hanson, who would work in the Ontario prime minister's office during Robarts's second term. "He'd say, 'Me and a bunch of other young guys went up against the best in the world and we beat them. When we came back, we knew we could do anything.'"

One year after winning re-election, John and Norah Robarts adopted another child, this time a son, whom they named Timothy Parmenter Robarts. Tim was two weeks old when he joined the Robarts household. He was constantly fighting health problems, particularly eczema. He was so often covered in ointment that he could never go to the beach. But John Robarts wanted a son, and Tim it would be. The decision would ultimately bring heartache to the Robartses.

Back at Queen's Park, Robarts was starting to get restless. It's true he initially showed little interest in a cabinet job in order to get his law firm established. But, having accomplished that, Robarts was now wondering whether he figured in Prime Minister Frost's plans. No doubt causing him great consternation was the promotion given to one of his best friends, Robert Macaulay, the MPP for Toronto's

Riverdale riding. Macaulay had known Frost since his childhood. Besides being a rising star in the Frost government, Macaulay had good Tory bloodlines. His father, Leopold, had been a cabinet minister in the governments of Premiers G. Howard Ferguson and George S. Henry. Leopold Macaulay twice ran unsuccessfully for the party's leadership. And now, Frost was asking Robert Macaulay to join his executive council.

The gossip of the day was that Robarts was a bit stung by Macaulay's elevation ahead of his own. For the most part, he kept his complaints to himself. But before long, his patience ran out. He told Eddie Goodman that if he did not get into cabinet soon, he would get out of politics altogether. Goodman told Robarts to relax, that he would do what he could to work behind the scenes for his friend. His first conversation was with Alec McKenzie, who had breakfast with Leslie Frost in the Royal York Hotel every morning, and thus had frequent and direct access to the one man who could improve Robarts's status. Goodman was blunt. "You've got enough assholes in cabinet," he told McKenzie. "You can make room for someone of his abilities." McKenzie assured Goodman that the prime minister would find a place for Robarts, not to worry. Goodman told the prime minister's top adviser that it was not he, Goodman, who was worried, but rather Frost and McKenzie who should worry, because without some movement Robarts was gone.

Frost continued to be nervous about Robarts's penchant for the nightlife. Nevertheless, on December 6, 1958, two weeks after Goodman's conversation with McKenzie, Frost called Robarts in London to tell him he was in, albeit at the lowest rung on the cabinet ladder. Robarts would be a minister without portfolio, essentially serving as a liaison between the cabinet and the water resources commission.

Robarts's elevation to the cabinet also made his friend Ernie Jackson's next decision that much easier. Jackson knew two Londoners were not about to be appointed to the cabinet. And so, satisfied that he could make a significant contribution in the back rooms and simultaneously boost his friend's prospects, Jackson decided not to seek re-election. The Tories would choose John White to carry their colours in London South in the 1959 election campaign.

Robarts also knew John White well. White owned a construction equipment rental company in London and had worked on Robarts's municipal campaign back in 1950. He was eight years Robarts's junior but shared a background in the navy. And in another coincidence, John and Bea White, like the Robartses, had also adopted two children, Martha and Emily.

Outwardly, all seemed blissful in Robarts's life. He was a popular up-and-coming politician. His two children gave him the patina of a good family man, to balance those rumours of late nights, partying in swank establishments. But Robarts's lengthy absences in Toronto led to significant problems back home in London. The truth was, Norah Robarts was starting to drink a lot to make up for the loneliness in her life. "We thought they were a star-blessed family," says Bev Shrives. "Two attractive people, two great kids and lots of money."

It was at this point that Norah made what would turn out to be the most crucial decision of her life, and by all accounts she made a bad decision. With her husband now spending more and more time in Toronto, Norah and the children found themselves increasingly on their own. Robarts, and many of his friends and colleagues, begged Norah to move to Toronto so the family could be together more. But Norah refused. Her life, her family, her friends, her bridge partners, and her status were connected to London, and she wanted to preserve it all. Toronto was foreign to her, and public events requiring the presence of the wife of the minister held even less appeal.

For her part, Robin Robarts remembers that her mother was "most assuredly not everyone's cup of tea." But she insists Norah Robarts was not a spiteful person. "My aunt Peg used to say she never heard her utter a mean word about anybody," Robin says.

Today, interestingly enough, Robin has nothing but fond memories of that time.

"For me, it was totally normal," she says. "I didn't know anything else, and as a child you're pretty self-absorbed. It was school, friends, and homework. I don't know that many children who knew their fathers were around, even when they *were* there."

On June 11, 1959, the people of Ontario went back to the polls and re-elected the Frost government, albeit with a reduced majority. The Tories lost twelve seats, almost all of them going to the Liberals. But Robarts was returned, and about to experience a stellar promotion. If Frost's concerns about Robarts's reputation delayed his entry into cabinet, then evidently the prime minister's views changed significantly once he saw the London MPP in action. On December 8—almost exactly one year to the day after he joined the provincial cabinet—John Robarts got another call from Frost, who wanted him to be minister of education—after finance, the most important portfolio in government.

So great was local pride in him that "when John Robarts was made education minister, they announced it over the public address system at London Central Collegiate Institute," remembers John Stoffman, who was a student at the school at the time and still lives in London today.

Andrea Robarts, the only child of Bob and Eleanor Robarts, echoes that story. For her Grade 7 current events class, her mother clipped the story out of the local paper of Uncle John becoming education minister. She presented the story of the family triumph to her class. Years later, she confesses she was not really sure why this was such a big deal, but that the adults around her certainly thought it was.

Now, on the home front everything would change. Robarts was effectively stuck in Toronto all week long and would only ever come home to London for weekends. He put his law partnership in moth-balls and bought a first-class ticket on the roller coaster that is politics, which was about to consume his life.

When Robarts came home over the weekend, Norah frequently opened up her home to numerous friends and threw wonderful dinner parties. Robin remembers many occasions when she would be wakened at three o'clock in the morning so her father could proudly parade her before his guests, then send her back to bed. As much as Norah detested what John's political career was doing to her home life, there is plenty of evidence to suggest that when he was around, things were pretty good. "We had lots of father-daughter talks about just life in general," Robin says. "He was quite a philosopher, so if I got confused about how the world was running, we'd have talks over that. And we did that from a very young age on. I remember sitting in his study asking normal questions, and he took them very seriously. I remember that. His answers were always very in-depth, and he was fascinating. He really was.

"My favourite picture is upstairs at home, and it's just him having a big belly laugh," she adds. "I've got great fond memories of him sitting with his silly little Christmas hat on, reciting *The Night before Christmas*."

Home movies also show a family very much enjoying themselves. Robin and Tim playing together at home. Tim hamming it up for the camera. Robin, with her fabulous carrot-top hair, combing a doll's hair. Tim skating and constantly falling. Backyard barbecues. Robin and Tim fishing at the cottage at Grand Bend on Lake Huron. A lovely shot of Tim feeding a deer. Robarts himself jumping off a boat into the lake. Robin and Tim on the observation deck of the Empire State Building.

The only thing Robin did not like about her father's being in poli-tics was the ministry he was charged with overseeing. She says, "I did ask Dad to get a different job because I didn't like the teasing." Robin frequently heard taunts, which would always begin with "You think you're so cool because your dad is minister of education ..." (Neil Davis, son of the future education minister William Davis, can confirm that in a schoolyard it is worse for your father to be the education czar than premier).

Perhaps mindful of that, Robarts refused to pose for the cameras with his son on the way into Tim's first day of kindergarten. "I do not want to create any difficulties for the passage of my child through school," the education minister told assembled members of the media.

Robarts got the education file at a time when it was becoming a hugely important issue for Ontario. The province was preparing to embark on a brave new decade. That huge demographic bubble of children born after the Second World War was about to graduate from the elementary panel into secondary school, and the system was not ready for it. So the government would start building schools with a vengeance.

Robarts's education department made several distinctive moves. Concerned about too many students dropping out of high school, he created the Ontario Scholarship. The government would give cash bonuses to students who graduated from Grade 13 with an 80 percent average or better. At the time, it was also thought prudent to begin to determine which students were academically, as opposed to technically, inclined. So the government began streaming students in the high school years: arts and sciences in one stream, technical, trade, and vocational in another. And unlike many ministers of the crown who lived in obscurity, John Robarts became virtually a household name, as his signature was on the high school diplomas of millions of Ontario students.

William Davis remembers one story that indicates Robarts may have been, from time to time, getting a bit big for his britches. "John received an honorary degree from Queen's University," Davis says, smiling as he remembers the occasion. "Robert Macaulay called his office. John's secretary was Miss Anderson. She answered the phone according to the custom at the ministry of education: "Dr. Robarts's office." Macaulay said, 'I've got a bad tooth, I'll be down there any minute for a little help.' That was the last time Miss Anderson answered the phone *Dr.* Robarts's office."

In May 1960 Ontario lost one of the all-time great political back-room boys when Alec McKenzie died. None of Frost's colleagues had any idea how long the prime minister intended to remain in office, but in hindsight, it seems certain that McKenzie's death hastened Frost's departure. In August 1961 the Silver Fox, as Frost was occasionally known, announced his intention to resign as prime minister, to be replaced at a leadership convention three months later. At that moment, John Robarts had given precious little thought to whether he wanted to replace Frost as prime minister of Ontario. But that was before the London Mafia, as the group called itself, got into the game.

3

THE SINGLE GREATEST DAY

HAVING RECENTLY FLIRTED with the notion of quitting politics altogether, Robarts soon came to an altogether different conclusion. Leslie
Frost, perhaps the most successful premier of Ontario in the twentieth
century (three elections, three consecutive massive majority governments), decided the time had come to retire from politics. Old Man
Ontario, as he was now known (he was seventy-six), had stayed in the
job for more than a decade. He was satisfied that the Conservative
dynasty begun by George Drew and continued so successfully by Frost
himself could be perpetuated under the leadership of one of his
younger cabinet ministers.

John Robarts was approaching his forty-fourth birthday. He had
not dreamed of being prime minister of Ontario since childhood. He
had never demonstrated the blind ambition so common in many of
today's leadership candidates. And there's precious little evidence to
suggest that even as Frost was approaching retirement, Robarts was
giving a possible leadership run much thought. Instead, it seems that

running to replace Frost was something both Robarts and his best friend (and future campaign manager), Ernie Jackson, did not exactly as a lark but not quite with much forethought either. The pair drove to Ottawa, got a room at the Château Laurier Hotel and started to laugh. "They thought it was so brash," recalls Ernie Jackson's second wife, Wilma, known to everyone in Tory party circles as Willie.

From their headquarters at the Château Laurier, Jackson began making calls to Conservative riding association presidents. The game plan was simple. Jackson would round 'em up, and Robarts would charm the hell out of 'em. "John Robarts was charming to everyone," says Gordon Walker, the London MPP first elected in 1971 and a cabinet minister in the Davis years. "There wasn't a time when he met a person that he didn't leave charmed, whether young ladies, old ladies, young men, old men. He had presence."

Robarts's colleagues saw a man not obsessed with leading his party or securing his place in history. Like Orson Welles's fictional publisher Charles Foster Kane who thought it might be fun to run a newspaper, Robarts seemed to think it might be fun to run for the leadership. Robarts and Jackson decided to test the temperature of the water they were about to wade into, and apparently they figured it tested warmly enough. Delegates in Ottawa looked favourably at Robarts's candidacy. He would have his hands full, considering who else was in the race. Most considered him a long shot. But his campaign team was taking shape quite nicely.

John Cronyn, one of Robarts's friends, was ideally situated to become most helpful. He was plugged into the London business scene in a major way, having been appointed to the board of directors of nine companies, including Labatt's, Canadian Cable Systems, and London Life. He was in charge of political donations at Labatt's (his paternal grandmother was a Labatt). He started as an apprentice brewer and worked his way up to executive vice-president. The world-famous Labatt's 50 and Labatt's Blue beers were his formulas. Cronyn was actually a bit late to the Robarts team. He and Robarts became friends after the war (Cronyn went to the University of Toronto). They lived two doors apart in London, but he remained uninvolved in politics until Ernie Jackson shamed him into getting active in 1951. His first job was to drive people to the polls to vote for Robarts. Cronyn's assistance was crucial if Robarts had any intention of being competitive during the leadership convention. His easy access to other business leaders meant fundraising wouldn't be an issue for the Robarts campaign, not to mention the organizational skills Cronyn could bring to bear. As another London friend, Nancy Poole, pointed out when asked about Robarts's chances for victory, "We didn't think he had a hope in hell."

And yet in August 1961 the Robarts for Leader organization was starting to come together. Besides Ernie Jackson, other supporters in on the ground floor included Bill Rudd, future general manager and chief operating officer of London Life and at this time secretary of the London PC Association. (Rudd used to joke that *he* ran London. "Joseph Stalin was general secretary of the Communist Party, and he ran Russia," he would say. "I'm general secretary of the London PC Association, so I guess I must run London.")

Fred Jenkins was also central to the operation. Jenkins was a London businessman and treasurer of the city's riding association. He operated out of a musty nineteenth-century office behind a local hardware store, from which he pursued potential campaign donors. Eventually, he took particular pride in the fact that no Robarts campaign ever failed to pay its election expenses or went into debt. Others on board included the MPPs William Stewart, a dairy farmer from Middlesex North; Charles MacNaughton, a seed merchant from Huron riding; James Auld, actually from Leeds in eastern Ontario but a navy buddy of Robarts's; and John White, the rookie MPP who had replaced Ernie Jackson in London South.

If you visit the main floor of the Ontario Legislature in downtown Toronto, you will see the names of every member of the provincial

Parliament impressively carved, in alphabetical order, in white marble stone on the walls. Ironically, the names of two MPPs in the twenty-sixth Parliament are almost identical, and are therefore situated one atop the other. They were both Conservative MPPs, then both Conservative cabinet ministers for Leslie Frost, and ultimately the only two contenders left standing on the last ballot at the convention to replace Frost as premier: John Robarts and Kelso Roberts.

Kelso Roberts was the odds-on favourite to win. He was the province's attorney general and represented a downtown Toronto riding at a time when the words *Tory* and *Toronto* were synonymous. (Today, in Premier Dalton McGuinty's Ontario, the Tories have exactly zero of the city's twenty-two ridings.) Roberts also had friends in high places—access to the barons of Bay Street—and therefore as much money as his leadership campaign would need.

But if Roberts had all that going for him, he also lacked some key ingredients. He wasn't all that well liked. You would never accuse him of exuding charm or grace. He was a bit of a stuffed shirt (maybe more than a bit). And quietly, behind the scenes, Leslie Frost let it be known that his attorney general wasn't the guy he had in mind to replace him. Frost was officially neutral, but several key members of his inner circle would end up working for Robarts. Frederick "Big Daddy" Gardiner, the first ever (and very influential) chairman of the new Metropolitan Toronto Council, was onside, signing up support in the legal community. So was Harry Price, the party treasurer, and another key member of Frost's inner circle, who mined his contacts in the business community for Robarts. "When you put Kelso Roberts next to John Robarts, it was no contest," says Nancy Poole, London friend of the Robartses. "John oozed charm. And it was Dickie [Dillon, Robarts's friend from UWO] and Ernie [Jackson] who knew how to work this."

Robarts's people skills may have been well honed, but he was sorely lacking the skills considered essential for today's political leaders. For one, he had a speaking style that hardly set the house on fire.

"Interestingly enough, I think he could be very boring at times," says Gordon Walker, who as a Conservative from London thought of himself as a disciple of Robarts's. "He had a rough, gravelly, monotonous voice that would drone on if he was reading some speech that was perhaps dry or dusty."

In addition, Robarts often had a terrible image on television. Early in the campaign, he gave an interview to the reporter Geoff Scott (a future Conservative MP from Hamilton), an interview noteworthy only for how bored the candidate seemed to be about his candidacy. "I could only say that I offer myself because I have experience and I have vigour and energy," Robarts said, in a speaking style that betrayed no evidence of vigour and energy. But the education minister's next statement to Scott was bang on:

"I have, I think, the physical stamina to do the job, and I have great interest in doing this," he said. "And I have confidence I can."

Stamina. Interest. Confidence. Robarts never lacked any of them.

The competition for the PC leadership was formidable. Besides Robarts and Roberts, there were five other cabinet ministers vying to become party chief. Robert Macaulay, the brilliant, flamboyant energy resources minister from Toronto's Riverdale riding, was considered the likeliest victor if the attorney general faltered. (Macaulay was actually the first energy minister in Canadian history.) His campaign manager was none other than William Grenville Davis, who would go on to become the longest-serving premier of Ontario in the twentieth century. Managing Kelso Roberts's campaign was the St. George MPP Allan Lawrence, who would be the last man left standing with Davis at the next Tory leadership contest ten years hence. Macaulay and Robarts were good friends, sharing an apartment in Toronto in the year leading up to the convention. Macaulay was not yet married, and Robarts needed a place to live.

A young lawyer named Alan Eagleson was at that convention helping Kelso Roberts. Eagleson practised law at Blaney Pasternak, where the High Park MP John Kucherepa—a Roberts supporter—often steered his constituents' legal work. "That's why I helped Kelso," says Eagleson, who, despite supporting Roberts, had met Robarts and was impressed. "He was a man's man and a lady's man," Eagleson says. "He had all the ingredients. I liked him right off the bat."

Other candidates were the provincial treasurer, James Allan, the MPP for Haldimand-Norfolk; the health minister, Matthew Dymond, the MPP from Ontario riding east of Toronto and a future chairman of the Ontario Science Centre; the reform institutions minister George Wardrope from Port Arthur; and Rev. Alfred Downer, the MPP from Dufferin-Simcoe. "Everyone thought Kelso or Macaulay would win," recalls Eagleson, who would become a future Conservative MPP and party president. "Then it was Jimmy Allan. There was reverence for him because he'd looked after everyone."

Robarts started the campaign with very few of the things one traditionally needs to win. His home base was sleepy London, not go-go Toronto. He was less well known than the others in the race. While the education ministry was one of the government portfolios with the largest budgets, Robarts lacked the legislative accomplishments many of the others had. But the marriage of Ernie Jackson's strategy and John Robarts's personality would soon prove more than enough to overcome the traditional shortfalls.

Eventually, Robarts picked up the endorsements of five of his cabinet colleagues—the most of any of the candidates. And the quintessential Tory back-room boy, Eddie Goodman, soon joined them. "I had to decide between Macaulay or Robarts," says Goodman. "I liked Kelso, but I didn't consider him. I thought Macaulay might be intellectually smarter than Robarts, but Robarts would be a better premier. He was level-headed. Macaulay had some fantastic ideas and some that weren't so fantastic."

Goodman called Macaulay. "Bob, this isn't easy," he told him. "I've decided to support Robarts."

Shortly thereafter, Goodman would introduce another future key player in Robarts's political life to the candidate: Richard Rohmer, who would become Robarts's right-hand man in government (and one of Goodman's least favourite people in Conservative Party circles).

The federal Conservative prime minister, John Diefenbaker, had a presence at the convention in the person of his young executive assistant. Henry Best first met Robarts in Oakville while the candidate was making the rounds, chatting up party members. Best, the son of Charles Best, one of the co-discoverers of insulin, now had a tough decision to make. He had attended Upper Canada College with Kelso Roberts's son, who was obviously hoping his school chum would support his dad. "Kelso was okay but didn't have a feel for the people," Best says.

And then there was Best's older brother, Charles Alexander (Sandy) Best, three years his senior, and the MP for Halton, who had instructed his kid brother to vote for Macaulay. "My brother said Macaulay was the most intelligent, and I didn't disagree," Best recalls. "But I didn't think he had the best judgment. So I worked for Robarts. My brother was not amused."

At the policy sessions a couple of days before the leadership vote, Best recalls a farmer from Grey-Bruce making some point about agricultural policy. Macaulay interrupted the farmer, telling him he did not know what he was talking about.

"A city boy telling farmers how to do things?" Best recalls the incident with incredulity. "This confirmed my judgment about Macaulay."

On October 25, 1961, delegates gathered at Varsity Arena on Bloor Street West in Toronto to replace Leslie Frost. Waiting for them on convention day was a state-of-the-art campaign organization, the likes of which they'd never seen before. Professor Keith Brownsey of Mount Royal College in Calgary refers to the '61 convention as a turning point in Canadian political history. The British influence and model for running campaigns was about to die. In its place would come more modern, American-style tactics.

Ernie Jackson had made two important contacts on the American political scene: Robert Teeter in Detroit and Richard Wirthlin in California. Jackson made the Park Plaza Hotel—just a block away from Varsity Arena—the Robarts campaign headquarters. He then borrowed the latest tactics from his American counterparts by parking a trailer outside the arena, equipped with telephones, and paid for by Labatt's, courtesy of John Cronyn. In these days well before the widespread use of cellphones, campaign workers could dash out of the arena to the trailer and pass on vital information to headquarters. Similarly, HQ could instruct workers on the convention floor, giving the Robarts team an advantage over its rivals. "That was also the first time we tried to use computer punch cards," remembers Cronyn. "Everybody we approached, we put on punch cards for second and third choice. It was the first attempt at a more scientific basis for a campaign."

Improved communications. A delegate-tracking system. It was very new stuff at a Canadian political convention. There was also some of the very old stuff, such as overzealous security guards. Bev Shrives remembers convention day well. She almost missed all the action. Her husband, Walter, was a voting delegate, but she wasn't and convention officials refused to let her into Varsity Arena until one of the candidates' wives happened to pass by. "Norah, I can't get in," Shrives said to Mrs. Robarts.

Norah took off her identification badge and gave it to her friend. "Here," she said. "They'll damn well let me in!" Shrives marched in, and has kept the badge to this day.

Darcy McKeough was at that convention, working the floors for Robarts. At one point, McKeough found himself talking to a bear of a man, the Suffragan bishop of Huron, William Townsend, who was also chairman of the London Board of Education.

"He was supporting John," McKeough recalls. "So much for the separation of church and state."

At one point, someone came over and interrupted their conversation. "We've got a problem with two or three people up in Grey [County]," the man said.

The bishop didn't miss a beat. "Give me their names!" he bellowed, upon which he left, presumably to remind these confused delegates that there might not be a place in heaven for fairweather friends.

After the initial results were announced, the education minister surprised all observers by coming second on the first ballot, well ahead of expectations, but behind Kelso Roberts. He then overtook Roberts on the second ballot. Again, on the third, fourth, and fifth ballots, it was Robarts in first, Roberts in second, but still no victor. However, after the fifth ballot, the third- (and last-) place candidate, Bob Macaulay, was forced to drop out. Kelso Roberts hoped his fellow Torontonian might choose to crown him king, but it did not work out that way.

What Kelso Roberts did not know was that even before a single delegate had voted on the first ballot, the decision in the Macaulay camp about what to do in this situation had already been made. Although hoping to win, Macaulay's campaign chairman, William Davis, was realistic enough to know his candidate needed a Plan B, just in case. While Davis now says there were no prior negotiations or deals with the Robarts side, there was apparently an understanding where Macaulay would go if he fell off the ballot.

So, after the fifth ballot, Macaulay followed the script. He marched up to Robarts, pointed to one of Robarts's buttons, and said, "Hang it on me, John." As Robarts attempted to oblige, Macaulay took the button and did it himself. "I put the button on so it would be evident where I wanted my supporters to go," Macaulay recalls. "I didn't want to have to tell dozens of people, so the most logical way was to show them how I felt about it." Despite the disappointment he must have been feeling, Macaulay says this final gesture "was not at all difficult. I joined John out of emotion."

For all intents and purposes, the marathon convention was over. Macaulay played kingmaker, and on the sixth and final ballot, by a delegate count of 967 to 633, Robarts became king. During his victory speech, Robarts was unequivocal in describing the significance of the moment. "This has been the single greatest day of my life," he said in his typically calm, understated, non-dramatic fashion.

Robarts celebrated his win at Ernie Jackson's home. Barbara Prevedello, Jackson's daughter and at the time a high school student, remembers the new leader having to wade his way through a horde of press photographers to get inside.

A few years earlier, John Robarts had thought of quitting politics entirely. In two weeks, he would be sworn in as the seventeenth prime minister of the province of Ontario.

4

THE PRIME MINISTER OF ONTARIO

THE ARRIVAL OF BOTH a new decade and a new prime minister at Queen's Park signalled one of the most significant generational changes in Ontario's history. In January 1961 Americans had entrusted their future to John Fitzgerald Kennedy, a handsome, vigorous Second World War hero who was only forty-three years old. Canada's biggest province was about to do the same thing. On November 8, 1961, the forty-four-year-old Second World War veteran John Parmenter Robarts became prime minister of Ontario.

Robarts was different from his predecessors in so many ways. Although he had seen plenty of frightening action during his military service, his reference points were the war years of 1939–45, not 1914–18. His immediate predecessor, Leslie Frost, had sustained a hip wound near the end of the Great War so serious that he spent seventeen months in hospital and never fully recovered. George Drew, in the office from 1943 to 1948, had sustained permanent damage to an arm from the war. T.L. (Tom) Kennedy, Ontario's premier after Drew left provincial politics to lead the federal Conservative Party, had been wounded in the arm and face by flying shrapnel. Mitchell Hepburn, premier from 1934 to 1942, had been in the flying corps. There were other distinctions as well. Just as Robarts won the leadership of his party with newfangled techniques, his approach to governing would be similar. He referred to himself as a "management man," the ideal hand on the tiller in a new, technocratic age.

After he'd won the leadership, Robarts's supporters staged a raucous celebration at Toronto's favourite Tory hangout, the Albany Club. During the festivities, someone knocked over a sculpture of Sir John A. Macdonald, Canada's first prime minister and founder of the club. The bust smashed into several pieces. Robarts, ever the steady hand, told the assemblage not to fret, that there were plenty more of those sculptures at Queen's Park, and in one of his first decrees as the new prime minister, he would be pleased to send one down to the club to replace the destroyed one. Robarts's eye for historical detail may not have been as keen as his generosity. "Six months later," says Tom Hockin, a former Mulroney government cabinet minister and MP for London West, "some other folks are having a party at the club, and someone asks, 'Why is that bust of Wilfrid Laurier there?'"

Robarts's legendary charm had helped him win the leadership, but charm can only take you so far in government. In one of his first moves as prime minister, Robarts displayed a loyalty and humanity to one of his former rivals that was unprecedented in partisan political circles. Conservatives across Ontario were becoming increasingly acquainted with a rising star in the party, a lawyer from Brampton. This rookie member of the legislature, Bill Davis, had run Bob Macaulay's leadership campaign, which under most circumstances would have been reason enough for the new premier to exclude him from his plans. Then again, this campaign manager delivered a huge percentage of Macaulay's delegates to Robarts on the final ballot, ensuring victory for the education minister. Some reward or special consideration was clearly in order.

This should have been the best of times for MPP William Davis. He was married to the love of his life, had four wonderful children, and had managed to win the 1959 election at the tender age of twenty-nine, in the riding of Peel, despite a local issue that nearly torpedoed his campaign. The Diefenbaker government had just cancelled the Avro Arrow fighter plane, considered a marvel of Canadian design, engineering, and technology. The A.V. Roe manufacturing plant was in Davis's riding, and virtually everyone assumed the voters would target their wrath on the next Tory to stand for office. Davis, however, squeaked in by just eight hundred votes and assumed his place on Leslie Frost's backbench.

Then tragedy struck. Davis's thirty-three-year-old wife, Helen, contracted cancer and died, leaving him a widower with four very young children to raise on his own. John Robarts knew all this. And he knew, because he was a man of good judgment, that someday Davis would be a significant player on the political stage. Aware that Davis needed time to get his personal life together, Robarts did something highly unusual. When he swore in his new cabinet, he kept the education portfolio for himself. At the time, no one could quite figure out why the new premier wanted to keep his old job as well. But a year into Robarts's premiership, it all became clear.

Bill Davis remembers it this way: "While he never said anything to me directly, it became apparent to people that he was keeping the portfolio himself with the thought I might be asked to assume it when my life settled down somewhat," Davis says. "And that's what turned out."

It was one of Robarts's better decisions. Together Ontario's seventeenth premier and the man who would become the province's eighteenth transformed the education system in as dramatic a fashion as anyone ever had, before or since.

Ironically, one of the places where Robarts's skills really shone was where no members of the public could see him—inside cabinet meetings. He demonstrated an uncanny knack for knowing when to lead and when to listen, he allowed ministers to carry the ball when he trusted them, and he cut them off at the knees when he thought they were out of bounds. Of course, he who controls the agenda controls the meeting. So Robarts's secretary to the cabinet, J. Keith Reynolds, demanded that any items ministers wanted to discuss at cabinet had to be in his hands four days before the meeting was to take place.

As in cabinet meetings today, those in Robarts's time did not take formal votes. However, perhaps somewhat unusually, Robarts did not have anyone keep minutes of the meetings either. That gave the prime minister a strategic advantage when it came to determining what, exactly, the executive council had decided. "He'd allow debate, then say, 'Gentlemen, it appears the consensus has been arrived at,'" recalls Keith Reynolds, who attended those meetings. "Often I'd ask him afterwards what it was!"

Robarts also established a rapport with opposition politicians, which by today's cutthroat standards seems either quaint or downright foolish. He refused to vilify his political opponents and told his caucus to behave similarly. "He felt it was important to have a strong opposition—that was how you got good government," says Margo Carson, who years later would become Robarts's secretary after his political career was over. "He made sure the opposition got funding. He didn't disparage them. He never got personal. He used to say, 'Don't acknowledge the people out to get you. Just do what you're trying to accomplish.'"

In fact, this unfavourable view of overt partisanship began while Robarts was minister of education. Remarkably, one of his speechwriters at that time was A.A. (Alex) MacLeod, who was on retainer to the department of education and had been one of just two Communist MPPs in Ontario history (the other was Joe Salsberg).

MacLeod got elected in 1943 under the Labour–Progressive Party banner, because being a Communist was from time to time in Canadian history illegal. But Robarts did not seem to care about his Communist ties. He cared more that Alex MacLeod could write a good speech.

The Co-operative Commonwealth Federation (or CCF, which would become the New Democratic Party in time for Robarts's first election as premier in 1963) held just five seats in the legislature when Robarts became premier. Then CCF leader Donald C. MacDonald, the MPP for York South, confirms Robarts's generosity to the opposition. "He was the first one to recognize that a strong, vigorous opposition was essential in a democracy," says MacDonald, who recently turned ninety years old and is still a community activist in Toronto. "He gave us extra money and resources for research so we could be effective."

"It was a hugely different time," remembers Stephen Lewis, the former Ontario NDP leader. "There were intense exchanges but without malevolence. He definitely set a tone of civility and dignity, which I more and more came to value."

A onetime Hamilton Mountain MPP, John Smith, remembers those less partisan days with fondness. Robarts once led a delegation of all MPPs from all parties on a train trek to northwestern Ontario. No advance men. No media. Just a big bonding session among politicians, forging links with local leaders. "He'd talk about moose calls with the mayor of Hornpayne," Smith says. "It was one of the most wonderful experiences. All the members of all parties socialized. The mean-spiritedness of today just wasn't there. And Robarts did it because he thought it was important that we all understand that Ontario was made up of isolated, remote places."

On another similar northern excursion in 1965, Robarts opened the Noden Causeway in Rainy River, which completed Highway 11 all the way to Toronto, where it is called Yonge Street, the longest street in the world. After dedicating the causeway (named after William Noden, MPP for Rainy River from 1955 to 1967), Robarts and several others were invited to the local Tory bagman's home, high up on a hill overlooking Rainy River. Robarts surveyed the scene and with a great sense of history remarked, "Just think, three hundred years ago, we would have seen the coureurs de bois going by here on the way out west."

Political life was so very different in those days. The presidentializing of Canada's high political offices had not yet happened. The occasionally oppressive security around our politicians and our Parliament buildings was completely unknown. On one occasion when Quebec premier Jean Lesage visited Robarts at Queen's Park, the Ontario prime minister decided to show his counterpart how his province's treasury department put together the annual budget. So, with no fanfare or advance notice, Robarts and Lesage left the Ontario legislature alone, dodged traffic across Queen's Park Crescent and made their way to the Frost Building to survey the scene. Lesage was shocked that no security people walked with them. Similarly, Robarts found it completely natural to leave the legislature unaccompanied in the wee small hours of the morning and walk to his suite in the Westbury Hotel. Such trips would be unheard of today.

Duff Roblin, premier of Manitoba from 1958 to 1967, met Robarts for the first time at a Dominion-Provincial Conference, the name previously used for first ministers' conferences.

"He made a very favourable impression," remembers Roblin, who at eighty-seven still goes to his Winnipeg office most days. "He was a very agreeable man. Eager to listen. Approachable. We became quite good friends."

Robarts invited Roblin to join him for a weekend at his cottage in Grand Bend. The Manitoba premier, who always drove his own car, was impressed at the difference in protocol. Robarts had a car and a driver provided by Ontario taxpayers, but even then, not all the time. On this occasion, after the weekend was over, Robarts asked Barbara

Prevedello, the second eldest of Ernie Jackson's five children, to drive the two premiers to the airport at Grand Bend. Prevedello was still a teenager who often babysat Robarts's children for twenty-five cents an hour (and thirty-five cents on New Year's Eve). "They trusted me a lot," she remembers. "I drove them to the airport at 6 a.m. because he didn't have his car and driver. Those were the days. Just the two premiers and me."

One of Roblin's favourite stories about Robarts centres on his grandfather R.P. Roblin, who was also a Conservative premier of Manitoba (from 1900 to 1915). The elder Roblin was born in Picton, Ontario, so Robarts thought it would be nice to honour him by erecting a plaque in his hometown. "He called me and told me he wanted me to come down to Prince Edward County and unveil the plaque," Roblin recalls. "He didn't have to do that. It was a very human thing to do."

At his core, John Robarts plain and simply wasn't a very partisan politician. He loved governing but wasn't much on campaigning. "He felt he was leader of all the people," says Bill Rathbun, who was a journalist at Queen's Park with Canadian Press and radio station CKEY in the early 1960s and went on to become a speech writer for Robarts. "The moment the polls closed, he felt he'd won everyone's vote. It was a non-political office. No one had to be a Tory to get service. Robarts took great pride in running a non-partisan office."

Mind you, there were exceptions. One day around the cabinet table, Robarts tried to push through an eastern Ontario highway program of dubious economic merit. He ran into some stiff opposition from some ministers. Robarts shot them down. "You just remember," he noted, "that in the dark years of Hepburn, eastern Ontario voted Tory and I've never forgotten it!"

"He had a long memory," says Darcy McKeough, the former Chatham-Kent MPP and cabinet minister, who witnessed the tongue-lashing, "and a great sense of history."

Interestingly enough, the public's first opportunity to render a verdict on Robarts's premiership did not go particularly well. A remarkable winning streak came to an end in 1962. For the first time in nineteen years, the Tories lost a by-election. The former Liberal premier Harry Nixon had died while still a member of the legislature. The seat, which he had held for forty-two years, was now in play. But his son, thirty-four-year-old Robert Nixon, kept Brant riding in the Liberal (and Nixon) family. (Thirty-one years later, Robert Nixon's daughter, Jane Stewart, would be the MP for Brant, becoming the third generation of Nixons to represent the area.)

Incidentally, it was Robert Nixon who began to make an issue of what people actually called the leader of the government of Ontario. At Confederation and for the next seventy years, Ontario's first minister was called the premier. However (and here's a little-known piece of Ontario trivia), after his first term, Mitchell Hepburn changed the title to prime minister, which it remained until William Davis officially changed it back to premier. So, technically, Robarts's title was prime minister of Ontario. If you called his office, that's how the secretary answered the phone.

"Nixon rode him hard about this," recalls Darcy McKeough. "Mr. Robarts would always say, 'That was the name on the door when I got here, and it's going to cost money to change it, so I'll stick with prime minister.' I always thought probably it had something to do with his building a relationship with the *premier ministre* of Quebec. And premier does translate into French as *premier ministre*."

(Perhaps unusual for a man who spoke absolutely no French at all, Robarts was keenly interested in the nationalist movement in Quebec. He would forge close relationships with his Quebec counterparts Jean Lesage and Daniel Johnson Sr. He wanted, as one of his advisers said, "a partnership with Quebec in fact and spirit and purpose.")

Fortunately for the new prime minister, his predecessor Leslie Frost retired early enough in his third mandate to give Robarts ample time to put his own stamp on the province. (For the record, Robarts and Frost appear to have had a good working relationship after the transition. Roger Graham writes in *Old Man Ontario* (University of Toronto Press, 1990) that Frost liked sitting on Robarts's backbench, offering advice when asked and never embarrassing the new leader.

Robarts's agenda was remarkably ambitious. There was more money for Toronto's subway system, more roads, more parks, portable pensions, a higher minimum wage, an Ontario Arts Council to better fund the arts, collective bargaining for civil servants, a provincial health insurance plan for those not covered by private plans, and more seats in the legislature for Ontario's cities, where an increasingly larger portion of the population lived.

Besides the ambitious agenda, Robarts was also becoming a better performer, a less ponderous speaker. "He was a speed reader," remembers Bill Rathbun. "He could scan a page in the blink of an eye and carry it." Mind you, Robarts still had his troubles. "He wandered off the text a lot," says Rathbun. "He worked the crowd by turning around, away from the cameras. I'd mark the text and say, 'For God's sake, stay still and look at the cameras here!' He uh'd and ah'd a great deal, but got a helluva lot better as he went along." In fact, Robarts gave one of his most memorable speeches in the legislature just before sending Ontarians to the polls in 1963, in search of his own mandate. One by one, Robarts barked out the items on a checklist of promises made under his leadership. After each item, Conservative MPPs would shout, "Done!"

Even though Robarts had inherited a solid majority government (seventy-one of ninety-eight seats), he did want to improve on the seat count and that meant trying to attract new, appealing candidates to run under the Tory banner. The logical place to begin looking was on the list of candidates who'd just been defeated in the April 8, 1963, federal election. Robarts's officials noticed that a twenty-nine-year-old lawyer running in York West had lost to the Toronto Maple Leaf legend Leonard "Red" Kelly by a whopping seventeen thousand votes. However, that same candidate also garnered the third most votes of any Tory candidate in Ontario. He had supported Robarts's rival, Kelso Roberts, in the leadership campaign, but no one was holding that against him at this stage. The candidate's name was Alan Eagleson. "I thought that running federally was fun, but I had no thought in my mind of running again," he says.

That was before Robarts's campaign team came calling. Dalton Bales, the MPP for York Mills and the man charged with finding Toronto candidates, wanted Eagleson to have lunch with Robarts. Eagleson's future political contacts would become the stuff of legend, but at this stage he'd never been to Queen's Park before. "We'd like you to run, but there'll be no guarantees about the nomination," Robarts told him in a gruff voice.

What does Eagleson remember about the meeting today? "Robarts was forty-five. I was thirty. I was in awe of the guy," he says. Eagleson defeated two other candidates to win the PC nomination in Etobicoke-Lakeshore and was soon on his way back to Queen's Park to have his picture taken with the premier.

The next time Eagleson and Robarts would meet was at a football game in London: the visiting University of Toronto Varsity Blues (Eagleson's alma mater) versus the University of Western Ontario Mustangs (Robarts's old team). The two men jokingly agreed to bet one dollar on the outcome. The Blues won, and Eagleson went off to a U of T post-game party to celebrate.

Given how the 1963 election started, no Tories were making too many bold predictions about the outcome. Leslie Frost and A.D. McKenzie had assembled a true Tory juggernaut. Over three elections, Frost won an astonishing 81 percent of the available seats up for grabs. With just ten days left in the 1963 campaign, Robarts looked hard pressed to get close to that. The Conservatives and Liberals, led by the Waterloo North MPP John Wintermeyer, were neck and neck.

Wintermeyer was gaining traction, with assistance from the Roman Catholic Church, on the issue of separate school funding. Both Robarts and Bill Davis, as education ministers, had so successfully built up the public school system that the Catholic system was starting to resemble anything but the separate and equal school system promised by the Fathers of Confederation. And so, in the dying days of the '63 campaign, Robarts promised a major extension of funds to the Catholic system—full public funding to Grade 9.

"It became a huge story," recalls Ab Campion, at the time a young Tory staffer who'd been seconded from party headquarters by Ernie Jackson to write speeches and advertising copy for the campaign. "The announcement took the sails out of the Liberal campaign."

Meanwhile, in London, Robarts had people such as Gordon Walker, the future MPP for London South, ensuring that the premier kept his own seat. One of Walker's jobs was to drive a campaign truck that blasted out the song "When Johnny Comes Marching Home Again." "The campaign team wanted that played up and down every street," Walker says. "I did it. Nearly drove me crazy."

Ontarians went to the polls on September 25, 1963, and gave the Conservative government a resounding endorsement. Robarts received a higher percentage of the total votes cast than any premier since the end of the Second World War—48.9—an achievement that still hasn't been surpassed. (However, his winning 71 percent of the seats doesn't come close to Frost's 88 percent, which Old Man Ontario had in 1951.) Robarts picked up an additional six seats in a legislature that was ten seats larger, to reflect the province's growing population. Conservative MPPs totalled seventy-seven. One of their new members was Alan Eagleson, in Etobicoke-Lakeshore.

The Liberals gained only two, for a total of twenty-four. And the newly named New Democratic Party now had seven, also a gain of two. One of their new members was a brilliant and fiery young orator named Stephen Lewis. "Robarts set a substantial tone for the legislature," Lewis recalls. "When he stood to speak, he spoke with a sense of gravitas."

"The house hasn't been the same since he left," adds Bill Reid, now a Toronto criminal lawyer but thirty-five years ago a page at Queen's Park. "He'd stand up and put his hand in his pocket. You could hear a pin drop. He commanded respect."

The Liberals had run a harsh campaign, criticizing the government for failing to make inroads against organized crime, which the Liberals alleged was running amok. In fact, in November 1961, one of the first speeches Robarts listened to in the legislature was a two-and-a-half-hour diatribe from John Wintermeyer, blasting the government for its inaction.

Jonathan Manthorpe, in his book *The Power and the Tories* (Macmillan of Canada, 1974), describes the background leading up to the Liberals' championing this issue. Apparently Harold Greer, a *Globe and Mail* reporter, had thoroughly investigated crime syndicates in Ontario and had written an article for the newspaper. But the editors at *The Globe* spiked the story, saying Greer hadn't proven his charges. He was so miffed that he quit the paper, took his story to Wintermeyer, and became a speech writer for the Liberal leader.

Wintermeyer suggested the provincial government and organized crime were virtually in cahoots. He claimed social clubs were being used for syndicate gambling, and that those clubs had received provincial government charters. "Organized crime was operating in Ontario under the government's nose" was how Manthorpe described the allegation. For his part, Robarts was so shaken by Wintermeyer's tough remarks that he decided to establish a royal commission under Mr. Justice Wilfred Roach. Roach launched a sixty-six-day investigation and in the end found only smoke but no fire.

Clearly, the public didn't believe the mud being slung and punished the Liberals. John Wintermeyer, who had become leader in

1958 and was the Liberals' best hope since Mitch Hepburn of winning an election, resigned after losing his seat. (However, Wintermeyer, who died in 1994, would live long enough to see his dream of a fully funded Catholic school system come to fruition. In 1984 Robarts's successor, William Davis, announced the government's intention to extend full funding. It was actually David Peterson's Liberal government that implemented the policy, in 1985.)

When the legislature reconvened in November 1963, the Tories had won so many seats that several Conservative MPPs had to sit on the opposition side of the house—there simply wasn't enough room for all seventy-seven Conservatives on the government side. Alan Eagleson sat in the last row of this "rump," which, in order to make its lack of status more palatable, called itself "The Chicago Gang."

"Next thing I know, I get a note from the premier," Eagleson remembers. Inside the note was a silver dollar and this: "Alan: to pay my bet from a warm October day. John P. Robarts." Eagleson still has the silver dollar to remind him of Robarts's warmth, charm, and a Blues football victory over the Western Mustangs.

With his election victory secured, Robarts got back to the business of running the government. One of the first orders of business was to get someone to set up his office and his life, both of which needed better organizing. That job went to Richard Rohmer. "I was his troubleshooter," says Rohmer, who occupied the office right next to the premier's.

"He was quiet and effective," adds Bill Rudd. "He was John's right arm."

Richard Rohmer was a bit of a legend in Canadian military circles. On July 17, 1944, he was leading a group of four Mustangs doing air reconnaissance over Caen, France, when he spotted a German officer's car on the road below. The gold and brass on the car was gleaming, even at fifteen hundred feet in the air. Rohmer was under orders not to attack, so he called in two Spitfires, which shot up the car. Severely wounded in the passenger seat was Germany's brilliant tank commander Gen. Erwin Rommel, the Desert Fox.

The fact that Rohmer was even alive to call in the attack on Rommel was a minor miracle in itself. Four days earlier, his plane had been attacked, bullets strafing an inch over his head in the cockpit. Had he been a little taller, he would have been killed. Instead, he survived thirteen bullet holes in his fuselage on July 13. There is no triskaidekaphobia—a fear of the number thirteen—in the Rohmer clan.

Meanwhile, given the solid mandate the MPP from London North had captured, a new nickname wasn't far behind. "The man was handsome, a large presence, a big man," says Rohmer. "And he ran the cabinet and government as if it were a business. So they called him Chairman of the Board."

"It was wonderful he was there," says London friend Nancy Poole, whose husband, William, was a law school buddy of Robarts's. "He could travel the world and never embarrass the province."

A promotional film shot at this time summed up the mood of the province. "Look out, world, here comes Ontario," it boasted. Stan Tkaczyk of Hamilton remembers seeing that film. As a teenager, he had immigrated to Ontario from his native Poland. By the time the 1960s came along, he was working at Stelco in Hamilton in a red-hot job market. "I just couldn't believe how impressive the place was," says Tkaczyk, who was at Stelco from 1958 to 1992. "The film made Ontario look like paradise. So many things happening." Tkaczyk saw Robarts at the Canadian National Exhibition in the mid-1960s. "This was in the days before there was so much security," he says. "I was a couple of feet away from him. He had the looks of a seasoned statesman." How does Tkaczyk, now sixty-seven, remember Robarts's time in government? Plain and simply, "The sixties were my best years."

They were for so many Ontarians. Canada's biggest province was about to blast into the stratosphere with unprecedented growth and spending. Prime Minister Robarts and his education minister, Bill Davis, once opened three new schools in Toronto in one day. How great was it being the education minister in those days? It was fabulous. Davis's department controlled almost seventy cents of every provincial tax dollar spent. In Ontario today, the two ministers responsible for education (the elementary and secondary, and post-secondary systems) spend twenty-six cents of every dollar.

Similarly, Robarts tapped Davis to initiate a building boom in the post-secondary education sector never seen before or since. New universities were popping up everywhere: University of Windsor, Trent University in Peterborough, York University in North York, Laurentian University in Sudbury. But that was only the half of it. Davis also spent millions creating a parallel community college system for those high school graduates inclined less toward academics and more toward a trade.

"He was very supportive of me when we developed the college of applied arts and technology," recalls Davis from his Torys law office in the Toronto-Dominion Centre. "He had a sense of its potential relevance within the education system and social and economic fabric of Ontario. And I think history will record that it was probably one of the more relevant decisions made and wouldn't have happened without the support of John."

And there was more. Robarts could foresee the population boom and subsequent urban sprawl that is the reality of Toronto today. So his government created Canada's first inter-regional transit system, GO Transit (the *GO* stands for Government of Ontario). The train and bus service has carried 750 million passengers since its creation in 1967.

He also moved to make the lives of emotionally disturbed children much better. At the time, critics were appalled at the treatment to which these children were subjected: they were dealt with in adult psychiatric wards, and in the education system there was nothing in the Education Act to provide for special needs kids. And most shockingly, when it came to corrections, youngsters—some as young as eight—were being incarcerated in penal institutions. The Robarts government changed all that.

"We had many difficult debates about these kids," says Stephen Lewis. "When Robarts decided, after a significant intellectual pummelling, to alter the legislation, he rescued a lot of kids in the process. There was a basic realization, albeit slowly and reluctantly, that it wasn't the end of the world to change your mind."

Robarts also wanted to make a statement about how modern and technologically advanced his province was becoming. And so in 1964 he commissioned Raymond Moriyama, a Toronto architect, to design the Ontario Science Centre as a Centennial project, in the suburb of Don Mills. Robarts officially opened the centre on September 27, 1969. Other ministers and civil servants no doubt supervised these projects, but as Richard Rohmer points out, "He made the decisions. The Chairman of the Board. And they were great decisions."

"What I know is, we were building things," says Bill Rathbun. "If a problem was there, we tackled it. It was a pragmatic government led by a pragmatic man. Yes, government grew. But it was there to accomplish things for the people."

"He ran a good government, but he was also lucky," adds Allan Lawrence, the former St. George MPP. "In those days, to solve most problems, you just threw money at it. The revenues were unbelievable. Everything was flying high."

Don Stevenson, who spent almost three decades in the Ontario public service, remembers a small example that illustrates a bigger point. In 1962 he went to the treasury board to get half a million dollars to publish an Economic Atlas of Ontario. The idea was to "take a geographic entity and discover what makes it tick," Stevenson says. Every library in the province got one. The atlas won the Leipzig Book Fair Award for most beautiful book in the world.

"He laid the foundations for the socioeconomic development of Ontario for the next thirty to forty years," says Richard Rohmer.

As much as Robarts loved making bold decisions, he was also cautious when it came to tackling delicate subjects. For example, when the child welfare system wouldn't allow Alan Eagleson's sister to adopt a Catholic baby (referred to as an "interfaith adoption"), Eagleson got up in the legislature and made a stink. The issue hit the headlines, and the Catholic Children's Aid Society responded with a scathing denunciation of Eagleson's position.

A week later, Eagleson was summoned to Robarts's office for a private tête-à-tête. The premier assured Eagleson that the changes he was seeking would eventually happen, but not just yet. "Alan," he said, "I'll give you a quick view of my political philosophy. When in doubt, don't."

"He stuck with that," Eagleson explained. "He had an understanding of what the public would accept." (In the late 1960s, the policy did change, allowing interfaith adoptions.)

Robarts's caution on some issues became an increasing irritant to his close friend and colleague Robert Macaulay. "I wasn't very happy being in cabinet," Macaulay says. "I thought there were stronger things we could be doing. And you're not well accepted if you're at all critical of the premier." After the leadership convention, Robarts did his best to bring Macaulay onside. He offered his competitor the choice of any portfolio he wanted. Macaulay, true to his nature, opted for something bold and dramatic. He asked Robarts to create a super-economics department for him, which would include economics, commerce, development, housing, trade, and industry.

"Macaulay was a human dynamo," says Don Stevenson, his director of economics. Stevenson joined Ontario's economics department in 1959, when Leslie Frost was still prime minister. He was there when Frost brought in the province's first sales tax in 1961. It was 3 percent (today it is 8 percent). And he helped write Ontario's first billion-dollar budget in the same year. Still, none of that prepared him for the likes of Robert Macaulay. "No one kept up with him," Stevenson says.

He remembers being at home one Sunday afternoon when he received a phone call from Macaulay. The minister had to testify the following day before the estimates committee of the legislature, and Macaulay wanted to be prepared. So he drew up a list of 250 hypothetical questions he thought the committee might ask and had Stevenson go over to his house to put him through his paces.

Macaulay would spend his time in cabinet bombarding the prime minister with new, adventurous ideas for boosting the economy— everything from setting up provincial trade offices in Europe to the Ontario Development Corporation, a banker of last resort for promising but risky ventures. In 1964 Macaulay established the new Ontario Housing Corporation, the vehicle through which the province built and managed socially assisted housing projects. He also created the Economic Council of Ontario to offer fiscal advice and do big-picture economic research that the civil service of the day could not do.

"He'd always been a whirling dervish," Stevenson says. "His blood pressure was always at a boiling point, and he had quite a swear-word vocabulary. But I liked working for him because he was intelligent and had ideas."

Robarts went along with many of Macaulay's ideas but never forcefully enough for the impatient economics minister. "I was disappointed in how things were going," Macaulay recalls. "We weren't showing enough leadership. We weren't a strong enough alternative to Frost and Drew."

And so Macaulay resolved to quit the cabinet and did it in a very dramatic fashion. On March 5, 1963, on his way into the legislative chamber, something happened to him. In his biography on Robarts, A.K. McDougall writes that the economic development minister "gasped, threw his papers in the air, and crumpled to the floor."

Rumours abounded that Macaulay had had a heart attack or a stroke. Even today, more than forty years after the episode, he is slightly evasive in describing the events of that day. He confirms he suffered neither a heart attack nor a stroke but will not say what it was. Maybe it was exhaustion mixed with the flu. Less charitable observers thought Macaulay faked the whole episode as a theatrical way to get out of cabinet. Whatever it was, it worked. He left the executive council, held his Riverdale seat six months later in the general election, then quit politics altogether.

"This was his way of having a dramatic departure," explains Don Stevenson. "I was sorry to see him go, although it made life a lot more peaceful."

"We had a tendency to do things the way they had been done," Macaulay says. "It was unimaginative. There were so many things we could have done more on. Put it this way: if you're a creative man, you'd be disappointed to be a garbage man."

Macaulay did go on to have a fascinating career outside politics. He taught law at the University of Toronto, moved to Holland, and served as counsel to the World Health Organization, then moved to London, England, again to teach law. He returned to Ontario and wrote a seven-volume, ten-thousand-page legal text, and served as legal counsel to a federal royal commission on the Toronto waterfront. In 1988 Premier David Peterson hired him to review Ontario's regulatory agencies. Unfortunately, he has suffered a series of strokes over the past few years, one of which cost him the sight in his right eye.

NOTHING IN ROBARTS'S POLITICAL LIFE dimmed his passion for what he had learned at his father's side—hunting and fishing. Opportunities, however, were obviously difficult to find. Robarts would occasionally go to great lengths to pursue his passions, regardless of the agenda at hand. For example, the prime minister of Ontario liked nothing more, while touring northern communities, than to command his pilot to land in the middle of some lake for an impromptu bit of fishing. If one thing upset him more than anything, it was having the solitude of those moments interrupted by a call from Queen's Park or the Ontario Provincial Police, indicating someone in downtown Toronto needed him back sooner than planned.

Don Matthews was one of Robarts's favourite fishing buddies. The two men met in 1950, during Robarts's run for London City Council, his first political office. Matthews was working for the city of London's engineering department, and one day he brought a proposal before council. Matthews thought his presentation of the proposal had gone rather well. But when it came time to count the votes, only the mayor and Robarts supported it. The idea died, but Matthews's friendship with Robarts bloomed.

After Robarts became prime minister, he invited Matthews to join him at a ceremony opening a new bridge. As the two men drove in their suits and ties down Number 3 Highway near St. Thomas, Robarts suddenly instructed his driver to pull over. "We're going to go fishing," the prime minister announced, apparently unconcerned about his pending ceremonial duties.

Matthews was a bit stunned. Neither man was dressed for fishing. Nor had Matthews brought along his fishing pole. But within minutes, the two men were changing out of their suits and getting into a couple of pairs of coveralls that Robarts had hidden in his car along with two fishing poles.

"We fished for an hour," Matthews says, laughing. "He had it all figured out."

The people of Moosonee, perhaps the most isolated outpost in all of Ontario, located about twenty kilometres from James Bay, can thank Robarts's love of fishing for some of the largesse they received from the government. The majority of Ontario premiers have never visited Moosonee. Robarts went twice, and, truth be told, his trips probably had as much to do with some nearby lakes that were superb for fishing as with his wanting to help the desperately poor native community there. Moosonee was the only native enclave in Ontario that was not under federal jurisdiction, and Robarts felt it was his responsibility to improve living conditions there. He poured money into the community for roads and health care.

One time, there was a ceremony at the local church, the only hall in the town, to announce a provincial program. Robarts was urged to attend to help legitimize the event, which he did. The ceremony was ten minutes long, and he spent much of it checking his watch because he wanted to catch a plane ride to a nearby lake and go fishing. Remarkably, he did not speak at the ceremony. But shortly afterwards, he did fish.

Up to this point in its history, Ontario did not have an official flag. After Lester Pearson's government retired the red ensign in favour of the red maple leaf flag in February 1965, Robarts made his move. He took the red ensign, stuck the Ontario coat of arms on it in place of the Canadian one, and voilà. On April 14, 1965, Ontario had an official flag.

The premier defended the move, particularly the inclusion of the Union Jack, which the Canadian government had just rejected. "The Union Jack in the flag does not give it any colonial aspect," Robarts told MPPs on second reading of the bill to create the new flag. "It covers the history of our province. I recognize and feel, from the bottom of my heart, that what we propose today will be a unifying step for the people of this province."

Later, in a private moment, Darcy McKeough asked the premier, "Is this just stirring up the flag debate again?"

"No," Robarts assured him. "We don't have a flag. We should have a flag. And besides, Darcy, it's damn good politics!"

It was during cabinet meetings that Robarts's vaunted reputation as the Chairman of the Board really shone. "He always listened to everybody at cabinet," says Rendall Dick, a former deputy minister. "He had his agenda. But he was casual. Not an emperor king."

Well, perhaps not always. One day, Robarts arrived late for cabinet and asked the chairman in his absence, York West MPP Henry "Les" Rowntree, what was being debated.

"We're discussing Green Stamps, sir," said Rowntree. "We can't decide what we're going to do about them." Retailers used to buy S & H Green Stamps and give them to their customers. The more purchases you made, the more stamps you got, eventually redeemable for household goods. In the days long before Club Z points, the NDP leader, Donald MacDonald, didn't like the Green Stamps program. He feared low-income people were being lured into spending beyond their means, and he wanted Green Stamps eliminated.

"Well, I'll tell you what we're going to do," Robarts said. "We're going to do nothing."

Darcy McKeough remembers what came next. "There was a great, stunning silence in the room," he recalls. "And finally someone said, 'Why?' And he said, 'Norah likes Green Stamps.'" End of discussion. "And the funny thing was," McKeough concludes, "we did nothing about Green Stamps, and Donald MacDonald ranted and raved but the whole issue disappeared."

Yes, he was a conservative, but Robarts also saw himself as a modern man. Go into a restaurant in Ontario at this time and patrons were not permitted to have alcohol with their dinner. Robarts changed that.

How he reformed the alcohol-availability situation in Ontario is a story in itself. One year at the opening of the Stratford Shakespearean Festival, the prime minister found himself playing host to HRH Prince Philip, the Duke of Edinburgh. Robarts knew two things. He knew the Conservative party's support base in rural Ontario shuddered at the thought of liberalizing the province's alcohol laws. He also knew that the prince would almost certainly want a drink at whatever event he was attending.

Stratford provided Robarts with an opportunity for action. When Philip asked Robarts for an alcoholic beverage at the festival's opening, the prime minister sheepishly had to admit he could not offer His Royal Highness one because serving alcohol at public events was illegal. "What kind of place is this where you can't get a drink?" Prince Philip asked. It was exactly what Robarts wanted to hear. He used the prince's comments as ammunition against those who opposed opening up the system, and before long, Robarts made it happen.

As government became bigger and more involved in the lives of Ontarians, people expected more from their politicians. But MPPs frequently complained about the lack of resources to do the job properly. Many members would have to share one secretary or office space. Seeing constituents at the legislature was tough. Money flowed freely for public projects, but the notion that politicians needed bigger budgets to do their jobs better hadn't yet reached the prime minister's office. That changed under Robarts.

"John White rented a room in the YMCA for all the London ridings," remembers the Hamilton Mountain MPP John Smith. "Every Saturday afternoon, people would come to see him. They'd wait in the hallway to go in. It was the beginning of the concept of constituency offices. We'd never had them before that."

White got the idea from Bob Macaulay, who, before getting into politics, would open his law office one day a week and serve those who could not afford to hire a lawyer. White even paid for the "clinic" out of his own pocket. Given Robarts's province-wide responsibilities, White found himself taking care of not only his own constituents but also those in adjacent London North, Robarts's riding. Smart alecks of the day called White "Robarts's messenger boy," but the insult seemed to roll off him.

"Robarts certainly took the Ontario government out of the pre-war stance, and he modernized it," says Dick Dillon. Dillon was perhaps Robarts's friendship of longest standing. The two met as students at the University of Western Ontario in 1938. Both went off to war (Dillon has been nicknamed "The Boy Colonel" his whole life), returned to London, and stayed close friends throughout Robarts's premiership. One day, Dillon's name came up during a cabinet meeting. He was in line for an appointment as executive director of Task Force Hydro, but his name wasn't ringing any bells with Les Rowntree, the minister of financial and commercial affairs from York West. "Who is this Richard M. Dillon?" Rowntree asked rather imperiously of no one in particular.

"I'll tell you about Richard M. Dillon," answered Robarts. "Richard M. Dillon is the dean of the engineering school at the University of Western Ontario in *London*. He's a former warden of Bishop Cronyn Memorial Anglican Church in *London*. He's the former president of the *London* Club in London, and former president of the *London* Progressive Conservative Association." The room went quiet. "Now, Mr. Rowntree," the prime minister concluded, "is there anything else you'd like to know about Richard M. Dillon?" There was not. Apparently, Rowntree's inquiry had been answered satisfactorily.

Despite the fact that the government was growing by leaps and bounds, Robarts instituted some very personal touches in the way he ran his office. "He signed every letter that went out," says Bill Rathbun. "There was no 'auto-pen.' He looked through invitations personally and decided which ones to take. He'd say, 'Surely people can't expect I'll return every letter personally, but they can expect a signature.' Every one was a bold signature, not scrawly. He used a big fat fountain pen that must have held a quart of ink. And he always signed John P. Robarts. He felt that obligation to people."

For a man with a relatively conservative, middle-class upbringing, surrounded almost exclusively by the ambitious, testosterone-oozing boys' club that was Queen's Park in those days, Robarts often demonstrated remarkable tolerance. "I remember a discussion once, and I have no idea who it was about," says Darcy McKeough. "Somebody said, 'Well, he's a queer,' which is a word you'd never hear today. And Robarts paused for a minute and said, 'I've never had a problem with that.' And we moved on. That was a very tolerant thing to say."

The Liberals spent the 1960s going through a succession of leaders, looking for a worthy challenger. In September 1964 Andy Thompson claimed the leadership over Charles Templeton. At this point in Thompson's political life, he was a brilliant young orator and not the embarrassment he later became when he was appointed to the Senate (his attendance record was pitiful, and it later emerged that he spent most of his time sunning in Mexico). But Thompson's health took a turn for the worse. Only two years into his tenure as leader, he resigned.

On January 6, 1967, Liberals selected a thirty-six-year-old farmer and science teacher whose main claim to fame was a father who had once been premier. The next time John Robarts would send Ontarians to the polls, he would be challenged by Bob Nixon, the man who wanted Robarts to take the words *prime minister* off the door of his office. In ten months, Nixon would find out just how tough that would be to do.

5

THE PRIVATE MAN

THE 1960S MAY BE REMEMBERED today as a wild decade, with anti-war demonstrations, political assassinations, tie-dyed shirts, and widespread experimentation with drugs. But the Age of Aquarius did not make much of a dent on life in London, Ontario, particularly on the upper middle class, which the Robarts family was part of. As a community, the London of the 1960s was very inward-looking and conservative. Women stayed home, looked after their children, and tended not to have careers. Men went to work, and if they were members of high society, they attended black tie dinners and stags. "And the men got away with it," says Willie Jackson, Ernie Jackson's second wife, laughing. In the wider world, Woodstock had not happened yet. The war in Vietnam was still years from dooming Lyndon Johnson's presidency. And, of course, when John Robarts won re-election in 1963, Watergate was still a decade away.

When he was at home, Robarts's family life was quite possibly unlike anyone else's in the city. Whenever Andrea Robarts would go over to visit her first cousin Robin, she was always struck by how often the phone rang, and the feeling of importance that permeated the home. "I remember thinking, God, I'm glad I don't live in this house, and I'm glad my father doesn't do what this man does," Andrea recalls. "It was really odd to be in a family that enshrined one person and elevated him to superhero status."

But if there was one place on earth where Norah, John, Robin, and Tim Robarts were able to be as close to a normal family as is possible, it was at the family cottage in Grand Bend.

Grand Bend calls itself the Sun Fun Capital of Ontario, and not without merit. Situated on Lake Huron, about forty-five minutes north of London, the town boasts gorgeous beaches and spectacular sunsets. It also became the unofficial headquarters for most of the London politicos who made John Robarts prime minister of Ontario.

In 1919 a furniture factory owner from Wingham built a golf club, inn, and dining room in Grand Bend and called it Oakwood Park. It was homey and rustic, and people came from all over to buy a lot and build a cottage. Ernie Jackson's family had a place there. One hundred yards down the road was Richard Dillon's gang. Then John Cronyn's family. Then Don and Joan Smith, who, despite being big players in the Ontario Liberal Party, were admitted to the Robartses' social circles there. Two doors down from the Smiths were Nancy and Bill Poole. In spite of all of that, Norah Robarts and her kids loved going there. At first, the Robartses rented a cottage belonging to John Cronyn's parents. But after he became prime minister, Robarts decided he wanted his own place. Cronyn's mother had bad arthritis, and the conditions in Grand Bend were too damp, so the Cronyns sold the place. Col. Doug Weldon, a Tory back-room organizer and fundraiser, put together a group of friends to help finance the purchase. And the Robartses rechristened their new getaway Oakhaven. The bulbs that John

Cronyn's father planted decades ago are still growing in the garden at Oakhaven.

In 1955 the London rainmakers and their families gathered to open Ernie Jackson's cottage and started what became a wonderful tradition—the annual get-together at the Jacksons'. Once, as many as thirty-two people showed up. The tradition has continued for more than fifty years.

Oakwood Park, the cottage complex, was a different world. There were no reporters or photographers. Interference from Robarts's political life was kept to a minimum. And it was the one public place where the prime minister did not have to act like the prime minister. Even though many of his friends took to the links and played golf there, Robarts declined to join them. "I spend all week in a highly competitive environment," he once said. "Why should I compete on the weekends too?"

When the weather was warm, the Robartses could be found at Oakhaven every weekend. And true to form, there was a party every Saturday night and a brunch every Sunday morning.

"We were so secure there because the Ontario Provincial Police prowled there all the time," says Nancy Poole. "You knew nothing untoward would happen."

"We'd have all-night parties in the backyard," recalls John Cronyn. "Right on the lake, surrounded by 150-year-old white pines. And we watched the best sunsets in the world." Norah Robarts loved playing charades in the Cronyns' living room, whose vast sliding glass doors afforded a magnificent view of the water. What the crowd loved the most was the atmosphere, which allowed John Robarts to be the fun-loving guy they all knew rather than the constantly on-duty politician he had by necessity become in Toronto or London.

From time to time, freighters would dump oil in Lake Huron. It would wash up on the beach, angering the Oakwood Park Cottagers' Association, whose meetings Robarts dutifully attended. "Old biddies would say, 'Mr. Premier, the oil is on the beach, and it gets on our feet. What are you going to do about it?'" recalls Don Smith. "And he'd say, 'I get kerosene or coal oil, and it gets rid of the oil pretty well.' His answer was so good because he would separate being premier from being a cottage-goer."

"He used to invite our kids over all the time," recalls Bev Shrives, who used to be next-door neighbours with the Robartses at the previous cottage the prime minister's family rented. "He'd say, 'Bev, our peanut butter is just as good as yours.'"

"The job didn't change him," marvels John Cronyn. "He kept the common touch with everyone. On one New Year's Eve, he was leaning back in his chair as if he were the chairman of the board. Then he fell over backwards. He said, 'That'll teach me to feel so important.'"

On another New Year's Eve during Robarts's premiership, Don Smith arrived at his cottage late and noticed the prime minister's car was there but nobody else was. Smith suggested his wife, Joan, call Robarts to see if he wanted to come over for dinner. "You don't call the premier and ask if he wants to come for dinner at 7 p.m.," Joan Smith told her husband.

"I do," came Don Smith's response. "I called. 'Sure,' John said, 'I'll be right over.' He brought a bottle of rye. He chatted with all our kids about politics."

"He was just totally unpretentious," adds Joan Smith.

By all accounts, John Robarts loved being a father, even though he was very much a part-time one. Still, for a man who lived away from his children for most of the week, he was as involved as he could be, often by telephone. One story indicative of his strong desire to be a good parent starts in Switzerland, from where Robin once called home, complaining of homesickness. The call came at a time when Robarts was stranded in a snowstorm between Toronto and London and had to stay overnight in a gas station, somewhere on Highway 401. "Apparently someone got my message to him," says Robin. "He asked to go directly to the airport, and he flew to Switzerland to make sure I was okay. I didn't know he was coming. But it was great. It was great to see him."

Robarts and his best friend, Ernie Jackson, may not have been the most dutiful family men, living apart from their families as much as they did. But they tried to make up in quality what they obviously lacked in quantity. For Barbara Prevedello's eleventh birthday, Ernie, her father, brought her to Toronto for a private tour of Queen's Park. They went onto the floor of the legislature, and Jackson showed his daughter where the prime minister of Ontario sat. They also saw Jackson's picture on the wall, along with all the other elected members of the twenty-fourth Parliament. Then it was off to the then fashionable Westbury Hotel for lunch. Many years later, Barbara Prevedello tells the story with pride.

For her seventeenth birthday, when Prevedello was boarding at Bishop Strachan School in Toronto, Jackson again came up with a memorable plan. He took his daughter and the prime minister of Ontario to dinner at the Westbury, followed by a National Hockey League game at Maple Leaf Gardens, just a block away from the hotel. Bob Pulford was her favourite Maple Leaf, and she watched his every move. Prevedello remembers it was a playoff game in April, and the federal opposition leader, John Diefenbaker, sat two rows in front of her. "Talk about feeling important!" she says, recalling how the two most influential elected Conservative politicians in the country (and the most notable back-room boy, her father) sat so close to her.

Robarts and Jackson were also members of the last-minute club when it came to buying Christmas presents for their wives. It was standard operating procedure every year on December 24 for the two men to enjoy a lengthy lunch at the London Club, then roll into Nash Jewellers around 5 p.m., rather well lubricated. They would keep the staff there long after regular closing hours, wrapping gifts for their wives. After a few years of that, the jewellery store stopped offering gift-wrapping services.

Even though he loved being prime minister of Ontario, Robarts had to acknowledge it was a hard job that took its intellectual and emotional toll. All the more reason why he loved going to Oakhaven, or getting out in the middle of the water in a boat with friends. "John didn't know a damn thing about sailing boats," says Dick Dillon, who frequently went sailing with Robarts. "He loved to sit there and steer the boat, but he never could pay much attention to where we were. He didn't give a damn about that, really."

There are numerous stories attesting to Robarts's love of—and lack of skill in—a boat. "One time," Dillon continues, "we were in Goderich harbour. And the wind came up. And I told him, 'John, you've gotta be careful here. You're heading straight for the pier.' I had to put my foot out at the last second and push the bow off just in time. Then the guy on the pier said, 'Jesus Christ, that's the prime minister of Ontario!'"

Another time, Robarts ran aground on a sandbar. Fortunately, the mayor of London was nearby and pulled the boat off the reef. Then everyone retired back to Oakhaven for a corn roast. "But he wasn't embarrassed," Dillon says. "Nothing like that ever bothered him."

Ernie Jackson's son George recalls once being with the prime minister on Transportation Minister James Auld's boat, the *Island Clipper*. Auld wanted to make holding tanks mandatory on boats so yachtsmen could not dump raw human waste into the water. "Another boater came over and we offered him a Scotch," says George Jackson. "Then he started angrily saying, 'I can't believe this fucking minister of transportation wants us to stop dumping raw sewage into canals.' Ernie stood up and said, 'I'd like to introduce you to the minister of transportation. And here's the prime minister.' And the guy *still* stayed for a drink!"

Stories about the prime minister's fun-loving side are legendary. Once while at Robarts's cottage in Grand Bend, he and Richard Dillon, by then dean of the engineering school at the University of

Western Ontario, discovered some UWO students carousing at the cottage next door. Dillon got the bright idea to "inspect" what was happening. He entered one of the other cottage's bedrooms and found a young couple doing something not quite consistent with academia. "Oh my God, it's the dean of engineering!" one of the students said, prompting somewhat of an exodus by the other partygoers. They dashed out of the cottage, only to see Robarts waiting for them on the street. He was brandishing a fancy old cane, out of which he pulled a sword. He thrust it forward, à la D'Artagnan, only to hear, "Oh, my God, it's the prime minister of Ontario!"

As much as members of the Robarts family prized their time in Grand Bend, the reality was that John Robarts was away most of the time. While Robin says her father's absences did not disturb her, they certainly had a greater impact on her more emotionally sensitive younger brother. And the distance between London and Toronto became toxic to Norah. "One of the things I felt sorry about is his wife didn't like Toronto," says Rendall Dick, the former deputy minister in the Ontario public service. "He had a suite at the Westbury Hotel and it was hard on him. Norah wasn't interested in government at all."

"Norah felt that she had to keep her young children in London, where they were brought up," offers Dick Dillon. "And she would not do as the majority of members of the house did and that was come and join him in Toronto."

Even William Davis, who possessed a remarkable ability to be oblivious (and sweetly naive) about the finer points of his colleagues' private lives, remembers it this way: "I was, and am, still fond of John and our relationship," Davis says. "Back then, I said to a mutual friend of ours one day that I wished Norah were in Toronto." Ironically, being the wife of the prime minister of Ontario afforded Norah Robarts an entrée into society circles she otherwise would not have got near. And yet, rather than immersing herself in her husband's career as so many political wives have done over the years (particularly in those days), Norah even went so far as to ridicule the circumstances in which she would often find herself. "I sat beside her at several dinners," recalls Hugh Hanson, who worked in Robarts's office during his second term. "She was vulgar in the nicest way. Positively irreverent. Clearly she didn't enjoy that life. It was obvious because she didn't participate in it."

"Norah was highly intelligent," insists Nancy Poole. "But she wasn't always the most tactful. She was very blunt. She was deadly with her tongue." Poole remembers a time when Ontario's first couple was invited to open a new branch of a public library. "Norah said quite loudly, 'I find these things incredibly boring.' And John would smile. What else could he do?"

One thing was certain: more and more people could not help noticing that things were becoming increasingly difficult for Robarts on the home front. "I think on occasion he remarked on my good fortune at having a family life that could support a politician, and he didn't have any," recalls Robert Nixon, Robarts's Liberal opponent and the father of four. "My own observation was that his wife seemed to resent him somehow. I didn't know her well, but on rather formal occasions when Dorothy [Nixon's wife] and I would be with them, she was dangerously critical of him. Unnecessarily critical."

Eric Dowd, the veteran journalist, covered the Robarts years at the Ontario Legislature and is still on the job at Queen's Park. Like Nixon, he remembers an encounter with the prime minister, who marvelled at Dowd's home life. "How is your lovely wife and those five lovely children?" Robarts once asked Dowd in the corridors at Queen's Park.

"Fine, Mr. Robarts, but how do you know about my family?" Dowd asked.

"Don't you remember?" Robarts replied. "When we returned from the retreat up north, they were all waiting for you at Union Station. That was a really charming sight."

Almost four decades after the conversation, Dowd still recalls the sadness in Robarts's voice. "It struck me afterwards," Dowd tells me, "that here he was, the second most powerful man in the country, and he had some wistful envy of a young unimportant reporter who had an obviously warm family life. It was well known that his own marriage wasn't warm and loving."

"It's hard to be the wife of the premier, so I don't condemn Norah," says Willie Jackson.

But Ernie Jackson's daughter, Barbara Prevedello, is more critical. She saw her mother, Barbara, Ernie Jackson's first wife, demonstrate the same disdain for politics that Norah displayed. "Dad must have asked Mom a hundred times to move to Toronto," Prevedello says of her parents. "She wouldn't. The men were out there doing their thing, moving on, living the fast life, and meeting new people. The women wanted their staid, boring lives in London. It was stupid of them not to move to Toronto. They had little kids, and it would have been a big move, but lots of people do it."

J. Keith Reynolds, who was Robarts's secretary to the cabinet, put it even more contemptuously: "Norah was loath to give up her twice-weekly bridge games."

(Interestingly, Nancy Poole says of John Cronyn's wife, Barbara, "She was everything the other two wives weren't. She moved to Toronto for John," unlike Norah Robarts and Barbara Jackson. By all accounts, the Cronyns had a wonderfully close marriage until her death a few years ago from leukemia.)

But not everyone saw it that way. Bea Hamilton, who at the time was married to London South MPP John White, supported Norah's decision. "I thought she was right and the criticism was wrong," Hamilton says. "If she wanted to stay in London, that should have been fine. She fundamentally couldn't and didn't want to uproot herself. I didn't think it was selfish."

"Norah was pretty stiff," says Andrea Robarts, her niece. "When she was around, a blanket was tossed over a type of fun that existed when she was not there."

In some respects, although no one would ever discuss it at the time, there was another constant presence in John Robarts's life and in his marriage. The influence of this other force was hard to gauge, but it was omnipresent: alcohol. "When John became premier, he lived a rather different life in Toronto," says Nancy Poole. "Alcohol became a major part of his life." Norah's too.

"My first wife and I spent a couple of weekends at Grand Bend, and hunting and fishing at Griffiths Island," recalls Fraser Elliott, whose law firm Stikeman Elliott would hire Robarts after his political career was over. "Their lifestyle was a little tougher than mine. They had a drink every morning. It didn't show, but he was a hard drinker. I couldn't begin to keep up with him."

"Ernie and John could drink anyone under the table," says Willie Jackson. "I was concerned his liver would give out."

"I've been associated with some pretty tough navy guys," says Al Hurley, Robarts's friend from their days playing football for the University of Western Ontario Mustangs. "But I've never seen anyone handle his Scotch like John Robarts. He'd just keep putting 'em back."

What set Robarts apart from virtually everyone else he knew was his ability to consume vast amounts of booze without it ever affecting his ability to do his job.

"There's no question there are stories about his capacity to go out and carouse at night, and probably bury everybody else in the room," says Gordon Walker, who replaced Robarts as the Progressive Conservative member for London North in 1975. "And the next morning, he'd be at his desk at eight as if nothing had happened the night before. And he'd only been home for a couple of hours' sleep."

"I think John did relax and enjoyed himself, but it never inter-fered with his work," confirms Bill Davis. "Certainly I never had any difficulty with his approach to his personal life in terms of my responsibilities or my functioning within government."

Ernie Jackson was the same way. "He said, 'Never have too much to drink that you couldn't go to work the next day," Barbara Prevedello remembers his telling her. "And he never did."

Ian Macdonald, future chief economist for Ontario, attended numerous federal-provincial conferences with Robarts. Frequently discussions would persist into the wee small hours of the morning. "I was often amazed," Macdonald says with a smile. "I'd come to the meeting the next day feeling bedraggled and weary, and there he'd be, polished and shining and himself as always."

"Everyone in government was terrified they'd be invited to a party at his place and have to drink all night long with him," adds Dick Dillon.

Robarts was also an inveterate "borrower" of booze, particularly at the family cottage at Grand Bend. "Up at the lake, he'd bum booze," says Nancy Poole. "He'd come with Tim and say, 'You don't happen to have an extra bottle of Scotch?' Well, you don't say no, but you knew you'd never see it again." But, she insists, "I never saw John as an angry drunk, or drunk, period. These chaps who came back from the war were very heavy drinkers. But they never appeared drunk. During the boredom of war, they drank to keep their sanity."

Prime Minister John Robarts was never much of a fan of the opposition leader Robert Nixon. Nixon constantly chided him for keeping the prime minister appellation, rather than changing the title to premier, considered a little more populist and less pretentious. In fact, it was Nixon's father, Harry, prime minister of Ontario for a few months in 1943, whom Robarts really did not care for. But the sins of the father appear to have been visited on the son. But (and just to demonstrate how different politics was forty years ago) Robarts did invite Robert Nixon up to his suite at the Royal York Hotel for a drink, after the conclusion of a formal dinner.

"Well, both of us had had a couple of cocktails before that," Nixon remembers. "And I can remember having a little difficulty leaving the suite, on my hands and knees."

Fraser Kelly, the former journalist with *The Toronto Telegram,* CFTO-TV, and CBC-TV, once took Robarts to the annual press gallery dinner in Ottawa. After the festivities on Parliament Hill ended, Kelly took the prime minister to the *Telegram*'s hospitality suite at the Château Laurier Hotel. The place was teeming with other journalists, politicians, and businessmen. By three o'clock in the morning, Robarts was still feeling no pain, enjoying a drink with Kelly and Ian Sinclair, then president of Canadian Pacific. At one point in the conversation, Robarts put his hand on Kelly's shoulder. "I know why we're here," he told Kelly. "This is an endurance contest. So, Fraser, there's only one thing to do. Let's win it!"

Andrea Robarts recalls being at several all-night parties at her home, watching her uncle demonstrate a remarkable capacity for imbibing, and remembering every detail the next day. One evening, she had a rather intense conversation with him, amid considerable partying and drinking. When Andrea woke up at seven o'clock the next morning, Uncle John was still there, having pulled an all-nighter. She remarked to her father that he no doubt would not remember any of their important conversation of the previous evening. Her father challenged her assertion. "Go ask him and see," Bob Robarts told his daughter. "I bet you're wrong."

"Sure enough, to my great surprise, John was very clear in all the details of our conversation the night before," Andrea remembers with amazement.

On another occasion, Robarts led a group of men on a trout fishing expedition at Echo Beach, near Ottawa. The governor general of the day, Roland Michener, was there. Everyone called him Roly. At breakfast one morning, John Cronyn offered Michener some champagne and orange juice, which he declined. "Then, in bounces Robarts," Cronyn says. "You'd think he'd had twelve hours of sleep."

"Where's the champagne?" Robarts asked no one in particular. "Roly, will you have a champagne and orange juice?"

"Yes, absolutely," Michener says. "Let's pour one for everyone else too."

The moral of the story: "It taught me the difference between being Robarts and being me," Cronyn says, laughing.

In Toronto, Robarts loved to bar-hop, and he became more sociable with strangers while knocking back the booze. "John and I were coming back late one night to the Westbury Hotel, so we went to a bar for a nightcap," recalls John Cronyn. "John would see someone and stick out his hand and say, 'I'm John Robarts.' One time, the other guy (a tad incredulous) said, 'So am I.' And John just put his face in his hands. It was the only time I've seen him stuck for a response."

"He was, in many ways, a lonely guy," says Alan Eagleson, a one-term Tory MPP from 1963 to 1967. "But he was so gregarious. His driver used to take him from bar to bar some nights."

While John Robarts could handle his hard liquor, it quickly became apparent that his wife could not. "My dear Norah liked her Scotch," admits Nancy Poole sadly. "Once at a dinner party at the lake, she was in great form. Rather obnoxious. He dragged her home. The demon rum interrupted their lives," Poole continues. "That whole group drank pretty hard. I, as an observer, was never terribly comfortable with this part of it. But by the end of it, I thought Norah was becoming an alcoholic. He and Norah verbally sparred. Alcohol played a large part in that. And she didn't bite her tongue."

"He wasn't an alcoholic," insists Don Smith. "I never ever saw him high. However, Norah was in that atmosphere and subject to becoming it."

Many people in London noticed that Norah was starting to decline. "It was after Tim's arrival that Norah began her downhill slide," says her niece Judith Grieve. "After she refused a move to Toronto, Robin was sent to school there. But Tim, alone with his mother, bore the brunt of her alcoholism."

And things between Norah and John began to deteriorate significantly. "John took Norah and the kids to Tokyo," says Eleanor Robarts, his sister-in-law. "John gave Norah an opal bracelet. She tossed it aside. He hands her a parcel, she unwraps it, and never says a darn thing." It was not unusual for Robarts to return to London after a week in Toronto bearing gifts, in hopes of patching things up with his wife.

But the combination of significant amounts of booze and endless nights away from his family had a predictable effect on Robarts and his marital vows. "It was like John Kennedy," says Willie Jackson. "He was a man's man. The reporters were all men. They all looked the other way. He and Ernie both crossed the line."

There is a well-known picture of Robarts during festivities surrounding the Grey Cup, Canada's annual football championship. The prime minister is in the middle of a conga line, behind Miss Toronto Argonaut, with his hands on her waist, clearly shimmying his hips. Two things come to mind. We almost certainly know what Robarts was thinking at that moment. We also know no politician today would dare be photographed so provocatively with a scantily clad woman half his age. "There was never anything untoward that came to public attention," says Bob Nixon of Robarts's wandering eye. However, Nixon adds this obvious caveat: "Mind you, you purveyors of public attention were a lot more circumspect then."

"The man knew what he was doing," says Richard Rohmer. "And in those days, the media were still protective of a person of his stature. So there wasn't the real need *not* to party, *not* have a good time, *not* be seen. So that's the way it went. But he knew he was on thin ice, and he was a big man skating on thin ice."

Today, Robarts's London friends insist they had no knowledge of his extracurricular exploits—with one significant exception. "Norah knew he was promiscuous in Toronto," says Nancy Poole.

Later in her life, Robin Robarts no doubt knew about her father's dalliances and came to understand and accept them. One day in the summer of 2001, she came to the TVOntario studios in midtown Toronto to examine some old video clips of her father that were stored in the TVO archives. The screening was a revelation to Robin, who was in her forties at the time. "It was the first time I've ever been able to look at my dad objectively, and I can certainly understand why the women went crazy," she acknowledges. "I mean, he'd have given Rock Hudson or Clark Gable a run for their money if he'd have been on the big screen."

In the fall of 2003, the NBC news anchorman Tom Brokaw appeared on *The Late Show* with David Letterman to discuss the revelations about Arnold Schwarzenegger. "The Terminator" had just won the California governor's job, but all the media buzz focused on his history of inappropriate sexual behaviour. Brokaw pointed out that many political leaders had had dalliances before Clinton, but they weren't reported on. After their presidential terms were over, copious details emerged about sexual affairs conducted by Franklin Roosevelt, Dwight Eisenhower, and John Kennedy. Why weren't those affairs considered newsworthy at the time? Brokaw had an interesting thesis. He suggested, for example, that Americans were so pleased with how Roosevelt was handling the war that they wouldn't have wanted anything untoward to interfere.

The same might have been said about the prime minister of Ontario during the 1960s. It was a great time, in some respects a wild ride, particularly economically. And no one wanted to jeopardize it by publishing scandalous information that could destroy the prime minister.

David Peterson sums it up this way: "John Robarts couldn't live today as premier of the province as he did in the 1960s," he says. "But that's not to diminish his premiership because it was a stunning achievement and he was a very fine man."

6

THE DEFEATS

JOHN ROBARTS ENJOYED so many successes during his premiership that it's possible to forget two enormously controversial issues, one of which threatened to consume his newly elected government.

A year after Robarts became premier, Mr. Justice Wilfred Roach reported his royal commission findings on the state of organized crime in Ontario. His conclusion—that there was no organized crime, as in the Mafia or Cosa Nostra—appeared to defuse the issue. But only for a while. The Liberal leader, John Wintermeyer, focused on the subject with such intensity during the 1963 election campaign that Robarts felt he had to act soon after securing his own mandate to govern. So, in the first session after that '63 election, Robarts's attorney general, Fred Cass, introduced one of the most controversial bills in the history of any democracy anywhere in the world. But the story did not start that way.

Robarts continued a tradition started by George Drew and Leslie Frost of having cabinet ministers brief the caucus when a bill was about to be introduced. Cass came to caucus and unveiled a proposed law, Bill 99, Amendments to the Police Act. He assured the caucus that the bill was simply a housekeeping measure dealing with police procedures. In those days, bills were never printed before first reading, so MPPs essentially took the minister's word for what was in them. In this case, Cass's description did not begin to tell the real story of what was in Bill 99. In the end, the attorney general would pay for his deception with his job.

Bill 99 proposed an all-out assault on organized crime. The most contentious part—Section 14—would give the Ontario Police Commission the authority to force anyone to give evidence in secret or be jailed indefinitely if he or she refused. Instantly, some questions arose, the most obvious being that if there was no organized crime, as the government insisted and even as a judge confirmed, why did the police need these vast powers? Other more disturbing facts began to emerge. The public learned that the police commission itself had essentially drafted the bill because it *was,* in fact, having difficulty fighting organized crime.

And then Attorney General Cass walked into a lion's den. Actually, a press conference, but in this case, same thing. Cass described the bill with these words: "It's drastic, and it's dangerous, and it's new, and it's terrible legislation in an English common law country." Incredibly, these were the words of a minister defending his own bill.

Allan Lawrence was a backbench Conservative MPP in the Robarts government. He first came to politics in a 1958 by-election in the downtown Toronto riding of St. George, where he lived and practised law at McLaughlin Macaulay May and Soward (the Macaulay referred to Leopold and later to Robert, his PC caucus colleague). Lawrence acknowledges, "I was a bit of a bitcher and a bellyacher" in the Conservative caucus. "There were pretty heavy Tory majorities, and the opposition was woefully weak," he says. "So I intended to be a thorn under the saddle of the government."

For that reason, Lawrence was never one of Robarts's favourite caucus members, but the prime minister accepted him well enough. However, Bill 99 would test their relationship as nothing before ever had. While Cass was making his outrageous remarks at the news conference, Lawrence was sitting in the back row of the government side on the floor of the legislative chamber. Suddenly, he heard a huge hubbub in the members' lobby behind him. The door to the chamber burst open, whereupon several reporters tried to get Lawrence's attention. "Al, Al, can you come out here?" they said.

Lawrence exited the house, then witnessed virtually every member of the Queen's Park press gallery yelling at one another, trying to understand what Cass's bill was all about. One of the reporters described the terms of the bill. "It can't be that," Lawrence said. "People picked up without charge, incarcerated, denied a lawyer on the mere suspicion of the police? I don't believe it," he told them. "If that's the case, I'd certainly be against it," Lawrence continued. "It would be terrible legislation."

"That's exactly what Fred Cass said!" another journalist pointed out.

"Well, I'll be voting against it," Lawrence said. "I can't believe they'll try this."

All hell broke loose. Other Tory MPPs began to break ranks. Citizens' groups expressed their outrage. The NDP leader, Donald C. MacDonald, proposed a motion calling for the deletion of Section 14. Astonishingly, the motion was unanimously approved. Robarts felt humiliated.

"The thing just kept going instead of dying down, as Robarts hoped would happen," recalls Allan Lawrence. "It kept gathering steam. I still do not understand why Robarts did not immediately step in and can it." Lawrence recognized the intent behind the bill. He knew the police were frustrated at the size and scope of organized crime, which, despite protestations to the contrary, did exist in Ontario. "But how that bill got through the safeguards of government and the attorney general's department, I do not know," he says. Lawrence says he later learned from two cabinet ministers that there was precious little discussion in cabinet either. He is also convinced Robarts did not know what was in the bill to begin with.

A.R. (Rendall) Dick was the deputy attorney general at the time, having just been shuffled to that department before Bill 99 was introduced. Ironically, when Dick got the job, he'd had a private meeting with Robarts, who gave him an important piece of advice. "Rendall, we have our little problems from time to time. When you hear of one, the first person you tell is *me!*" Robarts barked. Dick did not have to follow that order this time. The news got to the prime minister's office fast enough. When Cass made his statement, Dick in truth still had not even read the bill. He was working on Ontario's first consumer protection bill, and joined Fred Cass at the press conference, he assumed to help answer questions about that.

"It was a fiasco," Dick recalls. "It blew up like a cannon. It was idiotic. The chairman of the police commission wasn't there. If someone knew about the bill, they could have stopped Fred and saved it. I was named as the drafter, but I wasn't. But I guess if you run with dogs, you get fleas."

Alan Eagleson was another Tory backbench lawyer who had major problems with Bill 99. The government's official position was that Bill 99 was conferring on the police commission the same powers as those given to every justice of the peace in the province and nothing more. But few saw it that way, including Eagleson. The attack on fundamental civil rights was something no lawyer could accept. Still, Eagleson liked Fred Cass and wanted to do right by him. "Fred Cass was very good to me," Eagleson says. "Some cabinet ministers were pricks, but he was a wonderful guy. Still, I told him, 'Fred, you can't do this.'"

Robarts heard about Eagleson's chat with Cass. Next thing you knew, the Eagle was called to Robarts's office. Robarts got to the point.

"We've got a problem we've got to solve," he told Eagleson. "This is *our* problem, not Fred's problem. We're not going to destroy Fred." Robarts was doing his best to save his attorney general, but the effort was falling on deaf ears.

"We had a tough week in caucus," Eagleson recalls. "Guys were not talking to each other. Guys were beating the shit out of each other. And Robarts stuck right by Fred. I suspect he'd had Fred's resignation on his desk for a day or two. But he was fighting for Fred Cass. He stuck by him longer than he needed to."

Cass also had problems on the other side of the house. His temper tantrums, launched at the opposition members, engendered him no support at all. "He told us what tortured fools we were," remembers Stephen Lewis, then a rookie New Democrat MPP. "His behaviour was indefensible."

Allan Lawrence agrees. "The key to Bill 99 was the character of the attorney general himself," he says. "Fred Cass was an arrogant son of a gun." Lawrence recalls a story that was vintage Cass. At the beginning of every year, the government of the day would release a list with the names of the lawyers receiving the Queen's Counsel designation. In truth, the list had become a bit of a joke. It generally did not reflect length of service in the legal community, or any particular legal brilliance, but rather who was a friend of the government of the day. In mid-December, Cass telephoned the backbench MPP for St. George.

"Lawrence, you're going to be on the New Year's list," Cass informed him.

"Thank you, Mr. Attorney General," Lawrence replied, "but I'd just as soon not get my QC. It's a little too early in my legal career, and politically it'll do more harm than good. Senior lawyers in my constituency would feel affronted if I got it." Lawrence was not being overly modest. Bay Street, and all its well-connected, well-heeled lawyers, was in his riding.

"You misunderstand me," Cass shot back. "I'm not asking you. I'm telling you. I don't give a shit if you want to be on it or not. Let's see if you've got the guts to make a fuss after the list is out." And with that, the attorney general hung up. That was Fred Cass.

Soon after the controversy over Bill 99 broke, Robarts called Lawrence into his office for a chat. "Come on out into the hallway and walk around with me," the prime minister said. "I need some exercise and we can talk." Lawrence was no dummy. He knew Robarts wanted to be seen by the press gallery, in public, with one of his chief critics, discussing a possible resolution to the scandal. And Lawrence told the prime minister in no uncertain terms that the government had to withdraw or significantly amend the bill, or he would cross the floor and sit with the opposition.

Eventually, Robarts had no choice but to drop the offending bill, because as many Tories as Liberals and New Democrats opposed it.

"I remember the capitulation," says Stephen Lewis. "They scorned us, and then they caved. It was considered by us to be a great victory."

However, even as he killed Bill 99, Robarts defended it. He then accepted the resignation of Fred Cass as attorney general. "I wasn't at the meeting but I'm sure Fred, who was a fine man, resigned," says Rendall Dick. "John didn't fire him."

"Robarts showed a momentary lapse of political judgment," offers Stephen Lewis. "He should have seen the firestorm coming."

"I was absolutely flummoxed by his indecision," Allan Lawrence says of the prime minister. "Once the fat had hit the fan, he obviously didn't know what to do. He didn't want to admit the whole thing was wrong."

What came next has been described as the most significant long-term contribution the Robarts government made to the rights of citizens not just in Ontario but around the democratic world. Fred Cass was out. In his place, Robarts tapped a most unlikely successor. Arthur Wishart had made some money on the uranium

boom in his hometown of Sault Ste. Marie. He'd begun his professional career as a classics teacher in New Brunswick, and his seat in
the legislature—the very end of the very last row—didn't suggest to
anyone that he was a future influential player in government. But
that is precisely what he would become. On March 25, 1964, exactly
six months after his first election, Arthur Wishart became attorney
general of Ontario. The prime minister and his new minister had
met for the first time when Robarts chaired the Ontario Water
Resources Commission ten years earlier. Apparently, Wishart had
made a favourable impression.

The first order of business for Robarts and Wishart was to sweep
away the ashes of the police state bill and do something progressive to
give the public the impression the government was not as draconian as
Bill 99 suggested it was. Less than a year into his first mandate,
Robarts's political career and the survival of his government hung in
the balance. His next decision could profoundly affect his province
and his party for generations to come. Once again, the Chairman of
the Board would make a good decision.

When Robarts and Wishart met to consider their options, they
agreed on the same approach and the same man to lead the effort. The
approach: a far-reaching royal commission on civil rights. The man to
lead it: Ontario's chief justice, James Chalmers McRuer. McRuer was
considered the perfect candidate for the job. He was Ontario's top
jurist. He had an impeccable reputation. And for icing on the cake,
he had ties to the Liberals. No one could accuse Robarts of seeking
political cover by handing the job to a crony. "He was a pain in the
butt in court because he was such a stickler for details," Allan
Lawrence recalls. "So he was the perfect guy for the job."

Robarts and Wishart met the chief justice on his turf. They feared
what the optics of summoning the chief justice to Queen's Park might
look like. Robarts was so confident he could convince McRuer to take
the job that the order-in-council appointing the chief justice to head

a one-man royal commission was already signed and on the prime minister's desk. On May 1, 1964, James McRuer gave up the most important job in the Ontario judicial system to begin an ambitious legal adventure that would take almost a decade and eventually produce three reports of five volumes, consisting of 2,281 pages and 976 recommendations.

In essence, McRuer's job was to examine the laws of Ontario to see how they affected the personal freedoms, rights, and liberties of Canadian citizens and other residents in Ontario. He held numerous public hearings. According to Patrick Boyer, whose book *A Passion for Justice* (University of Toronto Press, 1994) chronicles this time, some witnesses were mentally deranged, others obsessed with personal grievances. Yet McRuer was respectful and patient. He also travelled extensively to do research. The United Kingdom, Sweden, Africa, Australia, and New Zealand were all on his itinerary.

McRuer recommended laws be written in meticulously precise terms. The state should exercise no arbitrary powers in any statute. Above all, he wanted to protect citizens from the arbitrary interference of the state. There were limits on search and seizure. The powers of arrest were strictly regulated. And in a new departure, McRuer thought victims of crime should be compensated.

As Patrick Boyer describes it, "Queen's Park couldn't suspend the license of a used car dealer, a mortgage broker, or a pest exterminator without a hearing." John Yaremko, the social and family services minister, said, "You can talk about Magna Carta and *habeas corpus*. But if a person running a restaurant or operating a taxi cab can't get the little slip of paper, the permit, or license from government on which his livelihood depends, then what value are these more celebrated freedoms?"

When McRuer's first report was tabled on March 5, 1968, it represented the most comprehensive study of civil rights ever made in Ontario. James Renwick, the brilliant NDP member from Toronto's

Riverdale riding, called it "a first-class beginning for protecting the average citizen against the executive power of government."

The Toronto Telegram called the recommendations a "welcome reaffirmation of the importance of the individual and a chart for government to follow in protecting and restoring his rights." *The Globe and Mail* opined, "What Mr. McRuer is attempting is the restoration of justice to the individual who has lost a lot of it to a complex and indifferent society." *The Toronto Daily Star* had this to say: "It is possible to say now that Mr. McRuer has done a great service to the people of Ontario. His report seems certain to lead to wider and more secure liberty than the individual enjoys today."

Throughout 1968 and 1969, McRuer and the government enjoyed widespread approval for the report, and the Tories' willingness to implement its recommendations. It generated interest across the country and around the world.

Actually, McRuer's work was so thorough that it outlasted John Robarts's time as prime minister. While Robarts introduced one bill providing new protections for individual rights, it was left to his successor, William Davis, to introduce most of the new legislation arising from McRuer's work. On April 15, 1971, after McRuer tabled his third and final report, Premier Davis said, "The people of Ontario owe Mr. McRuer a very large debt of gratitude, and I see this more and more as the years pass by." Two months later, the Davis government introduced four new bills, all based on the recommendations of McRuer's third report. "When these bills are brought into force," Davis said at the time, "they will bring to the people of Ontario a code of administrative law procedure that will be the first of its kind in the Commonwealth." Fittingly, the new attorney general who introduced these bills was none other than Allan Lawrence, the MPP who led a backbench revolt against Fred Cass's Bill 99. At the time, Lawrence called McRuer's reforms "among the most progressive in the world."

Back in the spring of 1963, the Robarts government had a mutiny on its hands. A draconian bill, brought in by a well-intentioned but imperious attorney general, almost brought the government to its knees. On April 29, 1970, every member of the Ontario legislature who was a lawyer, including John Robarts and Arthur Wishart, hosted a dinner in McRuer's honour. The former chief justice was given a silver tray bearing the engraved signatures of each of the twenty-three lawyer MPPs. The tray might have been silver, but it was a gold-medal finish, it seems, for all concerned.

A year after his retirement from politics, John Robarts was attending spring convocation at York University in Toronto. Someone approached him and asked him what he thought his greatest accomplishment as prime minister of Ontario had been. Robarts answered with just one word: "McRuer."

THE RUCKUS OVER BILL 99 was easily the worst self-inflicted political disaster of Robarts's premiership. But there was another battle royal, brought on by outside forces, that infuriated the prime minister as almost no other issue did. The war was between Robarts's Conservative government and the federal Liberal governments of Lester Pearson and Pierre Trudeau. And ironically, the dispute saw Robarts, a progressive politician, take a firm stand against a policy that has turned out to be one of the most popular, if expensive, social programs in Canadian history: medicare.

Today, public opinion polls tell us that medicare is more than just the most cherished social program in the country. Many people see it as a cornerstone of what it means to be Canadian—essentially, that no one should go without health care because of an inability to pay. And yet, in the latter half of the 1960s, as the federal Liberal government was in the process of developing universal health care, its staunchest opponent on the Canadian political firmament was the prime minister of Ontario. In fact, medicare came to Ontario a year after it was enacted in most other provinces because Robarts fundamentally opposed it until he simply could not any more. The policy disagreement developed into the worst Ottawa-Toronto relationship since the bad old days of William Lyon Mackenzie King and Mitchell Frederick Hepburn three decades earlier.

Why would a progressive politician such as John Robarts oppose a health insurance plan that covered every Canadian, with the federal government even offering to pay half the costs? To answer that, we have to consider what was already in place. Medicare wasn't Ontario's first health insurance plan. Once upon a time, there was something called PSI, Physician Services Inc. Ontarians had their own health care plan—funded by companies and individual subscribers—that covered 100 percent of medical services. It was considered the best plan in the country. (There were two other plans in southwestern Ontario, run by doctors.) But across Canada, service was uneven. Prime Minister John Diefenbaker appointed Mr. Justice Emmett Hall to study health care nationwide. By the time Hall reported back, Diefenbaker was gone, but his successor, Lester B. Pearson, signed on to Hall's recommendations of a national, universal medicare system, along the lines of what Premiers Tommy Douglas and Woodrow Lloyd had developed in Saskatchewan in the early 1960s. However, according to Canada's Constitution, health care is a provincial responsibility, and Robarts took that responsibility seriously. He didn't like the notion of the federal government messing around in his territory. So when he got wind of the fact that the Pearson government intended to bring in a national health insurance plan, Robarts was furious.

"He was against it because he thought that the government of Canada was usurping what in John's view was a fairly comprehensive program here in Ontario," says William Davis.

"It wasn't that he opposed everyone being covered," adds Darcy McKeough, a member of the Robarts cabinet at the time. "We already had virtually everyone covered, and those that weren't got looked after."

Robarts found an ally for his position in fellow Conservative premier Duff Roblin of Manitoba. Like Ontario, Manitoba already had its own health plan, covering everyone.

"I thought it was better than the federal scheme, and I still do," says Roblin. "But my voice didn't go very far. So I thought the best thing was to get behind someone big and push." That someone was the prime minister of Ontario. Robarts opposed the substance of what the federal government was proposing, and it didn't help that medicare's champion was Lester Pearson.

"He wasn't that fond of Pearson," recalls Darcy McKeough. "Partially because of the medicare hassle, but also because he said, 'You go to 24 Sussex for dinner and he only gives you one drink before dinner! That's not my kind of person.'"

But the tide was turning against Robarts. In the Ontario legislature, the future NDP leader Stephen Lewis introduced a private member's bill urging the government to adopt medicare. Robarts, of course, opposed the NDP measure. "He was friendly rather than excoriating," Lewis recalls of his debates with the prime minister across the floor of the legislature. "He took my comments seriously, despite the fact that I was an opposition member filled with pugnacity and ideological vindictiveness."

Doctors opposed medicare with a vengeance, fearing they were all about to become government bureaucrats rather than self-employed professionals. But the tide in favour was unstoppable, and in 1966 Parliament passed the legislation creating the program.

But as far as Robarts was concerned, the fight wasn't over. In fact, from a rhetorical point of view, it was just beginning. "On one occasion, we were chatting together at two or three o'clock in the morning at a federal-provincial conference," says William Davis with a smile. "His faculties were all there, trust me. But it was late. The next morning, we went into the conference. I was exhausted, but he looked completely refreshed. And he did suggest to Mr. Pearson that the proposal that is now medicare was the most Machiavellian scheme he had ever seen."

"This is the end of controlling the costs of health care in Canada," Robarts ominously told Ontario legislators. (Three and a half decades later, his prescience is all too apparent.)

However, the Robarts-Roblin entente didn't last. The fact was, the federal government was offering to pay half the costs associated with medicare, and if you didn't sign on to the federal program, you got no federal funding for health care at all.

"I'm not exaggerating when he said it was one of the worst proposals ever put before the provinces by the federal government," remembers Robert Nixon, then leader of the Ontario Liberals. "And then a couple of months later, when Robarts realized that if he didn't go into it, Ontario was going to lose out on a lot of money, he said, 'Well, I've changed my mind and we're going to go into it.'"

Eventually, Manitoba joined medicare as well. "I took it because it was impossible to refuse it," Roblin says. "I was unhappy at abandoning our plan. But the country and the people wanted a medical insurance plan of some sort. This was like the Old Testament. You couldn't change anything. That's why we did it in Manitoba."

"Really, by using money, using blackmail, the Pearson government brought in medicare," says Darcy McKeough, referring to the tens of millions of dollars Ontario was forgoing by not joining the plan. On October 1, 1969, the province of Ontario signed on, after holding out for more than a year. Accordingly, to fund the plan the federal government put a surcharge on the income tax Ontario citizens paid.

For those quick to point to the medicare saga as an example of how out of touch Robarts was with the tenor of the times, it's important to remember one crucial fact. When Lester Pearson urged medicare on the provinces, the federal government paid fifty cents on the dollar to fund the program properly. Today, it pays fourteen cents. Health care has become the highest-spending portfolio in every single provincial budget in the country, and the federal government has continually scaled back its contribution. In Ontario alone, the government spends close to $30 billion a year on health services. The federal government, which was an equal partner in medicare in those halcyon days of the 1960s, isn't even a junior partner any more. That is still true, even with the first ministers' "Deal for a Decade," passed in 2004. If John Robarts deserves criticism for opposing Canada's most cherished social program, surely he deserves credit for seeing its unsustainable future.

7

THE NATION BUILDER

THE YEAR 1967 was one of the most momentous in the history of both Canada and Ontario. So much happened. The country observed its Centennial with a magnificent world's fair celebration in Montreal. The national Progressive Conservative Party finally replaced John Diefenbaker as its leader, after years of internal, internecine struggle. And John Robarts would cap off his political career with two marvellous achievements: the re-election of his Ontario PC government, and the staging of an unprecedented political dialogue that no other provincial premier could have pulled off. Midway through Robarts's first term as prime minister, Canadians found themselves going back to the polls for the third time in four years. Prime Minister Diefenbaker's massive majority government had the stuffing kicked out of it in 1962. Dief lost ninety-two seats but hung on to a minority government. Then, ten months later, voters were at it again, and tossed out the Conservatives altogether. Lester Pearson captured a minority government, which only survived for a year and a half. So, in

1965, Canadians were asked to exercise their franchise once more. For Diefenbaker, it was his last chance to return to 24 Sussex Drive, and he knew it. He desperately wanted to grab the coattails of the popular prime minister of Ontario. Trouble was, Robarts could see a sinking ship a mile away and wanted little to do with the increasingly paranoid Tory leader.

It was Eddie Goodman's mission to convince the Ontario prime minister to help the former Canadian prime minister take back the country's biggest province. "Robarts called me," says Goodman, peppering his recollections with a hearty laugh and profanities. "He was so fucking mad at me."

Goodman got all the Conservative premiers together for a meeting with Diefenbaker at Varsity Arena in Toronto, the site of Robarts's leadership triumph four years earlier. Photographers snapped pictures of everyone, and Diefenbaker gave a good speech. Still, Robarts wasn't convinced and promised to make Goodman's life miserable if he made too many commitments to Diefenbaker's campaign on Robarts's behalf.

The election of 1965 would clarify nothing in the House of Commons. Pearson's Liberals were more popular, capturing 40 percent of the votes, compared with just 32 percent for the Tories. But the Liberals and Tories both won two more seats at the expense of the NDP and Social Credit. In essence, it was status quo. Pearson held on as prime minister. Diefenbaker was finished, and Robarts's lukewarm support for the federal leader was evidenced by the fact that the Liberals won more than twice as many Ontario seats as the Tories: fifty-one to twenty-five. The two men made some campaign appearances together, but when it really came to crunch time, Robarts's team would not help. Ernie Jackson even refused to give the federal party his list of campaign contributors.

Nineteen sixty-seven was also the year John Robarts turned fifty. He celebrated by travelling to Montreal to open the distinctive-looking Ontario Pavilion at Expo 67. He also unveiled a new provincial theme song, whose catchy tune would emanate from the lips of an entire generation of people. Ontario was now "A Place to Stand," and a place to grow.

Also growing in 1967 were the ambitions many Conservatives had for John Robarts, particularly at the national level. Ontario's economy was percolating beautifully. Annual growth rates were higher than a white-hot 8 percent. Predictably, the federal Tories dumped Diefenbaker after his second consecutive election defeat. And the obvious candidates to replace him were the three Conservative premiers, all of whom looked untouchable on their respective home turfs: Robarts in Ontario, Duff Roblin in Manitoba, and Robert Stanfield in Nova Scotia. The PC Party president, Dalton Camp, whose efforts to create a regular leadership review mechanism led to Diefenbaker's ouster, was bullish on all three men. He called them "contemporary Conservatives, men with philosophy behind their political actions."

However, none of those stars in the Tory firmament was showing much ambition for the country's top political office. At the country's Centennial celebration on July 1, all of Canada's first ministers found themselves on the royal yacht *Britannia,* going from Cornwall to Kingston, guests of Queen Elizabeth and Prince Philip. After dinner, the Conservative premiers and their spouses gathered privately to discuss the pending leadership convention. They all agreed that one of them should run for leader.

Robarts may have boasted to his wife years earlier that the prime ministership would be his someday. To which prime ministership had Robarts been referring—the national or provincial job? As far back as anyone can remember, Robarts's political orientation was always provincial, never federal. And even now, he was hardly exhibiting any interest in pursuing the top federal prize once he'd become prime minister of Ontario. And he said so on the *Britannia.* "A number of us told John, not that it was his for the asking, but he'd be an excellent person to lead the party," Bill Davis recalls. "But Ernie Jackson probably said, 'Who needs it?'"

And, of course, Robarts didn't speak any French at a time when bilingualism would become an increasingly important asset for national political leaders.

With Robarts taking himself out of the picture, that turned the spotlight on the premiers of Nova Scotia and Manitoba. Trouble was, neither Stanfield nor Roblin was showing much appetite for the job either.

Davis liked Stanfield. Just as Robarts had in the first year of his premiership, Stanfield held both the premier's job and the ministry of education portfolio simultaneously. Davis, in his capacity as Ontario education minister, had frequent contacts with Stanfield, got to know him, and became immensely impressed with his decency and humanity. Eventually, Stanfield jumped first, but it took a while. The Queen Mother was visiting Canada, and Stanfield did not want his announcement to take anything away from her tour. Further consistent with Stanfield's respect for others, the candidate wanted to speak to John Diefenbaker personally, to let the Chief know he was entering the race. But Dief was on vacation and unavailable to speak. Finally, on July 19, almost three weeks after the discussion on *Britannia,* the Nova Scotia premier announced he was in.

That he was able to maintain his political focus at all was something of a minor miracle. Like William Davis, Stanfield fought through terrible personal tragedy. In 1954 his first wife, and the mother of his four children, had been killed in an auto accident. But Stanfield had endured that tragedy, remarried, and, as *The Toronto Telegram* described it, the leadership became his "Centennial project."

"Roblin kept dithering," remembers Bill Rudd, one of the original Robarts supporters from way back. "So I joined Stanfield and ran his London organization." Curiously enough, even though Roblin was biding his time on the issue, his would-be campaign team was miffed at Stanfield's announcement. Backed by advice from Leslie Frost that a late entry would give his campaign an added boost of energy, Roblin's forces were waiting for the right moment to announce their candidate's intentions. They preferred July 26, one week after Stanfield. But Charles de Gaulle's *"Vive le Québec libre"* speech at Montreal City Hall, where the French president expressed his solidarity with an independent Quebec, so dominated the headlines that the Roblin forces thought they should wait even longer, lest their announcement be completely overshadowed by the controversy. Finally, on August 3, Roblin too decided to join the fray, but his delay in entering cost him valuable organizational support.

Robarts's ambivalence on whom to support was confirmed when so many of his cabinet members and close associates began publicly backing other candidates. And what a full field of contenders it was, particularly from Ontario. From the federal scene, there were many former Diefenbaker cabinet ministers: former trade and commerce minister George Hees from Northumberland; former labour minister Michael Starr from Ontario riding, just east of Toronto; former finance minister Donald Fleming, MP for Eglinton in midtown Toronto; and Malcolm Wallace McCutcheon, a Diefenbaker Senate appointee from Ontario.

There were others: former justice minister Davie Fulton, the MP from Kamloops; former agriculture minister Alvin Hamilton, from Qu'Appelle, Saskatchewan; and, of course, there was Diefenbaker himself, making a last grab for the job.

Having concluded he had no interest in the federal opposition leader's job, Robarts faced the next hard decision: whom to support. The federal PC leadership convention was to take place in the middle of Robarts's provincial re-election campaign. Despite that, several high-ranking Ontario Tories took time away from the hustings to participate in the national drama to replace John Diefenbaker.

Eddie Goodman was co-chair of the convention and, as a result, stayed neutral. Somehow, Goodman managed to corral Bill Davis into taking an official role as well. "Goodman made me chairman of the policy conference because he knew I supported Stanfield," Davis says. "He wanted to make me neutered. I wasn't allowed to support anyone till the policy discussions were over."

Other Ontario Conservative MPPs were not so restrained. Alan Eagleson and Bert Lawrence of Carleton East backed Davie Fulton. (So did future prime ministers Brian Mulroney and Joe Clark). Five cabinet ministers lined up behind Stanfield: economic and development minister Stanley Randall, attorney general Arthur Wishart, labour minister Dalton Bales, minister without portfolio Tom Wells, and of course, eventually education minister Bill Davis too. Robert Macaulay was campaign manger for George Hees.

But it was the Manitoba premier who had much of Robarts's organization behind him. In the front rooms, Allan Lawrence, the MPP for St. George in downtown Toronto, was for Roblin. So was Ward Cornell, the Londoner more famous for hosting *Hockey Night in Canada* from 1959 to 1972. (Cornell went on to have a lengthy career in the public service. He was agent general in London, England, after leaving *Hockey Night,* then became an Ontario deputy minister in the 1980s.) And Kent West MPP Darcy McKeough, a minister without portfolio, moved Roblin's nomination at the convention at Maple Leaf Gardens.

Robarts's team was also all over the back rooms of the Roblin organization. Dick Dillon and John Cronyn wanted to get deeply involved but were dismayed when they discovered an organization in disarray. Within hours of getting through the front doors of Team Roblin, they took over the premier's convention day unit and outlined a plan to save the dying campaign to a group of thirty-five supporters at the Royal York Hotel after midnight, the night before the vote. The effort no doubt saved Roblin from embarrassment the next day. Of course, the biggest prize Roblin's team was desperately hoping for never materialized. Ernie Jackson, Robarts's closest friend and confidant, tried over and over to get the Ontario prime minister to put on a Roblin button. But he never did.

On convention day, Bill Rudd's job for the Stanfield campaign was to make sure his friend John Robarts did not get any last-minute ideas to publicly back Roblin. Ironically, Roblin's forces were on the verge of badly overplaying their hand in an effort to get the prime minister of Ontario's endorsement. The Roblin people said they wanted to distribute to every delegate a picture of their man and Robarts together. The clear hope was that delegates would assume that Robarts had finally come out for Roblin. When Robarts heard about the scheme, he was livid. "John said if they did that, he'd march right over to the other guy [Stanfield] and put his arm around his shoulder," Rudd recalls. "No one was going to push John Robarts around."

Many of the conventioneers probably assumed Robarts was backing Roblin because Ernie Jackson was. But Bill Davis insists that would be an incorrect inference. "Just as people wrongly assumed that whenever Hugh Macaulay did anything, he was acting for me, it was the same for Ernie Jackson," Davis says. "John was careful not to indicate to anyone who he favoured. He quietly stayed neutral."

And how did Roblin deal with Robarts's lack of endorsement? "I didn't take it personally," the former Manitoba premier indicates from his office in Winnipeg. "It didn't change my opinion of him one jot. If he decided to take that position, it would have been carefully considered on his part. In public life, there are currents afoot, and you can't always explain them." By that, Roblin meant he assumed many of Robarts's ministers were for Stanfield, and therefore pressuring him not to endorse anyone. In the end, Robarts did indeed sit this one out.

Whatever the state of the Roblin organization, it obviously improved significantly after Ernie Jackson et al. got involved. Roblin managed to come second on all five ballots at the September 9, 1967, convention, capturing 46 percent of the votes on the last ballot. It was close, but in the end Stanfield took the top prize.

Could an endorsement by Robarts have made the difference for Roblin? Obviously, no one knows, but this much is certain. Robarts himself was not a Stanfield fan, and ironically, his unwillingness to endorse Roblin ensured that Stanfield got the job.

(The following year, the new Liberal leader, Pierre Trudeau, sent Canadians to the polls. Robarts made a few appearances with Stanfield during the election campaign. But he was more concerned about staying on good terms with the man at the centre of Trudeaumania. In fact, Robarts was so lukewarm about the federal Tory leader that he once told his pilot to delay landing in Thunder Bay, thereby missing a Stanfield event and guaranteeing no pictures of the two of them together. With that kind of backing from the Ontario prime minister, it's no surprise Trudeau led the Liberals to election victory nationwide, and a thrashing of the federal Tories in Ontario, sixty-four seats to just seventeen.)

With the federal leadership now out of the way, Robarts and his team could focus all their attention on re-electing Ontario's Progressive Conservative government. But this would be a much more difficult campaign than the heady days of 1963, when Robarts captured a post-war record percentage of the votes cast. In February 1967, less than a month after his fiftieth birthday, Robarts's health took a turn for the worse. He suffered a severe hernia and was incapacitated for the first time in his life. His knees and ankles hurt from old football injuries. He now lumbered when he walked, and because he was drinking more, his gut was all the more pronounced. His marriage to Norah was also foundering. But politically, he had a bunch of things going for him.

Item one: the Liberal leader, Robert Nixon, had only just got the job as opposition leader earlier that year. As Nixon knew then and freely acknowledges today, a thirty-six-year-old farmer and former science teacher didn't quite have the political heft of the Chairman of the Board. "Robarts seemed a bit unsure of himself, and there was no reason why he should be," Nixon recalls. "I was right off the turnip truck from the farm and dumped into a campaign in 1967."

Item two: a reinvigorated NDP. Conservatives at Queen's Park have always done well when the opposition is more evenly split between the Liberals and New Democrats. (William Davis made an art out of strategically propping up the NDP around election time. It helped prevent the Liberals from winning any elections during his tenure as premier, and also made securing the confidence of the house much easier during Davis's two minority governments in 1975 and 1977.)

Robarts was the star of provincial parliament, but the NDP had also had a pretty good four years after the 1963 election. Thanks, in part, to the respect Robarts showed the opposition, the NDP was treated more seriously than it had been in the past. Donald C. MacDonald was now into his second decade as party leader. And firebrands such as Stephen Lewis, Ken Bryden, and James Renwick— all MPPs from Metropolitan Toronto—gave the New Democrats a patina of "cool."

Furthermore, one of the most controversial men ever to stand for public office was preparing to take a run at the Tories—and he was a Tory! Morton Shulman became Toronto's chief coroner in the same year John Robarts won his first election, 1963. But he did not just break the coroner's mould. He utterly smashed it into smithereens. He was an activist like none before him. Not content to publish reports that sat on dusty shelves, he called press conferences to draw attention to social injustice. He took on medical quacks (those promising a cure to cancer), and the medical establishment (one woman died when her doctor left surgical instruments inside her abdomen). He crusaded against Canada's abortion laws by championing the stories of women who had died pumping Lysol into their wombs.

But here was the kicker. Shulman was also chief coroner for Ontario. He lobbied the Robarts government to adopt some recommendations on fire safety, but the government dragged its feet on the issue. So Shulman raised a ruckus and got himself fired. Next thing you knew, he decided to run in the 1967 election—for the NDP. "He decided he would be a thorn in their side in some other way," the current NDP leader, Howard Hampton, told the Ontario legislature four years ago when Shulman died. "I'm sure that every day after that, the Conservatives in this legislature wished they had never fired him, because during the whole time that he was in this legislature, he was nothing but torment to the Conservative government of the time."

Going into the '67 campaign, NDP prospects looked unusually good for a party that had broken double digits in the seat count just twice since its parent organization, the CCF (Co-operative Commonwealth Federation) was founded in 1932. John Smith, a Hamilton teacher, remembers that campaign well. It was his first run for provincial office. He didn't actually meet the prime minister until all the Hamilton PC candidates gathered for a giant rally—twelve hundred supporters—at a local school auditorium. "He was a colossal person, quite a presence," recalls Smith, who was only thirty-one years old at the time. "He was a fatherly figure. He had a calming effect." When Smith campaigned in the new riding of Hamilton Mountain (there were nine new ridings), he always identified himself as "the Robarts candidate," hoping the prime minister's coattails would help his own cause. The day before the Canadian National Exhibition opened, Conservatives gathered for another massive rally at the Ontario pavilion.

In Etobicoke, Alan Eagleson was getting nervous. Despite a couple of feelers from Robarts's office, he had actually declined an earlier offer to join the cabinet.

"I was asked discreetly if I would be a minister without portfolio," Eagleson says. "But you had to give up everything else, so I said no."

The "everything else" Eagleson refers to was a burgeoning legal career, highlighted by Bobby Orr's retaining him to be his agent, and the creation of the National Hockey League Players' Association. Rejecting a cabinet appointment and focusing on his sports career would bring Eagleson riches and fame (and infamy) in the years ahead. But it would also prove to be a fateful decision in terms of his future in elective politics. "If John had ever called me in as a follow-up and said, 'I'm making you *minister of this*,' I'd have had a lot of difficulty saying no," Eagleson says. "But it never came to that."

It's true that 1967 was an amazing year for Canada and for its biggest province. In some respects, Robarts would have to have screwed up mightily to lose the election that year—things were just that good. "Times were prosperous, people were content with the Conservatives, and he was reasonably progressive," says Robert Nixon. "He was not an iron man, right-wing, common sense revolution man. He, I thought, ran a practical government. He believed in democracy. The hints of scandal were distant and never amounted to anything, and that probably says quite a bit about him."

Nevertheless, Robarts did have his bad moments during the campaign. He's been compared to John Kennedy elsewhere in this book, but one area where Robarts could not touch Kennedy was in media relations. Kennedy loved the press, having at one time been one of them, and was the master of witty repartee during news conferences. Robarts tolerated the media but never seemed to like most of its members.

In 1967 Robert Fisher, today the dean of Queen's Park media observers, was a local reporter for CHWO Radio 1250 in Oakville. One of his assignments was to cover a garden party reception in Port Credit, now part of Mississauga, and get an interview with the prime minister of Ontario. "John Robarts was standing there," Fisher recalls. "I screwed up my courage, as much as an eighteen-year-old cub reporter could. I walked up to him, introduced myself, and asked, 'Mr. Robarts, I wonder if I could have a moment of your time for an interview.' He looked right at me and said, 'Fuck off.'" Fisher is still deeply incredulous as he relates the story more than three decades later. "I'll never forget the look on his face," says Fisher, now a CBC-Radio newscaster and frequent contributor to TVO's *Fourth Reading* program on provincial affairs. "He wore a navy blue suit and had a drink in his hand. I wilted away. I couldn't believe it. The week before, I'd interviewed Bob Nixon, and he walked across a whole field to get to me. I was in shock. Robarts had signed my high school graduation diploma. He was this God-like figure. I just couldn't believe it."

Other observers suggest Robarts's encounter with Fisher must have been a rare lapse on the part of the prime minister. Ian Macdonald recalls attending federal-provincial meetings with Robarts, and nary a curse word passed his lips. "In fact," Macdonald says, "he used to complain about Trudeau. He'd say, 'I wish that he didn't have to inject all those four-letter words all the time. I heard enough of those words in the football dressing room.'"

Robarts loved governing much more than campaigning, and it showed. It was also probably unreasonable to expect him to improve on his 1963 results, which were so good. So after all the votes were counted on October 17, 1967, there was mostly good news for Ontario Conservatives, but some disappointment as well. On the positive side, Robarts kept the Tory dynasty alive, winning a second consecutive majority government. But there were some big surprises. Despite having more ridings up for grabs, the PCs actually lost eight seats. One of the losers on election night was Alan Eagleson, the MPP for Etobicoke-Lakeshore, who watched Liberal support in his riding evaporate and move to the NDP candidate, Pat Lawlor. "Pat was a good pal," says Eagleson. "He practised law down the road. He attacked me for spending all my time trying to organize the hockey players association." Was Eagleson at all miffed at Robarts for not running a better campaign, or offering a more solid cabinet post? "It wasn't Robarts's fault I lost," Eagleson says. "I won because of him. He was my winning margin in '63. But there's no question he was not as popular in '67."

Alan Eagleson's career in elective politics ended that night. But of course his involvement in things political was only just beginning. Eagleson would win huge kudos for helping to organize the memorable 1972 Summit Series between Team Canada and the Soviet Union. He would also go to jail for defrauding the hockey players he claimed to represent. And worse, if that's possible, even the legendary Bobby Orr dropped him in 1980.

One of the other disappointments of the '67 election was that the PCs elected only two new members. One of them was John Smith in Hamilton Mountain. The other surprise—no, shock, actually—was the performance of the NDP. For just the third time since Ontario entered Confederation, the NDP/CCF hit double digits: twenty seats, just seven behind the official opposition Liberals.

Everyone would soon discover that the newest New Democrat MPP, Morton Shulman, marched to his own tune. At one point in his second term, Robarts's minister for financial and commercial affairs, Les Rowntree, needed an extended break from his duties, essentially to recover from alcohol-related troubles. After he returned, Rowntree was plenty nervous that he would not be able to stand up to the rigours of Question Period. So Robarts told Keith Reynolds to ask the opposition leaders to give Rowntree a break. Robert Nixon said no problem, that his members understood and would go easy on Rowntree. Donald MacDonald said virtually the same thing, with one notable exception. "I can deliver my people," he told Reynolds, "except Mortie Shulman."

For Robert Nixon, the conclusion of the 1967 election was not as devastating as the results might have indicated. "I enjoyed the campaign probably more than Robarts did," he says. "But he was very successful and very dignified and was not resorting to campaign crapola tricks." Nixon would lead the Liberals into two more elections—1971 and 1975, both against William Davis—and victory would elude him on both occasions. However, he would become treasurer of Ontario in 1985 in David Peterson's government and be the first treasurer to present a balanced budget since the Robarts years.

Now that Robarts had secured re-election, he was in a position to fulfil a commitment he had made in May 1967, which would turn out to be one of his most important legacies to the country. Ever since he had become prime minister, Quebec had fascinated Robarts. He saw nationalist and separatist factions gaining prominence and genuinely wanted to understand the motives behind them. "John didn't speak a word of French, but he was the second most popular politician in Quebec," says David Peterson.

"I think John had a sense that the relationship between Ontario and Quebec was important to the rest of Canada," says William Davis. "While he had no facility in the language, that didn't preclude his genuine affection for the people of Quebec."

Robarts's idea was to get all of Canada's first ministers together to discuss the state of play between English and French Canada and to look at the promise for improved relations into the next century. This was no ego trip. Robarts actually offered the chairmanship of the proposed conference to Prime Minister Lester Pearson, but the feds were showing little interest in participating in a provincial initiative. Still, this was a file Robarts had a history of taking deadly seriously.

"I remember one cabinet meeting," says Rendall Dick, the former deputy attorney general. "One of the ministers got up, talking about tactics in anticipation of a federal-provincial meeting. He urged John to attack Pearson on patriating the Constitution. John slouched, looked at the guy, and said, 'Do you think I want to play political football with the Constitution?'"

In the mid-1960s, Robarts feared that Ontario's public service couldn't keep up with the talent he was seeing in Ottawa or Quebec

City. He would often go to federal-provincial meetings and look across at all the impressive advisers the federal and Quebec governments were bringing. He would look at his own contingent and could not help feeling he was missing something. "Robarts was very frustrated with the thin element of his office from the time he came in," remembers Don Stevenson, who would spend nearly three decades in the Ontario public service. "He was really stranded."

As a result, Robarts put on a full-court press to convince several high-profile Ontarians to join the public service, to help get him the best advice he could. "He had the vision to put together a top-flight public service to go toe-to-toe with the feds," says Fraser Kelly, who watched it all from his perch as a reporter with the now-defunct *Toronto Telegram*. "They could take on the federal finance department and be just as good. Ontario hadn't had that before."

One of the officials Robarts attracted to the public service was H. Ian Macdonald. In 1965 Macdonald became chief economist of Ontario, but that title didn't begin to describe his role. A Rhodes scholar from humble beginnings in Toronto's Pape-Danforth neighbourhood, Macdonald was considered such a prize catch for the Ontario civil service that Robarts called a press conference to introduce him to the provincial media—something that had not been done before and has not since. Macdonald would become deeply involved in the negotiations with the federal government around Robarts's proposed French-English dialogue and a variety of other matters. In January 1965 he set up an advisory committee on Confederation for Robarts and staffed it with some of the top academic minds in the country. But things did not get off to a great start. The federal government was not at all keen on participating in any conference, or even that the conference take place at all.

That did not deter Ontario, and thus the decision was made to proceed with what became known as the Confederation of Tomorrow conference. Ultimately, Pearson rejected Robarts's invitation to chair the event, or even to attend as an observer. But if the federal government thought that would end Robarts's efforts, they were mistaken. Negotiations continued. If the prime minister of Canada refused to be part of the event, Robarts hoped the national government would at least have some kind of presence there. He sent Ian Macdonald to Ottawa to discuss the matter with Gordon Robertson, clerk of the privy council.

"While we were discussing that, there was a rustle outside the negotiating room and the door was flung open," Macdonald recalls. "A chap came in with an open-necked shirt and sandals, and his right wrist in a cast. It was Pierre Elliott Trudeau, who was minister of justice. He sat down and partook of the discussion for a while. And I could detect in him extreme doubt. Even a bit of muted hostility to the idea." Eventually, Macdonald got Trudeau to accept the idea of the conference, or at least to agree that it was not intended to be a constitutional conference, but rather a less formal taking of the nation's temperature. "When I reassured him it wasn't about the Constitution, the atmosphere relaxed," he says.

"My thought was not to decide anything but to have the discussion," Robarts told an interviewer at the time. "Let's hear what people think. Where are we in conflict? Where do we agree? Where is compromise possible?" Exquisitely simple questions, but exceedingly difficult to answer. However, the prime minister of Ontario wanted to launch a good-faith effort to begin to find those answers. If Lester Pearson wouldn't come, he would invite all the provincial premiers to show up anyway. And almost all of them did.

One year before the conference would take place, Fraser Kelly began to get a real sense of Robarts's role on the national unity file, and from a most unlikely source. One morning, he and Pierre Trudeau had breakfast at the cafeteria on the fifth floor of the West Block on Parliament Hill. At this point, Trudeau was not yet the minister of justice, and had only been elected the MP for Mount

Royal a few months earlier. He was an unknown commodity outside the exclusive literary and intellectual circles he inhabited before standing for office. Kelly was perhaps the first journalist in English Canada to take him seriously.

"Trudeau felt John Robarts could be the single most important politician in the country," Kelly remembers Trudeau telling him. "And he was absolutely right. Robarts knew instinctively and intellectually that he had a critical role to play in the national unity debate. He was miles ahead of his caucus, the Ontario legislature, and even the whole province. He brought us all along. That's leadership."

In 1967 the prime ministers of Ontario and Quebec were as close as any two first ministers from those two provinces have ever been. When Robarts sent Ian Macdonald to Quebec City both to explain the concept of the conference and understand what Quebec's sensitivities might be, Daniel Johnson Sr. spent two hours with Robarts's envoy. But that was only half the story. As Macdonald left, he saw Claude Morin, Quebec's deputy minister for intergovernmental affairs. "Did you know," Morin asked Macdonald, "that when you were with Daniel Johnson, he had come out of a cabinet meeting and kept his ministers waiting two hours while he talked with you?" Macdonald did not know that. But he did know Johnson's extraordinary time commitment was not for him. "That's how much Daniel Johnson revered John Robarts," Macdonald says.

One thing became abundantly clear. The prime minister adored the national unity file. "Robarts once said to me he enjoyed nothing more than sitting around with the members of the advisory committee over cigars and drinks and listening to academics talk about the future of the country," recalls Don Stevenson, who had become the point man in intergovernmental affairs in Robarts's office. Early in Robarts's first term, Stevenson correctly predicted that relations with Quebec would become a white-hot issue, so he asked Richard Rohmer, the prime minister's right-hand man, if he could keep an eye on intergovernmental issues. Stevenson got the green light and had a front-row seat on some meetings where Ontario officials actually put the nation's welfare first. "Our advisers didn't think in Ontario terms," Stevenson says. "They thought in Canadian terms. Robarts's frame of reference was an unhappiness about Quebec in Confederation, and John said, 'This is a problem we've gotta help fix.'"

Quebec might have been going through its Quiet Revolution during the 1960s, but according to *Time* magazine, Ontario was undergoing something just as noteworthy. The year before the conference, *Time* featured "Prime Minister Robarts and the Whiz Kids" in a cover story titled "Ontario: The *Other* Revolution." Robarts was photographed with a handful of his top advisers, including Keith Reynolds, Ian Macdonald, Don Stevenson, James Ramsay, and Rendall Dick, all up-and coming public servants in their thirties.

On November 27, 1967, the other revolution was on display for the entire country to see at the Confederation of Tomorrow conference (a name, incidentally, chosen by Ian Macdonald). Robarts wanted to show how modern and powerful his province was. So, at Jim Ramsay's recommendation, he held the conference on the top floor of the newly built Toronto-Dominion Centre, the tallest skyscraper in the city. The place was so new that the carpet had not yet been laid. And best of all, he put it on television for everyone to see.

Quebec was still nine years away from electing a separatist government; nevertheless, Robarts was preoccupied with the Quebec question and had an unusually sophisticated level of interest on this issue, particularly for a unilingual anglophone from small-town Ontario. Ian Macdonald has a hunch he knows why. "I asked him how he came to feel so strongly about this," Macdonald says. "He said he'd been in the navy and in the bowels of a ship and the fella above him was a francophone from Quebec. And he said when all's said and done, we're all in the same boat, so to speak. More than metaphorical."

Charles Beer tells a similar story. Beer was raised in Newmarket, Ontario, and the son of the founder of Pickering College, the famed independent boys' school near Toronto. He attended the University of Toronto, then Laval University in Quebec City, and became a fluently bilingual anglophone, something of a rarity in English Canada in those days. When he was twenty-six, Beer's first job after leaving university was on the support staff of the Ontario Advisory Committee on Confederation, the body that advised the Ontario prime minister in the lead-up to the Confederation of Tomorrow conference.

During this time, Beer heard another story about Robarts during the war. He was on a destroyer, serving with a crew of European sailors, whose first language was not English. "Whenever he entered a room and they were speaking other languages, they switched to English to make him feel at home," Beer says. That made an impression on him." Years later, when he became prime minister of Ontario, Robarts apparently wondered what it was like for French Canadians who frequently did not receive public services in their own language, even in the nation's capital. It was an unusual thing for a unilingual anglophone from Ontario to care about, Beer thought.

Fraser Kelly agrees. "I do think it goes back to the war years," he says. "There were no provinces over there. It was the country. They were all Canadians."

The year before the Confederation of Tomorrow conference, Robarts demonstrated his concern for francophone issues. Ontario's French-language school system was in desperate financial condition. Robarts and his education minister, Bill Davis, found the money to bring those schools into the public system, while allowing the schools to maintain their unique French character and approach. "The French-language school system would have collapsed entirely without him," Charles Beer insists. "All the secondary schools were going belly up." There was certainly no pressure from the government's traditional base of support to address the issue. But for Robarts, Beer says, "He just had an intuitive, gut sense that this was the right thing to do."

Even so, Robarts was keenly aware of the tightrope every Ontario first minister walks on French-English issues. For Ontario voters, particularly Conservatives in more rural parts of the province, there are not—and have never been—many votes to be won trying to increase the electorate's sensitivity on French-language issues. Nevertheless, against the wishes of his cabinet and caucus, Robarts plowed ahead. Just a few days before he was to announce an offer of significant new resources to the French boards of education, Robarts went fishing with Tom Symons, the founding president of Trent University in Peterborough and his frequent adviser. He told Symons of his intentions, which delighted Symons, who thought it was both fair and necessary. Still, he wondered why Robarts would risk all the flak that would no doubt be coming his way. "The Queen can't have first- and second-class citizens," Robarts told him.

To this day, Symons remains impressed with the answer. "To me, that revealed the depth of his romantic Tory sentiment," he says. "His cabinet colleagues could either fall in line or make a scene, which wouldn't have done them any good."

In 1963 Prime Minister Lester Pearson established one of Canada's most historic panels examining French-English relations, the Royal Commission on Bilingualism and Biculturalism. When the commission published the first volume of its report, Robarts asked Ian Macdonald and Charles Beer to come to his office to brief him on its key recommendations. As far as the government of Ontario was concerned, the principal issue was the panel's desire to see the country's biggest province become officially bilingual. "Robarts banged the desk with his fist in frustration," Beer says, recalling the prime minister's reaction.

"They've gotta realize what I can and can't do," Robarts told Beer and Macdonald.

"It was a very human reaction," Beer now says. "He wanted to do things but felt limited."

For those who think Robarts demonstrated a lack of courage on official bilingualism for Ontario, let the record show that none of his successors, in the more than three decades since he left office, has implemented the policy either. There continues to be significant concern in every premier's office that a major anti-French backlash would result if that symbolic step were taken. The fact is, Premier William Davis's government expanded French-language services in areas of the province where numbers warranted. And Premier David Peterson's government expanded them even more with his own French-Language Services Act. Coincidentally, when that law came into effect, Peterson's francophone affairs minister, responsible for ensuring that the act was adhered to, was none other than the same Charles Beer, then the Liberal MPP for York North, who had advised John Robarts on French-English relations twenty years earlier.

In any event, a few months before his re-election in 1967, Robarts watched in amazement as Charles de Gaulle sent a Montreal crowd into a frenzy. He was determined to better understand this phenomenon. "A lot of people were suggesting that perhaps he was spending too much time on these matters rather than on local matters," Ian Macdonald remembers. "But he was determined to bring about a dialogue on that hundredth anniversary of our Confederation about where the country was going next."

To the future international affairs expert Janice Gross Stein, having John Robarts at the helm of Ontario was just what the doctor ordered. As an anglophone growing up in Quebec, Stein had watched events in her home province with increasing concern. "It was so comforting to know that just down the 401, there was a solid, comforting presence in John Robarts," says Stein, now chair of the Munk Centre for International Studies at the University of Toronto. "I'm sure that was part of the reason why Robarts was so popular in Quebec."

One of the more glamorous aspects of Charles Beer's job at this time was to brief Robarts on the major agenda items for the conference. One of the less glamorous jobs was to go to the prime minister's suite at the Royal York Hotel in the mornings, wake him up, get his notes in order, and make sure he was on schedule and ready to go. One morning, Beer was fortunate enough to eavesdrop on a very special moment. As Beer entered Robarts's hotel room, he saw that the prime minister and his predecessor, Leslie Frost, were engaged in a deep discussion about something.

"I was trying to pretend I wasn't listening," Beer admits. "But at one point, Frost put his arm around Robarts and said, 'John, it never ends. It's seven days a week, twenty-four hours a day.' "What an image," Beer thought. "They were obviously sharing a very difficult moment." Robarts would publicly acknowledge from time to time how much he loved being "centre front" on Ontario's political scene. However, he also remarked on how unrelenting the prime minister's job was. It's another reason why he loved getting away to Grand Bend as much as possible.

With the federal government if not quite openly hostile to the conference then at least very lukewarm in its support, it was an open question whether anyone would actually show up. But observers have called this moment in Canadian history the turning point, when the majority of provinces decided to begin flexing their muscles and get more serious about national issues. And it would not have happened without John Robarts.

In total, nine of Canada's ten premiers attended the Confederation of Tomorrow conference. In Quebec, Daniel Johnson of the Union Nationale had now replaced the Liberal premier Jean Lesage. His endorsement of the conference, without which it would have been stillborn, came happily. Robarts's friend Duff Roblin was in the process of retiring as premier of Manitoba. However, his successor, Walter Weir, would arrive just after the conference got under way.

Other premiers attending included Ernest Manning of Alberta, Ross Thatcher from Saskatchewan, Louis Robichaud of New Brunswick, George I. Smith from Nova Scotia, Alexander Campbell from Prince Edward Island, and the legendary Joey Smallwood from Newfoundland. Only W.A.C. Bennett from British Columbia failed to show, but he sent his attorney general to keep an eye on things. (Ian Macdonald remembers Bennett once telling Robarts, "You look after the Quebec problem. When I get over those mountains I'm gone.")

The federal Liberals eventually agreed to send two civil servants as observers. Robarts instructed Rendall Dick to sit them in the front row as a sign of respect. "I wanted to seat them in a barn, not in the front row," Dick admits.

Also invited were Ontario's two opposition leaders, Robert Nixon and Donald C. MacDonald. Nixon was on his farm milking cows when the invitation came. "I grabbed a quick shower and tried to get some of the farm off the boy," Nixon jokes.

By all accounts, the Confederation of Tomorrow conference was a triumph for the prime minister of Ontario and, more important, for the country. Writing in *The Globe and Mail,* Ross H. Munro suggested that "Mr. Robarts, probably more than any other English Canadian, helped prevent Quebec from retreating into a dangerous isolationism."

West of Ontario, Canadians got what for many of them was their first insight into Quebec society, thanks to television. Ottawa sustained a black eye for essentially taking a pass on the event. The feds had their reasons. They thought the conference was premature, as they were still trying to nail down their latest strategy for dealing with the Constitution. But for others, Robarts's efforts were well worth it. "He hosted what turned out to be, historically, the beginning of constitutional change," says William Davis.

"I think it *was* a success," adds Rendall Dick. "It forced the prime minister of Canada to face the issue. Before that, people west of Ontario weren't interested in Quebec at all. They were completely insular."

The rookie MPP John Smith of Hamilton was impressed with Robarts's accomplishment. "He saw things from a national perspective," he says. "Probably because he was in the war. He fought for the country. He wasn't narrow-minded."

"He was the fella that really set up a basis of understanding between the two founding races of this country," says Robarts's long-time friend Dick Dillon. "And he thought that was extremely important. I admired him for that."

As much as Lester Pearson wanted no part of the Confederation of Tomorrow conference, he had to acknowledge it was a success. And he did just that, leaving a message for Robarts to call him so he could offer congratulations. However, in the days before cellular phones, that was not such an easy thing to do. Charles Beer remembers wandering around the fifty-fourth floor of the Toronto-Dominion Centre with Robarts after the conference ended, looking for a pay phone so the Ontario prime minister could return Pearson's call.

Political careers are frequently touched by irony, and in this case Robarts would encounter his share. Just three months after the conference ended, in February 1968, Pierre Trudeau, while still justice minister, unveiled his first set of proposals on constitutional change. Two months later, Lester Pearson retired as prime minister and was replaced by Trudeau. Over the next fifteen years, Trudeau would come to completely own the constitutional/national unity file. Robarts's thanks for putting the issue on the nation's agenda was essentially to be relegated to the sidelines when things got much more interesting.

If Robarts was distressed at that turn of events, he hid it well. Charles Beer suggests Robarts's reaction was exactly the opposite of disappointed. "After Pearson left and Trudeau won, Robarts said, 'I don't have to play that role any more,'" Beer recalls. The clear implication was that with Trudeau sitting atop a majority government, with significant numbers of Quebec MPs, Robarts thought the French-English file was finally in good hands.

Still, Robarts wanted to establish institutions that would make permanent the gains he felt he had achieved with the premier of Quebec. So the two provinces signed an Ontario-Quebec Accord, establishing more formal links. One program saw university students from each province travel to the other to work in the public service and improve their second language. Another saw an exchange of civil servants from both provinces' bureaucracies. Even members of the Ontario legislature and the National Assembly and reporters in the respective press galleries established exchanges, each side getting a once-in-a-lifetime opportunity to gain knowledge and insight into their counterparts. Yes, there was the phenomenon known as Trudeaumania. But there were also these smaller, and maybe ultimately more important, gestures. It was a hopeful, optimistic time for French-English relations.

"I've known and covered nine prime ministers and many more premiers," Fraser Kelly says. "I believe that when it comes to providing visionary leadership when the country was at a critical time, Robarts ranks right up there on the list."

John Robarts might have been relieved of his national responsibilities on the French-English file. Nevertheless, future events could never take away from him the satisfaction he enjoyed from mounting that nation-building exercise in November 1967. Years later, another Ontario premier from London, David Peterson, found himself at Robarts's cottage at Grand Bend. As Robarts was giving his guest a tour, the two men happened on a picture taken at the Confederation of Tomorrow conference. "He told me it was his favourite picture," Peterson remembers wistfully. "All the premiers of the day hanging in the hall of his cottage. And he alluded to that as something he was most proud of."

8

THE LAST PRIME MINISTER

TOWARD THE END of the 1960s, the Progressive Conservative govern-ment of Ontario seemed to take on more and more barnacles. That is not to say the party had run out of political and policy victories, but something was different. Although Leslie Frost had held office well into his seventies, with huge majority governments and highly regarded by the populace, John Robarts faced a tougher time. Only in his fifties, Robarts was seen by increasingly larger chunks of the party and the electorate as out of touch. In addition, many of the cultural influences of the United States, which Ontario had managed to avoid in the earlier part of the decade, were starting to penetrate into Canada's biggest province. After his party had lost seats in the 1967 election, Robarts's difficulties were compounded by a shocking by-election loss less than two years later in his own backyard.

The 1967 election breakthrough for the New Democratic Party indicated that more and more Ontarians might have been open to new political options. Robarts had also been politically damaged by the medicare debate: he seemed to be on the wrong side of history, even if he was proven to be correct on many of the program's shortcomings. Then on September 18, 1969, Archdeacon Kenneth Bolton won a stunning victory for the NDP in a by-election in Middlesex South. The riding included the suburbs of London and farmland south and west of the city, and by all logic it should have been a safe Conservative seat. But voters heard the firebrand New Democrat MPP Morton Shulman call the Robarts government "old, mean, and malicious." Despite a last-ditch campaign stop by the prime minister and his treasurer, Charles MacNaughton, to keep the riding blue, it went NDP. Jonathan Manthorpe, in his excellent book *The Power and the Tories,* wrote that to be a "Robarts man" during this time was to be a "fat cat establishment figure, self-satisfied, manipulative and scornful of frustration in the party."

Yes, the Conservative Party itself was beginning to show significant signs of more than just fraying at the edges. Today's notion of the perpetual campaign, where the first minister and his cabinet are constantly holding fundraising dinners to keep the party coffers from depletion, was still years away. Robarts and Ernie Jackson, who ran the party apparatus for his best friend, believed in cranking up the fund-raising machinery every four years at election time. But during the intervening years, Robarts was frankly not much interested in those matters. He was dead serious about his responsibilities as head of the government. He was less so about his responsibilities as head of his party.

Government at this time was also getting bigger and much more complex. As the self-styled management man, Robarts began to rely increasingly on professional advice from the civil service. He started losing touch with the Tory grassroots, particularly younger members. But that was only part of the reason. The other part could be found on the other side of the tightrope that every Ontario first minister walks—the national unity file. Ontarians are ambivalent when it comes to the national unity issue. As citizens who think of themselves as Canadians first and Ontarians second, they want their leader to assume his rightful and influential role in affairs of state. However, if there are problems on the home front, the electorate would just as soon see their premier drop the file as if it were the proverbial hot potato. History will record that David Peterson made a significant contribution to enable the ratification of the Meech Lake Accord. For his troubles, he was booted out of office a few months later. Similarly, Bob Rae played a high-profile role in trying to gain acceptance of the Charlottetown Accord. But in the midst of the worst recession since the Great Depression, few seemed impressed. They wanted Rae focused on improving the economy, not the Constitution, and he earned few kudos for his efforts. Mike Harris, despite being a polarizing figure in Ontario history, declared when he came to power that his main tasks were to lower taxes, balance the books, and fix the economy. Any work Harris might have done on the national unity file was done quietly and usually behind the scenes. After seeing the issue hamstring his two immediate predecessors, Harris understood what his voters wanted and, perhaps more particularly, what they did not want him focused on. All of which is to say that John Robarts, for all his triumphs surrounding the Confederation of Tomorrow conference and his other contributions to national politics, was beginning to encounter a party membership that wanted him more focused on Job One.

The mass media of the time may have cut Robarts a lot of slack in his personal life, but such was not the case in his political life. The press was getting tougher, more critical, and giving voice to those who started to resent the London Mafia's influential role in the PC Party.

Robarts was also still hitting the booze pretty hard and not always in off-business hours. One night after the legislature had adjourned, New Democrat MPP Stephen Lewis returned to the chamber, having forgotten something in his desk. There, sitting in the front row in the two seats closest to the speaker, were the only two men remaining in the chamber: John Robarts and William Davis.

"Bill was perched on the edge of his own chair, his arm around Robarts's chair," Lewis recalls. "Robarts's words were slurred. Bill Davis was affectionately looking after him. It was a real moment of tenderness. I waved and said hello. Robarts yelled back, 'You have a future in politics, young man, and this fella beside me does too!' Davis looked vaguely embarrassed."

The PC Party's concern over its deteriorating condition culminated in the election of a party president whom Robarts did not actually oppose, but who, no doubt, was not his first choice. Some members began to articulate a concern that Robarts and Jackson were too old (the prime minister was only fifty-two), and the party's image needed revamping.

Enter Alan Eagleson. Even though he had been a casualty of the 1967 election, Eagleson kept in touch with some of his former caucus mates. His friends Darcy McKeough, Tom Wells, and Bob Welch were all cabinet ministers now. One day, a group of his former colleagues called to take Eagleson out to lunch, whereupon they told him that the next generation wanted its own candidate for the party presidency, and they wanted Eagleson to run for the job.

"I called John and told him I wouldn't run for presidency if he didn't want me to," Eagleson says, aware of the tradition that the party president and the leader be sympatico on major issues.

Robarts's response: "No, no. Go ahead." He might not have been crazy about the idea, but he recognized the virtue of allowing the presidency to go to "more youthful, vigorous hands," as he described it at the time.

"We visited every riding between September 1 and the end of October," Eagleson says of his campaign. "We met every executive member. We'd have breakfast with one, lunch with another, dinner with another."

George Peck, the former Scarborough Centre MPP who, like Eagleson, lost his seat in the '67 election, had been a Royal Canadian

Air Force pilot during the war. He had a plane and offered to fly Eagleson all over the province to help with the cause.

"We got lost all the time," Eagleson says. "Shit, we were so off course. One time I looked down and said, 'Those are apartment buildings at Jane Street [in Toronto] and we're supposed to be in Sudbury!'" Despite Peck's lack of orientation skills, Eagleson defeated two other candidates for the presidency in 1968.

Rumblings in the grassroots notwithstanding, Robarts was still the Chairman of the Board, and only a few months after Eagleson's victory, the prime minister created one of the most important advisory bodies of his entire premiership. With government becoming increasingly large and unwieldy, the Ontario Chamber of Commerce recommended the prime minister get some blue-chip advice on how to keep things as efficient as possible. Management man that he was, Robarts and his treasurer, Charles MacNaughton, created the Committee on Government Productivity to study the overall structure of government. Robarts wanted top executives from the private sector to meet with senior public servants to develop a plan to keep government lean and efficient.

It actually took almost ten months for the committee to get up and running because, despite the worthwhile goal, Robarts and MacNaughton were having enormous difficulty securing senior executives from the private sector to serve. G.R. Heffernan was one of the rising stars of the time in the private sector. He founded Co-Steel in Whitby, Ontario, one of the first ever mini-mill steel producers and scrap processors. Heffernan developed the technology and management of these mills, which now account for almost one-third of the world's steel output. (Heffernan has since received numerous awards for technological innovation.)

His first meeting with Robarts had taken place in 1964, late one night at Queen's Park. Colin Brown, the London insurance executive and a friend of Robarts's, thought the prime minister should meet this entrepreneur, who was going to build a new state-of-the-art steel business in the province. "As I came into his office, he had all the drawings for the Pickering nuclear plant in front of him," recalls Heffernan, a metallurgical engineering graduate from the University of Toronto's class of '43.

After they'd exchanged some pleasantries, Robarts said to Heffernan, "You're an engineer. Tell me whether I should do this or not."

Five years later, Jerry Heffernan got a phone call from Queen's Park. "The prime minister would like to see you in his office at ten o'clock tomorrow morning," the voice said. Heffernan showed up and proceeded to get the full-court press from Robarts. "We're setting up this Committee on Government Productivity," he said. "I want you to serve on it. It won't take much of your time."

Heffernan said no. "I'm really up to my eyeballs and overloaded with two companies these days," he told Robarts, referring not only to his steel business but also to a British Columbia enterprise called Peace River Mining, whose roots went back to the nineteenth century.

Robarts scowled. "If you guys won't help us straighten out this government, I never want to hear another word about government inefficiency," he said.

Heffernan was mute. "I couldn't turn him down," he says. (Ironically, Peace River Mining went broke shortly after Heffernan agreed to serve. "If I'd spent less time on COGP and more time on Peace River, it wouldn't have gone under," he jokes, three and a half decades after the godfather of Ontario politics made him an offer he couldn't refuse.)

Meanwhile, MacNaughton approached Robarts's friend and Labatt's executive John Cronyn to be chairman of the committee. But Cronyn declined the offer, saying as incoming president of the chamber of commerce, he did not want to put himself in a potential position of conflict. However, after months of fruitless effort to find a chairman, MacNaughton went back to Cronyn and in essence begged him to do it.

This time, Cronyn resigned his position with the chamber and accepted. (In fact, the advisory body was initially called the Productivity Improvement Project. But every time they bumped into each other in Toronto, Robarts began to tease Cronyn about the acronym. "*Pipping* again, are you, John?" Robarts would say. Cronyn asked for a name change and got a more dignified acronym: COGP, the Committee on Government Productivity.)

By December 1969 Robarts had his team in place. Besides John Cronyn and Jerry Heffernan, he had also signed up Alf Powis, the president of Noranda Mines; R.D. Wolfe of the Oshawa Group, the huge food and pharmaceutical marketing concern; and C.C. Hay, a director with Gulf Oil and president of Hockey Canada. And, in a major departure from the way things work in government today, almost all the members of the committee worked free—not even earning a dollar a day. "We donated our time because we thought it was a necessary thing for government to do," Cronyn explains. (Actually, the only member of the committee to receive per diems was Charles Hay. Although on the board of Gulf, he was technically retired, without the full-time income the others had, and so he requested compensation.)

The public sector members of the committee were five senior deputy ministers, including two of the prime minister's top advisers: his own deputy minister (secretary to the cabinet) J. Keith Reynolds; and the deputy minister of the treasury department, Ian Macdonald. (The others were the deputy attorney general, Rendall Dick, G.H.U. "Terk" Bailey, the deputy minister of lands and forests, and Carl Brannon, secretary of the treasury board.) Jim Fleck was the executive director.

The Committee on Government Productivity was so influential that it actually continued to sit well beyond Robarts's years in power. It wrote ten reports on streamlining government. Key recommendations included the creation of the management board of cabinet, which would have the power to scrutinize every government expenditure, much to the chagrin of free-spending ministers who wanted more freedom to do their own thing. The COGP also recommended the creation of a kind of inner cabinet—what became known as the Priorities and Planning Committee. Its job was to identify and initiate policy analysis on issues not being examined by any ministry or agency, and anticipate emerging issues in the longer term.

There was so much agreement on the usefulness of the committee's work that three months after William Davis became premier in 1971 the legislature implemented the recommendations after just a few days of debate, with support from all three parties.

The committee did such an authoritative job that members of the Ontario legislature were still debating its merits more than thirty years after Robarts created it. Even Peter Kormos, the maverick NDP member from Niagara Centre, and as anti-establishment an MPP as was ever elected, once quoted at length the COGP's recommendations, in its praise, during a 1998 house debate.

A postscript to COGP's work: there was also a warning about taxation levels a quarter of a century before Mike Harris's Common Sense Revolution would usher in an era of unprecedented tax cutting. "Since most major sources of revenues have been tapped," the report warned, "the emphasis must shift in the years ahead from finding new sources, to making the best uses of existing ones." It may have been the first major red flag raised by an Ontario government committee that taxpayers were becoming increasingly concerned about how much of their money was going to Queen's Park. Still, at this point in history, most Ontarians had to be content with the province's fiscal picture. The Tory government routinely balanced the books. The economy was so buoyant most of the time that the biggest decisions related to what to build rather than how to devise new methods of taxation to pay for services.

Government was getting bigger, but not so big that when a light bulb went on in the prime minister's head, he couldn't make something happen. One day, Robarts was driving back to Toronto from a cabinet retreat in Niagara-on-the-Lake with his treasurer, Charles MacNaughton, and deputy treasurer, Ian Macdonald. Perhaps for the first time, he truly became aware of the majesty of the Niagara Escarpment, a natural land mass in southern Ontario that the United Nations has now designated a world biosphere reserve. At one point in the drive, Robarts began to marvel at his surroundings and started discussing some ideas with his colleagues on how to preserve the escarpment. "These are our crown jewels," he told them. Before long, Robarts set the wheels in motion, which ultimately resulted in the creation of the Niagara Escarpment Commission, whose mandate is to control development on the escarpment. More than thirty years after its creation, its seventeen-member council still exists today.

In the late 1960s, the Robarts government had a notion to deal with several outstanding problems all at once. The province was less than thrilled with the Government of Ontario Building at the Canadian National Exhibition. It wanted to make a splash in the recreation sector. It hoped to create a lasting legacy for young people who had to stay in the big city during the summer. And it wanted to develop Toronto's dramatically underused waterfront. All those priorities came together in one megaproject: Ontario Place. Construction started in March 1969 and consisted of three artificially created islands connected by bridges. The showpiece of the project was the magnificent geodesic dome. All told, Ontario Place cost $29 million to build; it opened in 1971.

The cabinet minister who saw the project through to completion was Stanley Randall, one of Robarts's most colourful and controversial ministers. Randall, a self-made businessman who got his start selling washing machines, was personally recruited by Robarts to run for government in 1963 in the Toronto riding of Don Mills. After winning election, he replaced Robert Macaulay as minister of economics and development. Randall was a unique character who loved using folksy lines like "He stood out like a red wheel on a hearse." He was also, by today's standards, totally politically incorrect. In fairness, almost all the legislators of the time were, but Randall mixed his political incorrectness with irresistible humour. One time during Question Period, Randall was the target of some intense questioning by Elmer Sopha, the Liberal MPP for Sudbury, nicknamed "the Northern Gadfly."

"I want to know," Sopha began, "in this country of so many talented, wonderful, young Canadians, why the chief hostess at the Ontario pavilion at Expo 67 is a British woman."

"Mr. Sopha," Randall responded, "that woman wasn't chosen for her background, but rather for her foreground."

When Sopha took Randall to task for his sexist remark, Randall shot back, "I've got tears running down all four of my cheeks."

The antics aside, Randall was one of Robarts's most effective ministers. "Stanley Randall took hold of Ontario Place and made it great," says Darcy McKeough, a cabinet colleague. "He gave people something exciting to do in the summer, gave employment to lots of kids, and provided summer employment for members of the Canadian Opera Company, the Toronto Symphony, and the National Ballet."

Even though Robarts began the inexorable growth in the size of government, the numbers were still tiny compared with today's. In 1970, Robarts's last year as prime minister, his office budget was only $350,000. (By way of comparison, William Davis almost doubled that figure in his first year in office, and took it to $1 million in his second.) By the end of the 1960s, the Prime Minister's Office was still a fairly lean operation. Robarts had only five senior staffers doing most of the heavy lifting: J. Keith Reynolds, the secretary to cabinet; Hugh Hanson, who ran the cabinet office; William Rathbun, his speech writer; William Kinmond, his press secretary; and Don Martyn, his executive assistant, in charge of the political files, including keeping relations with Conservative MPPs running smoothly.

Reynolds had joined Robarts's office in 1964 in a kind of chief operating officer's role. He was subordinate to Malcolm McIntyre, who was Leslie Frost's deputy minister, and liked to remind Reynolds of the fact that when it came to the office pecking order, McIntyre was *numero uno*. Most accounts seem to suggest Robarts was more comfortable with Reynolds, whom the prime minister hired from the ministry of natural resources. The two often hunted and fished together. And like Robarts, Reynolds was a Second World War veteran, whose plane had been shot down and crashed in the North Sea.

Although the two men got on famously, Reynolds insisted during his job interview that there be clear lines drawn as to what he would, and more particularly would not, do for Robarts. "At the end of the interview I said I wasn't keen about the job but if I'm your man, so be it," Reynolds recounted in 2002, before being stricken with Alzheimer's disease. "But I told him I wouldn't be involved in partisan politics. He agreed." When McIntyre retired in 1969, Reynolds assumed his responsibilities and essentially was in charge of the office.

While Kinmond and Rathbun were former reporters brought in during Robarts's first term, Hanson and Martyn were second-term additions. Hanson was hired for his organizational skills, Martyn for his political savvy, and both for their youth. In fact, one of Robarts's first directives to Martyn was to go to London and "replace my fat, fiftyish friends on the executive with guys your age." At least on his home turf, Robarts was taking criticism about his fat-cat image seriously.

Don Martyn loved being a back-room political operator, but it was not his original career path. He had graduated from the University of Toronto with a degree in modern history, then wrote his doctoral thesis on Tory democracy in the United Kingdom in the 1880s—the beginning of modern Conservative politics. Martyn was actually a university instructor when he decided to become a candidate for John Diefenbaker's Progressive Conservative Party in the 1965 federal election. Lester Pearson's Liberals won both that election and the York North riding Martyn was contesting, but Martyn made it close. He came within eighteen hundred votes of knocking off the two-time Liberal incumbent John Addison and got almost as many votes as the much higher-profile Dalton Camp, who ran for the Tories in Eglinton riding but lost to Mitchell Sharp.

When Richard Rohmer left the prime minister's side, Robarts discovered he needed someone to run the political aspect of the office. Recommended by Darcy McKeough, the twenty-nine-year-old Martyn met with Robarts and Ernie Jackson at their favourite luncheon hangout, Winston's restaurant in downtown Toronto. Not only were Martyn's Tory credentials excellent, but his connections to the rising NDP were solid as well. He had gone to school with MPP Stephen Lewis and Gerald Caplan, a party adviser, and therefore could offer extra insight into the New Democrats' tactics and strategy. Martyn developed a close rapport with Robarts, to the extent that he began to call him by a nickname: "Fearless." Plainly and simply, Martyn saw a politician who never feared making the tough decisions required by the office he held.

It was a view echoed by Robarts's chief economic adviser, Ian Macdonald.

"I do remember one time we were dealing with a particularly difficult issue," Macdonald says. "I remember John Robarts saying, 'Sometimes governments have to take decisions, even if they do end up getting defeated.' And that phrase rang in the back of my mind. I wish we heard it more often."

Darcy McKeough says debating the politics of an issue always came at the end of cabinet deliberations. "A matter would be debated on its merits, and when a conclusion was reached, Robarts would say, 'Now we should discuss the politics,'" he says. (McKeough adds that during the Davis years, discussing the politics of a matter often came first. Part of the reason, no doubt, was the fact that Davis had a minority government for almost half his tenure).

Martyn used to tease Robarts by saying he felt he was doing a good job when the prime minister followed his advice 67 percent of the time.

"Donald," Robarts would answer, "that's where we're different. I only have to be right 50 percent of the time."

Hugh Hanson was recruited by Keith Reynolds after the 1967 election, and he called the prime minister "sir." Hanson was secretary to the Ontario Committee on Taxation, chaired by Lancelot Smith. The committee advised the government on many issues related to taxation, including how to make the property tax assessment system, which at the time was a hodgepodge of disparate and unfair rates, more equitable.

Hanson's first public service job was actually with Tommy Douglas's CCF government in Saskatchewan in the budget bureau. ("A great place to learn government," he says.) A few jobs later, he was working for the Ontario Committee on Taxation, before heading to Robarts's office.

One of the first political crises he observed on Smith's taxation committee dealt with religion. The committee recommended that the province eliminate the exemption from property taxes that churches then enjoyed. When church leaders found out, they predictably hit the roof. Shortly thereafter, Robarts convened a meeting in the cabinet room, of the heads of all the major churches in Ontario. "Gentlemen, I think we can cut this short because as long as I'm prime minister of Ontario, there'll be no change in policy," he said.

One skeptical onlooker challenged Robarts. "That's all well and good to say now," he said. "But we know what politics is like. How can we be sure this won't change?"

Robarts was not amused. "Gentlemen, you'll just have to have faith, a concept with which I believe you're all familiar."

After he moved to the Prime Minister's Office, Hanson started as Keith Reynolds's executive officer, handling the mail and telephone inquiries, and worked his way up to taking minutes at cabinet meetings and briefing the prime minister directly. He was ideally placed to see Robarts's policy side in action. One time, a government committee wanted to recommend a course of action but feared making that recommendation to Robarts because committee members doubted the prime minister could move it through the cabinet or bureaucracy. When Robarts got wind of this, he became furious. "He slammed the table," Hanson recalls. "He said, 'You recommend the best policy and I'll worry about the compromises.' He wanted the very best result, and if the committee recommended something less, he'd have to settle for even less."

On other occasions, Robarts would chide his more timid cabinet colleagues with expressions such as "We are going to lean over backwards so far we'll fall flat on our asses." But that is not to suggest that Robarts was always a risk taker. Other times, when he feared cabinet wanted to move too quickly, he would say, "We're getting so far out ahead, we'll look back and no one will be following us."

"He looked like and acted like and felt like a very prominent, self-confident leader," Hanson says. "He was a very good listener. He would hear people out. He once said whenever a decision was brought to him, he could almost toss a coin, because if there was an obvious decision, it would have been made already."

"I always remember in conversations his preoccupation was what's good for Ontario," Ian Macdonald says. "'I'm the premier,' he'd say, 'and I have a responsibility for all the people of Ontario. We've built a great society here. Now, how do we preserve it?'"

Hanson recalls once taking a flight from North Bay to Toronto with the prime minister, constantly pushing files at him for decisions. "That's it. I'm tired," Robarts finally told him. "When I'm tired, I'm apt to make mistakes."

Where Robarts and Reynolds shared a love of hunting and fishing, Robarts and Hanson had sailing in common. The prime minister once called Hanson into his office and asked his advice on nautical matters. "I'm thinking of buying Tim a sailboat," he told him. "What do you recommend?" Hanson suggested a fourteen-foot Albacore. It was easy to sail. Later, after Robarts's retirement from politics, Hanson would often accompany him on Robarts's thirty-one-foot sailboat *Trillium*, which he kept at Ontario Place.

In private with friends, Robarts was able to let his hair down. But it was a luxury he almost never afforded himself in public. Once, while fishing in the northern Ontario town of Geraldton, Robarts noticed a photographer approaching. He instantly reached for a tie, which he put on with his plaid fishing shirt. Other times, the prime minister attended summer festivals and, despite perspiring a great deal, refused to take off his jacket. He could not abide the informality of that gesture, much to the disappointment of all the other men in his company, who similarly could not get more casual if the first minister stayed formal.

Robarts once showed up at a formal event wearing a brown suit. He was so miffed at what he perceived to be a major faux pas on his part that he demanded his receptionists follow up each appearance request with wardrobe suggestions. Extra dinner jackets were kept in his office. The fact that he wore the same size as Don Martyn made things a little easier whenever the inevitable wardrobe exchanges were necessary.

Hanson and Martyn each had another much more personal reason for admiring, even adoring, John Robarts. Both young men had lost their fathers prematurely, and Robarts in no small measure represented a kind of father figure to them both. "He's one of the great memories of my life," says Hugh Hanson, whose father, Edward, died of an embolism when Hugh was in his early twenties. "I became very attached to him. In some ways, I thought of John as a substitute, in a minor but comforting way." Similarly, Murdoch Martyn died of a stroke while Don was in university. More tellingly, Murdoch Martyn and John Robarts even looked alike.

Robarts no doubt understood the paternal role he played in the lives of his two underlings. However, that did not stop him from enjoying himself in their presence. While neither man ever saw the prime minister incapacitated, they were both with him in circumstances where the booze flowed freely. Martyn once played bartender and disc jockey on a flight from Thunder Bay to Toronto. He ran the bar, put on the music, and watched Robarts and his pal, the cabinet minister James Auld, belt back the rye and port throughout the four-hour flight.

On another occasion, the mayor of North Bay asked the prime minister to come to the city and give a speech. Robarts did not want to do it, in part because he thought the mayor was a bit of a pain in the neck. So, even though he planned to be in North Bay, he turned down the invitation. And yet, surprise, surprise, when the invitation arrived in the mail, there was the prime minister's name listed as the keynote speaker.

As Robarts was flying to North Bay, he became even less enthusiastic about the prospect of having to see the mayor, who had manipulated him into giving the speech. So he asked the pilot whether there was anything that could be done to get him out from under this burden. The pilot, no fool, played along and suddenly "discovered" he had an engine fire. That information was radioed to the tower in North Bay, and sadly, the speech was cancelled.

For someone who was now routinely criticized as an establishment fat cat, Robarts was capable of doing some quite off-the-wall things. Ian Macdonald remembers the prime minister's receiving a courtesy call from the new German consul general toward the end of the 1960s. "I walked into his office, and they're both on the floor going over a map of the world," Macdonald says. "They were reviewing a naval battle in the Mediterranean where John had torpedoed the consul's boat. They'd both survived to meet."

On another occasion just after announcing his retirement, Robarts was to be the guest of honour at a testimonial dinner at the London Club. But the fates intervened, the weather turned foul, and Robarts's party got snowed in at the 401 Esso Service Centre between Ingersoll and Woodstock. It had all the makings of a public relations disaster, except for those who watched the local news the next night and saw the prime minister of Ontario sitting on the floor, leading a singsong at the restaurant and having a grand time. Meanwhile, Robarts's friend John Cronyn gave a tribute address to the prime minister in absentia (the text of the address is in the appendices). The next morning, Robarts left the scene on a snowmobile.

Toward the middle of 1970, Robarts started dropping hints to his closest friends that the end of his political career was nearing. In the summer, he discussed his possible retirement among very close associates in his backyard pool in London. He expected at least four of his MPPs to try to run for the roses: William Davis, Darcy McKeough, Tom Wells, and Allan Lawrence. Robarts was pleased with the notion of Davis, McKeough, and Wells taking a run at the job but was not a big fan of Lawrence's. Lawrence cooled his heels until February 1968 before getting the call to cabinet. Robarts considered him difficult, though in his political lifetime he had had little animosity toward others and few grudges. Despite the fact that Lawrence had been campaign manager to Robarts's leadership rival Kelso Roberts, and that Lawrence made the prime minister's life miserable during the Bill 99 fiasco, Robarts put him in cabinet (although in a rather unusual portfolio for a downtown Toronto MPP: minister of mines). "In some cases, a pretty vindictive guy would have cut me off, but Robarts certainly did not do that," Lawrence says today, with admiration.

Robarts also let slip that, much as he liked and respected Davis, there was something about his education minister that concerned him. "The trouble with Billy is he can't say no," Robarts told one of the people in the pool with him. (Robarts need not have worried. Davis would develop a thick skin and had no trouble saying no to separate school supporters when he led the Tories into the election campaign of 1971.)

"I could see the writing on the wall," says John Cronyn. "He used to say, 'I'm bored with the job.' I told him, 'You've been there ten years. You're on the top. It's time to get out.'"

Darcy McKeough remembers trying to get a meeting with Robarts at this time, but was having trouble. When he approached Keith Reynolds about it, the province's top civil servant bluntly said, "The ship of state is not being steered."

John Robarts almost did get out of provincial politics at this time, but for reasons completely unrelated to tiring of public life. In fact, in a story never before made public, new information suggests Robarts had his eye on a possible move to national politics. On June 25, 1968, Pierre Elliott Trudeau romped to a majority government victory over Robert Stanfield's Progressive Conservatives. The seat count was 155 to 72. The popular vote looked just as solid for the Liberals, as Trudeaumania captured 46 percent of the votes cast, compared with just 31 percent for the Tories. Two years later, Trudeau still looked strong, and as a result Stanfield was considering stepping down. It was at this moment that two close friends of both Stanfield and Robarts began considering options. Eddie Goodman was a bridge between the men. He had introduced Robarts to Conservative Party politics back in their days together at Osgoode Hall Law School. He also had enormous respect for Stanfield and was pleased to see him win the federal PC leadership in 1967.

Peter Hunter was to John Robarts what Norman Atkins was to William Davis—an advertising guru who knew how to translate a leader's image into maximum voter appeal. Hunter first met Robarts in 1959 when both men lived in London and he worked on Robarts's leadership campaign. He was chairman of McConnell Advertising in the days when advertising agencies had enormous influence in the back rooms, and not just at election time.

Goodman and Hunter were among many Tory partisans who felt a change of leadership in the national party might help Conservative fortunes against Trudeau. So, very quietly, Goodman agreed to approach Stanfield, and Hunter promised to talk to Robarts about a possible leadership switch.

"I will not aggressively try to move Bob Stanfield out," Robarts told Hunter. "I have high regard for him. But if he called me, we could work something out." Hunter was actually in Toronto General Hospital while all this was happening, having an operation to fix a stomach ulcer. His hospital room seemed more like a political war room, with phone calls going in and out all day long.

Meanwhile, Goodman had managed to talk to Stanfield, and the federal PC leader was apparently amenable to stepping aside in favour of the Ontario prime minister.

"Stanfield would draft him," Hunter now says of the plan, "and we'd all work out a procedure, because he didn't want Robarts to have to go through a leadership convention." Robarts was open to the scheme, but only on the condition that he not approach Stanfield. He didn't want to be accused of undermining the federal party leader. However, in a twist of fate worthy of a Hollywood movie, Stanfield *twice* called Robarts to offer him his job. But on each occasion, Robarts was unavailable to take the call. Eventually, Trudeau's popularity waned, the momentum behind the leadership switch faded, and both Stanfield and Robarts stayed put. "Robarts was high profile and very respected," Hunter says. "We don't make 'em like that any more. People thought he was the guy to knock off Trudeau."

When the results of the October 30, 1972, election were in, Robarts supporters were fit to be tied, just as the Liberals and Tories almost were. Trudeaumania had clearly ended, as the Liberals bested

Stanfield's Tories by only two seats—109 to 107. The popular vote was a virtual dead heat as well, with the Liberals edging the Conservatives 35.8 percent to 35 percent. "How history might have been different," muses Gordon Walker, the former London MPP and cabinet minister. "I suspect Robarts would have won that election."

A further examination of the 1972 election results suggests the claim is not without merit. In Ontario, the less popular Stanfield won forty seats to Trudeau's thirty-six. Robarts almost certainly would have done better. In Quebec, Stanfield won only two seats. Hard to believe Robarts would have done worse. Out west, Stanfield bested the Liberals forty-two seats to just seven. Even the NDP, with nineteen seats, did better in the west than the Liberals. Robarts likely would have kept the west in the blue column. About the only place one could argue Robarts would not have done as well was in Stanfield's home province of Nova Scotia, where he won ten out of eleven seats. But since the Tories won more seats than the Liberals in the three other Atlantic provinces, it is reasonable to assume Robarts would have been strong on the ground in Nova Scotia as well, particularly if Stanfield helped campaign for Robarts. Alas, for those who had greater ambitions for the prime minister of Ontario, none of it was to be.

In October 1970 Canada found itself in the throes of a full-blown political and military crisis. Prime Minister Trudeau invoked the War Measures Act in response to the kidnappings in Quebec of the British trade commissioner, James Cross, and the province's labour minister, Pierre Laporte, by the Front de Libération du Québec (FLQ). The last thing the country needed in the middle of the October Crisis was to have Quebec premier Robert Bourassa's closest provincial counterpart quit the scene. John Cronyn remembers being in Robarts's office in the midst of the crisis. "We were sitting around waiting for calls from Ottawa," he says. "Trudeau wanted to know whether we would go along with the War Measures Act. I said to Robarts, 'You've got a tough decision to make.' He said, 'What do you mean *I* have a tough decision. *We're* going to make the decision.' He was such a cool guy. You couldn't panic him."

Who knows how much worse the October Crisis might have been if the prime minister of Ontario had not agreed with the prime minister of Canada's approach. It's a hypothetical question the country never had to ponder. Robarts came out firmly and unequivocally for Trudeau. "There is absolutely no way we can allow ourselves to be blackmailed," Robarts opined at the time. "There is no way to survive as a society if we permit this." Eventually, the crisis passed, but not before Pierre Laporte had been killed, James Cross held hostage in fear for his life, and hundreds of Quebeckers arrested and detained as suspected FLQ sympathizers. It was a dark and frightening chapter in Canadian history.

With the FLQ crisis behind the country, Robarts felt liberated to deal more directly with his future plans. But not before teasing opposition politicians in a game of cat and mouse. In a rumour-filled legislature, the Liberal leader, Robert Nixon, asked Robarts directly if he was thinking of leaving. Robarts's response: "I must say, I never anticipated a question like this, so I will have to do some fast thinking on my feet here." Nixon grinned back. Fast thinking on his feet? Come on. Robarts's future was all everybody was talking about.

In November 1970 Robarts sent a message to Alan Eagleson that he wanted to have dinner at the Westbury Hotel with the Tory Party president. The two men polished off a bottle of wine, and then Robarts gave Eagleson his letter of resignation. He also told his party president he wanted his friends Ernie Jackson and Eddie Goodman to run the upcoming leadership convention to choose his successor.

But Eagleson, flexing his presidential muscles, was having none of it. "John, no offence, but Ernie and Eddie won't be running the convention," he said. "I'll be running it."

Robarts sat back in his chair, a bit miffed but undoubtedly not surprised at Eagleson's cheekiness. "Alan," he said, "I could have guessed that would be your response."

In the first week of December, John Robarts set in motion a series of events that would culminate in his departure from politics. At noon on Monday, December 7, he announced to his riding executive in London that he intended to cease being the member for London North after the current legislative session was over. He then drove to Toronto and posed for pictures with his office staff as he imparted the news to them that after nine years and one month, he was retiring as prime minister of Ontario. The following day, he told his cabinet and gave each minister a personally addressed and signed photograph. "There are only enough copies for each of you," Robarts told them. "The negative has been destroyed." There was not a dry eye in the room.

9

THE DEPARTURE

JOHN ROBARTS'S NEXT TASK was one familiar to every retiring party leader. He held the obligatory news conference to outline the reasons behind his departure, then confirmed that the party had agreed to hold a leadership convention to crown his replacement two months hence. "I have never believed that any one man or one group had a monopoly on ideas," Robarts told reporters. "I firmly believe it is necessary to provide opportunity for new approaches." In his letter to party president Alan Eagleson, Robarts added, "It is over nineteen years since I was first elected. They have been years of enormous growth and development in Ontario. May I say that in my view, our party is in good shape, filled with able people prepared and happy to give of themselves."

"He just thought the province needed new blood," his daughter, Robin Robarts, recalled in an interview in 2001. "He said he always intended to only stay for ten years if he was lucky enough to be able to stay in that long."

At fifty-three and in reasonably good health, Robarts suggested to a very small number of people that, in fact, under the right circumstances, he might have been persuaded to stay on. "Just as he was finishing his term in 1970," recalls Richard Rohmer, "he said, 'Richard, I have to quit. But if I could just take one year off and regroup and reconstitute my life, I could go on and on.' But it wasn't to be," Rohmer adds wistfully.

Interestingly, *The Globe and Mail* assigned the job of writing a summation of the Robarts years to Harold Greer—yes, the same Harold Greer who had previously quit *The Globe* to write speeches for Robarts's Liberal opponent in the 1963 election, John Wintermeyer. Even through his partisan prism, Greer had to acknowledge what every Ontarian instinctively knew: that the Robarts years had been good ones. "It is in many ways an impressive record, as good as or better than any other jurisdiction in North America," Greer wrote, then enumerated the achievements. "Legal aid, a massive social welfare program, the creation of a huge system of community colleges and universities, law reform, reorganization of school administration, a start on regional government, one of the best anti-pollution programs to be found anywhere."

But Greer also let the other shoe drop: "But it is not as good as it could or should be solely because Mr. Robarts is a cautious, consensus politician, without any gut feeling, unless it be a negative one, for what he has been about." Considering the source, it wasn't a bad write-up at all.

Indeed, a new era in Ontario politics was about to begin. If Robarts's yellow-jacketed leadership team set new standards for the conventions of the 1960s, the advertising gurus in the post-Robarts era would set even more modern standards for the leadership conventions of the 1970s. William Davis, the province's education minister, was considered the front-runner. He had the same portfolio Robarts had when the man from London made his own leadership run in

1961. At age forty-one, Davis represented the next generation, which had proved so important a formula for the Tories in previous leadership transitions. (Straying from that formula in two future leadership contests both resulted in the loss of power: Frank Miller in 1985 and Ernie Eves in 2003.) Furthermore, Davis represented the establishment voice in the party and seemed to offer modest change and continuity at the same time.

Because Davis had the party establishment in his corner, most of the new Tory back-room talent did not have a role in his campaign. "Davis's people told him they could make him premier without a highly organized campaign from Toronto," Allan Lawrence recalls. "They were probably right, except for the fact that they ran a terrible campaign for him. It was bloody awful."

Those left off the Davis team were a tremendously talented group of advertising executives and communications experts who could not wait to test their new ideas in battle. Trouble was, they had no candidate. They finally settled on the mercurial Allan Lawrence. Lawrence may have had the dream team on board, but he was hardly a dream candidate. His speaking style was awkward. He had run afoul of Robarts during the Bill 99 controversy (the so-called Police State Bill), even shaking his fist in the prime minister's direction during one debate in the legislature.

Robarts had wanted another Toronto voice in his cabinet, but the only vacancy was the mines portfolio. Still, Lawrence's appointment was not as bizarre as it seemed. He did having some mining experience, having worked in the Arctic and northern Ontario for Falconbridge, the three-quarters-of-a-century-old nickel-mining giant. "I was so astonished by the appointment, I didn't have the wit to respond," Lawrence says, recalling Robarts's pulling him aside after a January 1968 caucus meeting to make him the offer. Still, given ten years on the backbenches, Lawrence instantly said yes and ended up loving the job. Yes, it meant spending five days a week in the North, immersing himself in northern issues, and trying to resuscitate the Tory party in a region where it has rarely done well. But for an ambitious man with ideas, which Lawrence was, representing downtown Toronto and being the minister for the North was a fascinating combination.

One of the most difficult problems Lawrence's campaign team had was convincing the man himself to be a candidate. They assured him the campaign would not cost him a dime, that a first-rate organization was in place, and best of all, his wife, Moira, was onside. "All you have to do is say yes," they told him.

In December 1970 Lawrence was driving to Toronto from his cottage in the country, en route to a meeting with his campaign team to give them the green light. But during the drive in, he began to have doubts. "This is going to change my life," he thought. "And Davis is going to win the damn thing anyway. To hell with it." Lawrence arrived at the Albany Club, Toronto's favourite hangout for Tory types, and announced to his team that he was out. They were apoplectic. They pulled out all the stops, including a phone call to Moira, begging her to help change his mind. Ultimately, with her help, he did.

Now that Lawrence had apparently decided against simply ceding the race to Davis, others opted to enter the fray. Darcy McKeough, nicknamed "the Duke of Kent" after the county in southwestern Ontario he hailed from, was the ambitious and talented municipal affairs minister. His family had a very successful plumbing supply business in Chatham. He was also married to a sharp woman who had seen her fair share of politics over the years. Joyce McKeough's father was David Walker, the public works minister in John Diefenbaker's first government, later a senator after losing his Rosedale seat to Donald S. Macdonald. But McKeough was only thirty-seven, the youngest member of cabinet, for whom many had high regard, but they suspected he could wait until next time. (That view was heartbreakingly confirmed for McKeough when Charles

MacNaughton, the treasurer from nearby Exeter and a big fan of McKeough's, backed Davis.)

Two other cabinet ministers joined the race, although neither of them was thought by objective observers to have much of a chance: Bert Lawrence from Carleton East, and Robert Welch from Lincoln riding on the Niagara Peninsula. Don Martyn ran Welch's leadership campaign, ostensibly because the prime minister asked him to do it. Robarts wanted none of "his boys," as he called them, to be embarrassed, and he feared Welch might be without some help. Other Robarts confidants Ab Campion and James Auld were also persuaded to come to Welch's aid.

Despite all the negatives Lawrence brought to the table, he had some brilliant pluses in the persons of Dalton Camp, Norman Atkins, and Ross DeGeer, together later dubbed "the Big Blue Machine" by the columnist Claire Hoy. The BBM managed to remake Lawrence into a highly credible candidate. If his speaking style turned people off, the team used short snippets in smartly produced ads to make Lawrence seem more thoughtful. Since he had been a bit of a thorn in Robarts's side, it did not take much to portray him as the anti-establishment candidate. And his going to bat for northern Ontario in some well-publicized cabinet fights with the treasurer helped solidify his support in that part of the province. Before long, Lawrence's campaign was clearly on the move, and much of the anti-Davis (read anti-establishment) sentiment lined up behind him.

Robarts, as tradition dictated, played his preferences very close to his vest. He publicly endorsed no one and believed it was good for Ontario that so many qualified candidates were running. "He felt when he became leader he didn't have as much experience as he needed," says Bill Rathbun, Robarts's former speech writer. Rathbun notes that ministers in Leslie Frost's government had few opportunities to hone their Question Period skills in the legislature because Frost tended to want to answer every question. "Robarts complained he almost never answered a question in the house," Rathbun says. "These candidates were better. They sat in the house and they knew the province."

With much of the party establishment backing Davis, many at the time wondered whether Robarts secretly was supporting him as well. To this day, Davis says he is unclear how much Robarts might have done behind the scenes to aid his candidacy. "He did nothing to hinder my efforts," Davis feels confident saying.

But how helpful was he? Davis allows just a hint of irritation in his voice. "Check the number of ministers selected in his cabinet who supported me," the man from Brampton says. "The most," he points out, then adds a second later, "by far." A notoriously modest man, this is as close to a personal boast as Bill Davis ever gets.

Before the official leadership convention could get under way, two thousand delegates paid $10 each to attend a farewell dinner for Robarts in the Canadian Room of the Royal York Hotel. There was a video presentation filled with memorable news clips, evoking nostalgia throughout the room.

Bill Rathbun knew this would be the most important and memorable speech he would ever write. He also had a long-standing, set way of getting his speeches to the prime minister. The speeches were always written on 8½-by-11-inch paper and placed between blue covers with a plastic binding. Robarts did not like to carry the actual speech himself but preferred to have it waiting for him at the lectern. Rathbun made sure the speech was on the shelf under the lectern and had it taped down for extra security.

"That night," Rathbun remembers, "I also handed him a copy of it while he was being piped in. I said, 'Stick this in your pocket anyway.'" That was something Rathbun had never done, but for some reason something told him to do it on that night.

As party president, Alan Eagleson was the host of the affair. He introduced the film, after which the lights came up, and Robarts assumed his place at the lectern, preparing to speak. Suddenly, he looked over at Rathbun with a puzzled look on his face. Rathbun could not figure out what was wrong until he saw Robarts pull the speech Rathbun had given him earlier in the evening out of his pocket.

"The real speech?" Rathbun speculates. "Al Eagleson unpeeled it and walked away with it. And John didn't think it was an accident. There wasn't exactly the best rapport between them. They weren't great buddies at the end." (For the record, Eagleson denies he filched the speech to embarrass the prime minister. "If it did happen, I think I would have heard about it," he says.)

To say thank-you for a job well done, Ontario Conservatives bought Robarts a thirty-one-foot sailboat, designed in Port Credit by C&C Yachts and built by Belleville Marine. Don Martyn later sent Robarts a memo asking the prime minister what name he wanted on the craft. "The obvious one is *Trillium*," Martyn's memo read, "or you could do something more adventurous like *Rather Be*." That name was a play on the slogan found on every Ontario licence plate of the time: "Any other place you'd rather be?" Robarts circled the word *Trillium,* initialled it, and sent the memo back to Martyn. *Trillium* it would be.

There was another parting gift, this one from the London Progressive Conservative Association, where politically it all began for the Robartses. Members chipped in to send Norah and John to London, England, for a vacation. While there, John went to one of the world's foremost gun manufacturers and was specially fitted for a new hunting rifle, made to match his particular specifications.

The leadership convention to choose a new prime minister of Ontario took place on February 12, 1971, at Maple Leaf Gardens in Toronto. Where Robarts's leadership win in 1961 had become a marathon because it lasted six ballots, this event similarly seemed to go on forever but for very different reasons. The Tories tried to use newfangled electronic voting machines, which simply did not work.

Voting had to be redone, and many northerners, who had to get back home, could not stick around to participate in the final ballot, no doubt hurting the Lawrence camp's chances.

After delegates voted on the fourth and final ballot, but before the results were announced, Allan Lawrence left his box and went to the men's room. As he approached the urinal, who should be standing beside him but the outgoing prime minister. "He was absolutely drunker than a skunk," Lawrence says, chuckling at the memory.

"Congratulations on a great campaign," Robarts told him. "The whole thing would have been a lead balloon without you."

Lawrence thanked Robarts for the compliment, then got serious. "Look, this thing's going to be over soon, and Bill's going to win it," Lawrence said. "One of the first things he's gotta do is get my people onside because there's absolutely no antipathy toward him. They'll definitely want to work for him."

Robarts instantly sobered up. "You really mean that?" he asked. Lawrence confirmed it. And that's exactly what happened. In the days ahead, the Big Blue Machine would move seamlessly to embrace William Davis.

Finally, at 2 a.m., an arena filled with exhausted Tory Party members crowned Davis the new leader. But it was a much closer affair than anyone had anticipated. The Big Blue Machine managed to turn what was supposed to be a smooth and relatively easy win for Davis into a nail-biting, four-ballot affair, in which Davis prevailed by only forty-four votes. (Much of the credit can go to Darcy McKeough and his organization, which moved to support Davis after the Duke of Kent was eliminated on the third ballot. McKeough became king-maker. Davis became king.)

By the time the outgoing leader and the new leader took to the stage for the final arms-locked-and-thrust-in-the-air picture, it had been a very long night, and John Robarts had had plenty to drink. The look on the winner's face was classic Bill Davis: a frozen smile, with a hint of nervousness at what a very tipsy Robarts might say. In the end, the booze may have made Robarts somewhat more emotional than he otherwise would have been, but Davis need not have worried that the prime minister was going to embarrass himself.

"Well, ladies and gentlemen, my remarks will be very short because I've achieved my objective," Robarts told the assemblage. "I'm a has-been." Then, to his successor, he offered the following: "Billy, best in the world to you. You've got a great group to go with you." And finally, what seemed like a father's farewell good wishes to his sons: "My boys," he said to the other candidates, "I love you all."

Robarts was not uncomfortable with the notion of his education minister taking over the reins of government. But he did not vote for Bill Davis. At one point in the evening, Robarts walked by Darcy McKeough's section of the arena and said to the candidate's wife, Joyce, "I want you to know I voted for my godson's father." When McKeough heard about the comment later, he was moved. "I didn't win the convention, obviously. But I took that home with me and for the rest of my life," he now says.

A couple of days after the balloting, Robarts, Davis, and Eagleson found themselves on a stage at a public event. Eagleson introduced Davis. "Now, ladies and gentlemen, our new premier, Bill Davis," Eagleson remembers saying. "John tugs at my sleeve and says, 'I'm still premier for a few weeks.' So I got back to the microphone and said, 'Sorry, ladies and gentlemen—the new *leader,* Bill Davis.' John looked at me as if to say, You dumb shit," Eagleson says with a laugh.

The Robarts era officially ended on March 1, 1971, with the swearing-in of William Grenville Davis as Ontario's eighteenth prime minister. One of the first things Davis did was to change the name on the door that so exercised Robert Nixon. He would be *Premier* Davis, not prime minister. "I thought there should only be one first minister in the country," Davis says.

The best words on the Robarts years belonged, not surprisingly, to the outgoing prime minister of Ontario himself. In an interview with Rosemary Speirs of *The Toronto Star,* John Parmenter Robarts summed it up beautifully: "I'm a product of my times exactly," he offered, "and my time is finished."

Running for Office: The Robarts family (Timothy, Norah, Robin, and John) used this picture postcard as campaign literature for one of John's early runs for office. *(courtesy Robin Robarts)*

The Great Outdoorsman: Robarts goes fishing with his older brother, Robert (left). An unidentified man steers in the background.
(courtesy Eleanor Robarts)

The Single Greatest Day:
Robarts gives his victory
speech at the October 1961
PC Leadership Convention
at Varsity Arena in Toronto
after winning a thrilling
six-ballot affair.
(courtesy Archives of Ontario)

Proud Papa: This is daughter Robin's favourite picture
of her father, evidently delighting in something she said,
as her brother, Tim, looks on. *(courtesy Robin Robarts)*

A Partisan Tory: Robarts applauds
a speech by John Diefenbaker
during a 1965 federal election
rally at Maple Leaf Gardens.
(courtesy Julien LeBourdais)

The Godfather: Robarts was a personal and political hero of Chatham-Kent
MPP Darcy McKeough. The prime minister was godfather to Darcy and
Joyce McKeough's son, Jamie, pictured here at his christening
at Christ Church in Chatham in October 1968.
(courtesy Darcy and Joyce McKeough)

Robarts shares a 1969 Grey Cup victory moment with Ottawa Rough Riders' quarterback Russ Jackson. Riders' defensive captain, Ken Lehman (number 41) and team owner David Loeb (far right) look on. Ottawa defeated the Saskatchewan Roughriders 29–11 in Montreal.
(courtesy Archives of Ontario, F 15-7-2-6)

The Statesman: Robarts huddles with Prime Minister Pierre Elliott Trudeau and federal cabinet minister Jean Marchand.
(courtesy Archives of Ontario)

His Other Love: Along with fishing, Robarts loved nothing more than to go hunting. *(courtesy Archives of Ontario, F 15-8-2-14)*

Good times at Oakhaven: There were numerous parties at John and Norah's cottage near Grand Bend, Ontario. *(courtesy Archives of Ontario, F 15-8-2-4, item 10)*

A Fond Farewell: John and his first wife, Norah, at the outgoing prime minister's retirement dinner in February 1971. *(courtesy Julien LeBourdais)*

The Tory Firmament: Robarts is flanked by George Drew (left) and Leslie Frost (right), both former prime ministers of Ontario, at Robarts's farewell dinner in February 1971. *(courtesy Julien LeBourdais)*

The Successor: Robarts talks to the man who would replace him and continue the Tory dynasty for another fourteen years, William G. Davis. *(photo by John Harquail; courtesy Archives of Ontario, F 15-7-1-54)*

Mourning a Loss: Robarts's daughter, Robin (right), is overcome at her father's funeral. Robarts's second wife, Katherine (middle), and her daughter, Kimberly (left), stand alongside. *(courtesy Julien LeBourdais)*

The Chairman of the Board: No nickname ever fit its recipient more
appropriately. After a stellar career as prime minister of Ontario,
Robarts became a corporate lawyer, director, and university chancellor.
(courtesy William G. Davis)

10

THE TRANSITION

JOHN ROBARTS BEGAN the William Davis era at Queen's Park with a very amusing state-of-the-province summary. "I'm not going to bother you with a lot of advice," the former prime minister told his successor. "Besides, I've only left you two minor problems: Spadina, and the Bishop's Brief."

Robarts must have exhibited an ear-to-ear grin after uttering those words. He had not left Davis "two minor problems" but two giant headaches, either one of which had the potential to cost the Tories the next election. "Spadina" was the Spadina Expressway, which Metropolitan Toronto Council wanted to build to enable suburbanites quicker access to the city's downtown. But the expressway would have cut a swath right through some of the city's oldest and most politically influential neighbourhoods. Residents launched numerous protests and begged Davis to intervene. The "Bishop's Brief" was the burgeoning Roman Catholic community's demand for full public funding of the separate school system. Successive bishops had lobbied hard for more money for the Catholic system, which had become quite inferior to the public system, thanks to all the investments made by Robarts and his education minister, Bill Davis. While Robarts did offer an additional year's worth of funding to the separate system, he knew the Tory political base would look very unfavourably at funding the Catholic system right to the end of Grade 13. But with Catholics soon to become a majority of the population in Ontario, that political strategy was becoming increasingly risky. And now it was Bill Davis's problem.

Besides Spadina and the Bishop's Brief, Davis was inheriting a government that was unabashedly pro-growth and determined to play an increasingly bigger role in the development of the province. Today the province of Ontario is a $71-billion-a-year business, but when Robarts assumed the prime ministership in 1961, the entire provincial budget was only $1 billion. A decade later, as he was leaving office, Robarts's treasurer, Charles MacNaughton, presented a budget almost three times as big: $2.75 billion. Davis would pick up the baton and run with it, making government even bigger, although unlike Robarts, Davis would never balance any of his budgets during his fourteen years as premier. (Robarts joked to Davis's treasurer, Darcy McKeough, after his first budget in 1971, "Your *deficit* is bigger than my first budget!")

There is no wake-up call in politics that is quite so abrupt as what happens to first ministers who lose their crowns. A perfect example is what happened to Robarts shortly after he retired, and curiously enough, it happened on his home turf. A couple of dozen prominent Conservatives in London gathered at the home of Bill and Ann Rudd just prior to an annual general meeting. Bill Rudd was now president of the provincial Tories, and both he and his wife had backed Davis in the leadership convention to succeed their good friend John Robarts. At one point in the evening, Ann Rudd entered the living room from the kitchen and was surprised to find Robarts almost all alone with her husband and just two other long-time Tories. She later discovered nearly every other guest in her home was in the den. Many were sitting on the floor, balancing dinner plates on their laps. Why? Because the new premier, Bill Davis, was holding court in that room. "Where is everybody?" Ann Rudd asked Robarts.

"Annie, my dear," Robarts responded, "you have just witnessed what happens when power passes."

(Virtually the same thing happened to William Davis fourteen years later. Davis had just retired as the longest-serving premier of Ontario in the twentieth century and was planning to transfer power to his successor, Frank Miller. On this occasion on the second floor of the legislature building, Miller was mobbed by reporters and camera crews outside the premier's office. All of them wanted to know how the new premier's first day was going. Meanwhile, Davis and his deputy minister, Ed Stewart, stood nearby, by themselves, leaning against the door to the premier's office, watching the spectacle. Davis appeared to be chewing just a little bit harder on his omnipresent pipe, no doubt unhappily marvelling at what happens, as Robarts put it, "when power passes.")

Losing power also meant that John Robarts was now obliged to drive his own car, since his days of being chauffeured around the province courtesy of the taxpayers were over. "He was a terrible driver and it was frightening being with him," jokes his niece Andrea Robarts. "He'd be chatting away, not paying any attention to the road, his car weaving all over the white line."

Later in 1971 Premier Davis made what turned out to be a brilliant political decision, but one that appears not to have impressed his predecessor. After considerable debate, Davis heeded the wishes of those downtown Toronto neighbourhood groups and intervened to stop construction of the Spadina Expressway. With this one decision, he demonstrated some remarkable political acumen. He showed he was not afraid to reverse course and be his own man, not beholden to decisions of the previous government. He also showed an understanding of urban issues, which politically allowed the Tories to stay competitive in downtown Toronto. (No Tory leader has since demonstrated similar smarts on inner-city issues, as evidenced by the fact that the Ontario PCs held *zero* seats in Toronto after the October 2003 election.)

At this time, Robarts and Norah were in London, England, on a holiday. During that trip, Robarts hooked up with a contingent of Ontario government officials who were there on business for the province. The group included Keith Reynolds, Charles MacNaughton, Darcy McKeough, and Ian Macdonald, all of whom accompanied the Robartses one night to a theatre in London's West End. The Canadian actor John Colicos was starring as Winston Churchill in a play about the Royal Air Force's firebombing of Germany during the Second World War. During one scene, Colicos took his audience through the agonizing decision-making process Churchill experienced. There were tears in his eyes in the scene. "Robarts was really taken with this," remembers Ian Macdonald. "It really got to him—the dilemmas that the decision makers have."

His political career may have been over. But that did not mean John Robarts's days of playing politics were done. He wanted to do something positive for the federal Tory leader. So he called Don Matthews, his friend from his London days. "Somebody's gotta give Bob Stanfield the loyalty he deserves," Robarts said, as he lobbied Matthews to seek the presidency of the Progressive Conservative Party of Canada. Matthews had not intended to go for the job, but like so many others, he could not resist Robarts's powers of persuasion.

"When a guy says that to you, what the hell are you going to do?" Matthews says today. Ironically, the man who would become national PC Party president from 1971 to 1974 had and would have connections to other political parties. Matthews himself had been president of the CCF club at Queen's University for two years. His daughter Shelley married David Peterson, who would win his first election as a

Liberal MPP in 1975 and become premier of Ontario ten years later. Another daughter, Deb, is the current Liberal MPP for London North Centre.

After a very successful decade at the helm of Canada's biggest province, Robarts was now ideally placed to write his own ticket in the private sector. But where to work? Should he return to London's legal community, where it all started for him before politics? Or stay in Toronto, where so much of his life now resided? And if he did choose Toronto, which law firm should he join? With so many established blue-chip firms in town, signing up with one would most likely alienate the others, and maybe even raise unwanted questions about whether that firm had received preferential treatment during the former prime minister's last months in office.

Fraser Elliott's connection to John Robarts began the day the prime minister announced his retirement. The two men had no history at all. Elliott and his partner, Heward Stikeman, ran a prominent and successful law firm in Montreal and wanted to expand to Toronto. Elliott had touched base with Robarts five days before the prime minister's announcement, then saw him at his office at Queen's Park early on the day of the public statement. Elliott made him an offer to join the new Toronto office. "He had a choice of all the firms in Toronto," Elliott acknowledges. "He'd have put a lot of noses out of joint if he joined an established firm. We were going to try to take over their territory." Robarts resolved that if he joined Stikeman Elliott, he could avoid getting embroiled in any existing turf wars among the established firms.

"I guess he was a bit of a rainmaker," Elliott says of Robarts's responsibilities at the firm. "I didn't want him to be a detail man. He couldn't have done it anyway." Robarts's knowledge of the ins and outs of the law may have been more than a decade out of date. But his rainmaking skills were quite good. "He got us business we wouldn't otherwise have got," is how Elliott puts it. "He knew everybody. He knew where to go. And he was a kind, caring, intelligent person who was a team player."

Robarts instantly integrated himself into Stikeman Elliott's culture. In fact, the Toronto firm was renamed Stikeman Elliott Robarts and Bowman, reflecting his status as a heavy hitter. Far from simply using the firm as a place to hang his hat, Robarts attended all its social functions, enjoyed the partners' meetings, and had the Elliotts to his cottage at Grand Bend. "He was a positive addition to my life and this firm in Toronto," Elliott now says. "I didn't have a history with him. I landed on him when he was five days before the end of his premiership and gave him a new career."

"We used to see him roaming the halls," says David Brown, still a lawyer at Stikeman's today. "We thought of him as the big grandfather of the firm."

"He was fantastic," recalls Margo Carson, who at age twenty-one became Robarts's secretary at Stikeman's on the forty-ninth floor of Commerce Court. "He was very discreet and professional around the office. Quietly playful. He'd look out the window at the islands and the boats and say, 'I'd much rather be out there on a boat than ever going to a board meeting.'"

Within a year after his retirement from politics, Robarts found himself on nearly a dozen boards of directors. Abitibi. Canadian Imperial Bank of Commerce. Canada Steamship Lines. Power Corporation. Holiday Inn. They were a few of the bigger names. And he continued his interest in public policy, education, and his home-town of London by agreeing to serve as chancellor of the University of Western Ontario, his alma mater.

Robarts also linked up with Don Matthews by joining the board of the Matthews Group, a wildly successful development company in London, which would enjoy forty straight profitable years and whose annual revenues would one day approach $1 billion. One day after a board meeting, Robarts asked Matthews if he could use his office to make a few phone calls before heading out. Matthews agreed. Half an hour later, Matthews poked his nose into his office and found the former prime minister of Ontario going through his desk drawers. "I've always been interested in how people keep their desks," Robarts told him. "It tells me a lot about people." Robarts noted that Matthews had kept a drawerful of schedule books. "Why do you keep these things?" he asked.

"No real good reason," Matthews answered. "I live with the damn thing for a year so I don't want to throw it away."

"Well, get rid of them," Robarts urged him. "If someone wants to take a run at you legally, they can misinterpret all sorts of things in there." And with that, Matthews threw them all out.

Hunting and fishing still provided John Robarts with the peace and tranquility that was not a part of the rest of his life. To that end, Robarts became one of the founding members of an elite club on Griffiths Island, near Grey County in Georgian Bay.

"We bought the island," says J.J. Barnicke. "We borrowed $1 million from the Canadian Imperial Bank of Commerce, and the club had as many as seventy members at its peak."

Griffiths Island became Robarts's ideal getaway. And unfortunately for his marriage, you could add hunting and fishing to a list that already included politics and the social scene in Toronto as yet another kind of activity in which Norah Robarts had absolutely no interest.

Some habits of Robarts's did not change with his departure from political office. He still loved to hit the town in the evenings with friends, toss back a few drinks, and listen to music. On one occasion, he quite accidentally encountered a man who strung him along on a beautiful ruse, and who would later come to introduce him to a whole new segment of Toronto society. The man was Peter Widdrington. Strangely enough, he was a senior manager for Labatt's Breweries in London, Ontario, but Robarts did not know him. Then, just after Robarts's second election win, Labatt's sent Widdrington to California for four years to try to rescue Lucky Lager, a failing brewery the company owned there. From time to time, he would return to London or Toronto, get caught up in all the local gossip, then return to California. One night, Widdrington found himself alone and with a free evening in Toronto, so he hit one of the city's favourite nightspots. As he was watching the show, in walked John Robarts with a couple of pals; they parked themselves next to Widdrington. The gregarious Robarts personality quickly manifested itself. "Hi, I'm John Robarts," he said. "How are you?"

Widdrington happily joined in conversation, mentioned he was visiting from California, and before long, the two were discussing the latest details of provincial politics and the London social scene. Robarts was astounded. "Just who are you anyway?" he finally said, completely confused as to how this stranger would know so much about his hometown.

"I'm just some guy from California," Widdrington said accurately, although perhaps not completely truthfully.

"How does someone from California know so much about Ontario politics?" Robarts asked him again.

Widdrington was delighting in the spectacle of the former prime minister and his minions having no clue how this stranger would be so plugged in to local issues. "I never spilled the beans either," Widdrington told me last year, after recounting the story. "It was so amusing watching this gigantic captain of industry and head of the province get more and more puzzled."

In July 1973, after four years in California, Widdrington returned to London and became chief executive officer of Labatt's for the next seventeen years. A few years later, he and Robarts would cross paths again on the board of one of the most successful and influential companies ever created in Ontario: the Toronto Blue Jays.

If Robarts had an overall successful reputation after his political career was over, he was doing nothing in the private sector to diminish that. His star shone just as brightly, and his integrity was considered so unimpeachable that various governments tapped him to chair special commissions on matters of public interest.

The Davis government wanted to determine whether Metropolitan Toronto was still working as well as it could as a municipality. Twenty years earlier, when the Leslie Frost government created Metro Toronto out of thirteen disparate smaller towns, it was seen as one of the most modern, efficient municipal restructuring efforts in North American history. But in the early 1970s, the province was starting to hear the early rumblings of discontent. So Davis struck a royal commission on Metro Toronto and convinced Robarts to take the chairmanship. He was an ideal choice. As a native Londoner, Robarts could not have been accused of favouring one particular vision for the city over another because of past political ties. But as a man who had spent considerable time in the city since 1951, Robarts knew the issues well and would not need months of briefings to understand the difference between Maple Leaf Gardens and Allan Gardens.

One of the first things Robarts did was gather together some familiar faces for his new team. Richard Rohmer, his former right-hand man, became the commission's senior legal counsel. Robarts's former secretary at Stikeman's, Margo Carson, had since moved on to a promotion at another law firm, Fraser Beatty. But she was not enjoying her time there. "I called him up and asked if he needed a secretary for the royal commission," Carson recalls.

"Well, of course, Margo," Robarts told her. "Come on aboard." Carson became senior secretary and spent the entire four years the commission lasted on staff.

In June 1977 Robarts unveiled his prescription for making Metro Toronto work better. At this point in its evolution, Metro consisted of six (rather than the original thirteen) municipalities: Toronto, North York, Scarborough, Etobicoke, York, and East York. Emergency services such as police and fire were more efficiently organized than in the old days, when there had been thirteen different police departments, thirteen different fire chiefs, and so on. However, there were some unusual aspects to the situation. Members of Metro Council were not directly elected to it. In those days, voters in each local ward elected two councillors. The one with the higher vote tally sat on Metro Council as well. (The second-place finisher sat only on the local council.) In addition, the Metro councillors—not the general public—voted for a chairman, which meant the most powerful municipal politician in the country never actually had to face any *real* voters. Nevertheless, the system seemed to work relatively well. Voters were hardly taking to the streets, clamouring for a different system of governance. But some pundits and provincial politicians saw something strangely amiss in an entirely different level of government not actually being directly elected by (or some would argue, accountable to) the voters of what would soon be Canada's most populous city. Naturally, neither the Metro chairman nor very many of the Metro councillors saw anything wrong with the system, since they were the beneficiaries of it.

Robarts picked up on those nagging doubts about how democratic Metropolitan Toronto Council was and made some sensible recommendations. The Metro chairman should be elected by the public, he said, not just forty-odd politicians. The council itself should also be directly elected, Robarts thought, so the Metro Council job would have real meaning, not just be an afterthought for politicians, whose bread was still buttered in the local wards.

One other major recommendation related to the two smallest municipalities in Metro: York and East York. Residents in those boroughs seemed to like identifying themselves with a jurisdiction that was smaller and more distinctive than the four other bigger ones. But that independence came with a price. Neither York nor East York had much of an industrial tax assessment base, and as a result, homeowners paid much higher property taxes than those in the other constituent municipalities. Robarts felt any municipality with fewer than 200,000 residents really could not survive and recommended that York and East York be merged with their larger neighbours. Financially, it made perfect sense. Politically, it was a tough sell.

He made two other key recommendations. He wanted politicians elected on three-year, rather than two-year terms, which was then the practice. Two years was too short, Robarts thought. Politicians were perpetually campaigning for office, and two years just was not enough time to sink your teeth into major issues. Furthermore, the commission considered, and rejected, eliminating one tier of government entirely—in other words, creating one giant megacity. Torontonians were attached to their local municipalities and demanded a level of on-the-ground service that Robarts thought would be jeopardized if one enormous council were created.

Robarts's recommendations for the city were thoughtfully reasoned and aimed at making governance more democratic. But for the cautious Davis, who led only a minority government and had already been burned badly on the municipal restructuring known as regional government, Robarts's ideas were too ambitious. Davis moved on none of the major recommendations, except for lengthening the term of office to three years. (However, after Davis left provincial politics and David Peterson took over in 1985, his Liberal government implemented almost all Robarts's ideas, sensing an electorate that was much more open to change. While the Metro chairman would not be elected across the entire municipality, he would be forced to find a ward, win a popular election, and then be chosen by his colleagues on council. Similarly, the indirect election of Metro councillors would end. Candidates would now run for either the local tier of government, or the upper one, but not both. York and East York survived as political entities, however, and their residents continued to pay higher than average property taxes. As an interesting postscript to efforts to revamp municipal government in Toronto, it was the Mike Harris government of 1995 that eliminated local municipalities altogether and created one megacity council. Harris's reward for disregarding Robarts's advice was to be portrayed as a philistine, ignorant of inner-city concerns. Over two elections, Harris's Conservatives lost every seat in the old city of Toronto, and eventually, after the October 2003 election, which brought Dalton McGuinty's Liberals to power, the Tories lost every seat in the entire megacity as well. The Conservatives' unwillingness to show some understanding for the issues Robarts championed has left them a spent force in virtually every major urban area of the province.)

DURING ROBARTS'S SECOND TERM as premier, he wanted to pursue a big-ticket item that would both represent a Centennial project for the province and demonstrate Ontario's being on the cutting edge of the emerging knowledge economy. According to Martin Friedland, in his massive tome *The University of Toronto: A History* (University of Toronto Press, 2002), Robarts toyed with the idea of building a provincial library, just as it had a provincial art gallery (the Art Gallery of Ontario) and a provincial museum (the Royal Ontario Museum). However, he decided to go a different route, and opted instead for the Ontario Science Centre. It was a great decision, and thirty years later the Science Centre continues to delight young students and adults alike with its exhibits, designed to make science more accessible.

In 1968 Robarts did find some money for a significant new library, to be built on the downtown campus of the University of Toronto. Five years later, the $40 million edifice opened its doors and is now the third-biggest library in North America (measured by the number of books, its budget, and staff). It is named the John P. Robarts Research Library. Ironically, for an institute that was supposed to be a testament to its namesake's love of education, the Robarts Library was mired in controversy from the get-go. Surrounded by much smaller university buildings and residential neighbourhoods, the library is hardly consistent with the streetscape. Its massive size deeply disturbed the neighbours. Friedland writes that by the time the day came to open the building, both the major university and political figures of the day held no official opening ceremony, hoping to avoid further controversy.

Students and neighbours nicknamed the building Fort Book because of its monstrous size. The library's design is unique but also difficult to describe. If one stands to the south of the building, looking north, it sort of looks like a peacock spreading its feathers. Others have said it more closely resembles a turkey. Critics might agree for different reasons. If it was difficult to describe the building accurately, Robarts certainly had no trouble offering a clear, concise opinion of it. "The library is without a doubt the ugliest building I've ever seen in my life, and it's got my name on it!" he once said, while driving by en route to lunch at the York Club.

A portrait of Robarts hangs in the library, and there is a story behind that as well. After every Ontario first minister retires, it is the tradition for him to select an artist who will paint the official portrait to remain in perpetuity in the Ontario legislature. When Robarts and his friends saw the former prime minister's portrait unveiled, it is not an exaggeration to say they collectively gasped in horror. None of Robarts's qualities was present in the painting. Chairman of the Board? The man in the painting looked more like the prissy chairman of the local Scrabble club. Robarts asked that the painting be taken down, which it was, and stored in the attic at Queen's Park. The wheels were then set in motion to have a second work commissioned. "I think it's the first time in Ontario history I know of where the official portrait was changed because people wanted to see a portrait there, a living memory, that reflected what people thought about him," William Davis now says.

Eventually, Robarts's former deputy, J. Keith Reynolds, suggested the portrait nobody liked be sent to the Robarts Library, where thousands of students might see it. But none of them would ever have met

John Robarts, so it was thought that the offending picture could do less damage there. The second portrait, which hangs outside the premier's office on the second floor of the legislature, absolutely captures the Robarts his colleagues admired. It was painted from a photograph by the renowned Armenian-Canadian artist Onnig Cavouk, taken just before Robarts resigned as prime minister. The nerdy-looking pedant in a tweed jacket was replaced with a strong, vigorous-looking Chairman of the Board in a dark blue suit. It is the right portrait in the right place.

In 1976 JOHN ROBARTS joined a new board of directors that would pay him not very much money but offer him entrée into a new, exciting world: Major League Baseball. Back in 1976, the new American League expansion franchise for Toronto was owned by a triumvirate of Labatt's Breweries, R. Howard Webster, and the Canadian Imperial Bank of Commerce. Labatt's and Webster each appointed two members to the Blue Jays board, the CIBC one more. Webster used his two votes to put himself and the former prime minister of Ontario on the board. Robarts's appointment actually created a bit of a stir in the Blue Jay head offices. First, he knew nothing about baseball. Second, the city of London now seemed overrepresented on the board, given that the two Labatt's positions were held by Londoners, the other by Peter Widdrington. But Robarts did bring something to the table no one else did. "John Robarts gave legitimacy to the board," says Paul Beeston, the former accountant from Welland, Ontario, former Blue Jays money man and the recently retired chief operating officer of Major League Baseball in the commissioner's office in New York City, where he earned a multimillion-dollar salary. "He'd walk into a room and there was a presence there. He gave us presence."

The other members of the board were all individually much richer than Robarts, but he was the star. People returned his calls. And there was that gravelly voice. "How are ya, Paul?" Beeston says, doing his best Robarts imitation. "His secretary said he looked forward to the meetings of the Blue Jays because they were so fun and different. He showed up at every meeting, and for what we were paying him, it wasn't for the money."

Beeston says the Blue Jays board got on remarkably well. Besides the five ownership reps, there were three young baseball men—Pat Gillick, Peter Bavasi, and Beeston—who were like kids in a candy store. And remember, when Robarts was there, the team was reasonably successful at the box office, awful on the field, and still more than a decade away from playing in the SkyDome and winning the back-to-back World Series of 1992 and 1993. "That was a group that really got along very well," Beeston says. "From 1976 until 1991, when Mr. Webster died, there was never a problem. It was a collegial group that made decisions well."

The first major decision the new board had to consider was what to call the new team. Baseball fans sent in thirty-five hundred possibilities, and a group of sportswriters then narrowed down the choices to ten. Curiously enough, the name Blue Jays was not on that top-ten list. Board members knew that if Labatt's had its druthers, the word *blue* would appear somewhere in the team's name, playing off the brewery's successful Labatt's Blue brand of beer. But none of the best options at the moment featured that word. Some liked Toronto Towers, because of the proximity of the CN Tower to the team's home park at the Canadian National Exhibition grounds. For similar reasons, others thought the Toronto Exhibitions would work. Others still wanted to hearken back to the city's great baseball history by calling the team the Toronto Maple Leafs, paying homage not to the legendary hockey team but the minor league baseball team that used to play its games in Maple Leaf Stadium at the foot of Bathurst Street.

The discussion at the board continued, but none of the names was grabbing any support among the members. Then, apropos of absolutely nothing, Robarts started talking about his morning routine.

"I was shaving this morning and I saw a blue jay out my window," he told board members.

"That's an interesting name," one said. It was the first time anyone had mentioned the words *blue jay*.

"The Labatt's guys liked it," recalls Paul Beeston. "Then Howard's got the name all over his mouth. It just got going. And all of a sudden, we became the Toronto Blue Jays." Beeston then roars with laughter, recalling what Gerry Snyder, the former Montreal city councillor, who helped bring the Olympics and the Expos to Montreal, said shortly after the board agreed on Blue Jays: "It's a good thing Robarts didn't see a fucking sparrow."

In a final piece of kismet, who should become one of the senior executives in the Blue Jays organization, by virtue of his connection with Labatt's? Why, Peter Widdrington, of course—the same "California" man who baffled Robarts with his knowledge of Ontario years earlier in a Toronto bar. "I was on the Blue Jays board and saw him frequently and he never remembered that night," Widdrington says with a chuckle, still amused at the fast one he played on the former prime minister.

Robarts never did become a baseball fan. But he was wonderfully supportive of the young Jays' management. What Beeston really came to enjoy were the heart-to-heart talks he shared with Robarts. "What do you miss the most about politics," Beeston once asked him.

"Paul, the power!" Robarts said, using a word no Canadian politician would ever be caught dead uttering. (Tradition holds that politicians are supposed to be in the business of public service, not wielding power). "At that time, you could get anywhere. Doors were open for you. You will not ever understand, unless you were in the position, how much power there is."

J.J. Barnicke confirms noting those sentiments in his old friend. "Once you get into politics, they don't make a pill that makes you get over it," he says. "Once they get in, they're life long. They love the power, the fun, the action."

Beeston summarizes Robarts's involvement with the Jays: "It wouldn't matter whether or not he was the premier of Ontario," he says. "If he walked into a room with that voice, that moustache, that look, you'd say, Who's that? He had national fame, yet when you were with him, you felt you were with a friend. He made you feel quite relaxed. He was just a terrific person."

Paul Beeston still does something to this day because he saw John Robarts do it first. When Beeston's mother died in 1978, Robarts wrote him a note of condolence and signed it "John R." "So I started signing all my notes 'Paul B.,'" Beeston says.

IN NOVEMBER 1976, Canadians woke up to a new and shocking reality. The separatist Parti Québécois was elected in Quebec. For the first time since Confederation, Canadians had to give serious thought to the possibility that their country might fall apart.

Robarts had always enjoyed a good relationship with Prime Minister Pierre Trudeau. Even though their time as first ministers together only lasted two years, Trudeau retained a favourable impression of this former premier, who always enjoyed high approval ratings in Quebec. Within a year of René Lévesque's victory, Trudeau would bring Robarts back into public life and team him up with the former Quebec federal Liberal politician Jean-Luc Pepin as co-chairs of the Pepin-Robarts Task Force on Canadian Unity. Initially, Robarts had doubts about getting back into the national spotlight. He told Ian Macdonald at the time, "I'm not sure I can face more rubber chicken sandwiches at ten o'clock at night." He felt he was finally entitled to take life a little easier. But in the end, he acquiesced to Trudeau's entreaties.

Trudeau's co-chairs were a study in contrasts. In some respects, they were perfect stereotypes of Canada's two solitudes. Pepin was emotional, fiery, and loquacious. Robarts was the picture of a solid, pragmatic English Canadian. Yet each knew and liked the other, mostly from their serving on two boards together (Canada Steamship Lines and Power Corporation).

"He talked much less than Jean-Luc Pepin, but when he spoke, people listened," says Ron Watts, the former principal of Queen's University, now a professor at the university's Institute of Intergovernmental Relations. "He was enormously respected by the Quebec members of the task force."

Watts, one of the commissioners on the task force, recalls that one Saturday morning at a meeting in Ottawa, Robarts asked each of the French-Canadian members—Solange Chaput-Rolland (the Quebec commentator and writer), Gérald Beaudoin (dean of law at the University of Ottawa), and Pepin—to tell the entire gathering what his or her own experiences had been as a francophone in a country dominated by anglophones. "John was very much moved by what they said," Watts says. "That was all he could talk about. How different it was for them. He had a sympathy and an empathy for the French-Canadian members of the commission."

"When I heard he was going to be one of the co-chairs of the task force, my reaction was, Fantastic!" recalls Gérald Beaudoin. "He always told me, 'I'm ready to make constitutional reforms if that's what it takes to keep Québec in Canada.' He was in love with Canada."

"He was a good foil and balance to Pepin," adds Ron Watts. "Sometimes the press criticized him because he wasn't as dominant as Pepin, but he was very influential inside."

"He would sit for long stretches of time and say nothing—you'd wonder if he was even awake," recalls John Evans, the former University of Toronto president who was also one of the English-Canadian commissioners. "Suddenly, he'd contribute to the conversation. And I came to realize that his apparent silence and sleepy demeanour didn't mean his brain circuits were shut off. He seemed to listen, then pull out something that was central to the issue. Robarts didn't look fully engaged at all, but he was."

Robarts's lack of dynamism no doubt related to his health. He was not quite obese at this point, but he was definitely very overweight, no doubt a factor of constantly being on the road and touring the country. "The excesses of alcohol were apparent," admits John Evans. "He tended to lose focus toward the end of the day. The general impression was of a person who was tired or a bit burned out but had a lot of wisdom to bring."

However, Robarts impressed everyone with his firm view that no Ontario government should be too independent from the national government. He regretted how first ministers' conferences had descended into public bickering contests and found it unseemly when the provinces ganged up on the prime minister.

"Ontario can't afford to be anti-federalist," Robarts told Evans during a private conversation. It was a lesson Robarts's successor as Ontario premier similarly learned. During one particularly nasty spat between Ottawa and the provinces, Evans once asked Bill Davis, "Why don't you sock those bastards in Ottawa? It's so crazy what they're doing. And he said, 'Ontario will never take an anti-federal position.'

"John Robarts thought he was as important to making the federation work as the federal government was," Evans adds. "He was a father statesman. Unruffled. We appreciated his demeanour. Had a calming effect on people of different polarities."

According to Gérald Beaudoin, Robarts was open to major constitutional changes, with one exception. "He said to me, 'Beaudoin, you like constitutional law. You want to amend the Constitution. That's all right with me as long as we keep the Queen," Beaudoin recalls. "I said, 'John, that's fine. The monarchy was never part of the problem.'"

The task force criss-crossed the country, taking the national temperature in as thorough a fashion as had ever been attempted. Many critics feared the task force was a grand con job by Trudeau, designed to lower the temperature in the face of the Parti Québécois government's election. But Robarts and Pepin made sure it was nothing of the kind. They listened to endless deputations in every major city in the country, determined to give ordinary Canadians their say. When it came time to publishing excerpts from those presentations in the final report, the task force pulled no punches. "Why aren't those who have the power to change the situation that creates a disturbance here instead of you?" one submission from Vancouver asked. "Perhaps they have decided to enjoy their Parliament Hill cocktail parties."

"I had reservations about participating in this show. But after having been told by the media that our economic problem is the result of my living too high off the hog and the Quebec problem is the result of my not learning French, I come to seek out the real culprits of our malaise," said another in Winnipeg.

Robarts even heard out the separatists. "This task force is but another cog in the enormous propaganda machine set up by the Canadian bourgeoisie to deny the Quebec nation the right to self-determination," opined one Montrealer.

Or this from another Montrealer: "This task force is just a smoke-screen, a lot of humbug to make a shaky Confederation look good."

And there were the cynics. "We have a government which deals with a separatist threat by sending sixty highly paid people, living in luxury hotels, on a tour of Canada to see how much the average citizen can say in five minutes."

But there were others who offered submissions that had to warm the hearts of even the most cynical political observers. "I feel very lonely up here," one person said in Toronto, "because I don't belong to any particular group. I'm a worker. I pay my taxes so we can have this kind of thing. But I think it's worth it."

In St. John's, one presenter said apologetically, "I hope I haven't taken up too much of your time, but, as you see, I'm on crutches. I made a special effort to get here because Canada means a lot to me."

Someone from Moncton said, "I came here today to participate in this task force because as far as I'm concerned, it's the first worthwhile attempt made by the federal government to unite Canada since they built the railway to link the Atlantic to the Pacific."

The task force published all comments, whether they were positive or negative, laudatory or skeptical in the extreme. Then in March 1979, less than two years after the task force was struck, it published three reports on the state of Canada's unity and offered numerous recommendations for improving it. Three years before Pierre Trudeau brought the Canadian Constitution home from Westminster, Pepin-Robarts recommended a new Constitution with more decentralization, and unity through pluralism. It was not what the prime minister was looking for.

"Trudeau really dismissed it out of hand," says Darcy McKeough. "And that was the end of it. But if we'd listened to Pepin and Robarts then, there might have been a different story in the future." McKeough is referring to the failures of the Meech Lake and Charlottetown constitutional accords, both of which followed the spirit (and some of the letter) of the Pepin-Robarts recommendations. Both also received overwhelming support from the political leadership of the country, and both still failed to achieve passage.

However, despite the cool reaction from Trudeau and his Quebec lieutenant Marc Lalonde, Gérald Beaudoin for one thinks much of what Pepin-Robarts recommended has come to pass. The commission wanted a Charter of Rights and Freedoms. Canadians got one in 1982, when Trudeau initiated the patriation of the Constitution. Pepin-Robarts also favoured the equality of French and English in national institutions. Section 16 of the charter achieved that.

"As a jurist, I think what we proposed was taken care of," concludes Beaudoin. "In 1980, we weren't too happy with the government's reaction, but I was happy in 1982. So we didn't work for nothing."

More than twenty years later, how does Beaudoin look back at his association with the former Ontario prime minister? "I have only good words to say for John because he was so well intentioned," he says. "He was so sympathetic to the Quebec question. Everybody had great admiration for him."

Robarts's legal career was doing extremely well. He sat as a valued member of many boards of directors. His love of politics and public policy brought him the chairmanship of two significant royal commissions, one federal and one provincial. Everything in his life seemed to be going so well, with one critical exception. John Robarts was, perhaps, the most unhappily married man he knew.

"*Everyone* was aware that his home life was difficult," acknowledges Robert Nixon, Robarts's former political rival. Nixon remembers that back in 1967 many foreign visitors came to Canada to help celebrate the country's hundredth birthday. He and his wife, Dorothy, happened to be invited to one small state dinner, attended by perhaps a couple of dozen people. Robarts was there in his capacity as prime minister of Ontario, and Norah Robarts was there as well. Nixon could not believe what he saw. "I was always quite dumbstruck at how personally critical she was of John, in everything he was doing and saying," Nixon says. "I think it was sort of an attempt at emasculation."

"Being premier held that marriage together," says Joan Smith. "You didn't divorce if you were in politics then."

Don Smith remembers Robarts's opening Alumni Hall at the University of Western Ontario all by himself. "His wife lived three blocks away and didn't come," he says.

After Robarts's retirement from Queen's Park, he and Norah attended the annual press gallery dinner. In a skit that brought the house down, *The London Free Press* reporter George Hutchison performed the role of the outgoing prime minister and could not help noticing how much Norah Robarts delighted in seeing her husband lampooned. "She'd been so taciturn for years," Hutchison recalls. "She was laughing and having a great time."

Close friends of the couple were convinced that John and Norah Robarts loved each other. They enjoyed each other's company and opening their home to friends and family. But twenty years of prolonged absences were finally taking their toll. The marriage just was not working, and the evidence was everywhere. Andrea Robarts remembers that when she got married, her uncle gave the toast to the bride. Norah continually injected sharp little barbs from the side. Robarts did his best to ignore the comments, but in the end, his loving toast "turned into a sarcastic commentary on marriage," Andrea remembers with a smile.

Norah's refusal to move to Toronto when Robarts became prime minister—for what she saw as very legitimate reasons—in essence doomed the relationship. One of them had to yield, and certainly Robarts was not going to give up the premiership to practise law in London so Norah could raise her children in her hometown and enjoy that city's social scene.

After retiring from politics, Robarts asked his wife one last time to move to Toronto. He figured the children were older. His career, both at the law firm and on corporate boards, was inextricably tied to Toronto. With the income he was now making, the two of them could have a wonderful life in the provincial capital. But, just as Norah had dug in her heels on this same issue many years earlier, she was not about to change her mind now. "Norah just was never there, and John of course had to be there," family friend Richard Dillon says. "I think that was the basis of it. If there hadn't been that division, I don't think there would have been anything wrong because it wasn't that they didn't love each other. They did."

The two of them began to deteriorate physically. Robarts's weight hit 240 pounds. And Norah's alcoholism became all too apparent. John Robarts had made myriad tough decisions as prime minister of

Ontario. But this next decision was unlike any of those. It was deeply personal, not political. He decided his future was in Toronto, not London.

"He loved the life in Toronto," says Eleanor Robarts, his sister-in-law. "He outgrew his London friends."

The couple decided to separate. In some respects, the Robartses' breakup was a long time coming. Nevertheless, it was a great shock to high society in London, which was utterly unaccustomed to seeing such local luminaries' marriages end.

Interestingly, the couple's daughter was not shocked. Robin had lived away from the family for several years now, in Toronto and Calgary. "It didn't surprise me at all," she admits. "I guess perhaps I never thought they were meant to be together. They very rarely were. My mom's life always seemed to be in London with all her friends. And I saw my dad in Toronto when I went to Toronto. They just seemed to lead separate lives, so it wasn't a shock to me." Robin says John and Norah were typical 1950s parents. They didn't argue in front of their children or talk about money in their presence.

If Robin was independent and living away from London and therefore less distressed by her parents' divorce, her brother, Tim, was exactly the opposite. He lived in London. He watched his mother descend into the hell that was her alcoholism. He was a more sensitive kid to begin with. As Robin puts it, "It was very heart-wrenching for my brother."

John Robarts was not the only prominent Londoner whose marriage was ending. Coincidentally, the man who had been at his side for all the achievements of his political career would now join Robarts in having his marriage fall apart too. In 1972 Ernie and Barbara Jackson split up. Neither man would be single for very long.

11

THE WOMAN FROM ROME

PERHAPS THE WORLD should not have been surprised that John Robarts and Ernie Jackson both separated from their wives around the same time. Their lives had essentially been mirror images. Robarts left London to become a political star and discovered he loved the new life he created for himself in Toronto. Jackson also left London for Toronto, and for the same reason—to make John Robarts a star.

The two men, at some level, both loved their wives and unconditionally loved their children. But they hated the constant loneliness of too many evenings in the capital city because their wives refused to leave their old lives behind. Perhaps not surprisingly, both men discovered that alcohol and other women could fill some of that chasm.

Darcy McKeough continued to serve as a cabinet minister in Bill Davis's government after Robarts retired. He kept in touch with Robarts and expressed the sentiments of many in the political world: "I think there were a lot of us who obviously felt bad [about the breakup]. Normally, it's easier to feel bad if you can blame it all on one side or the other. But in this case, you couldn't do that."

Although Robin Robarts was not surprised once her father had made up his mind, Ernie Jackson's daughter, Barbara, was. "I was shocked when they split up," she says. "People didn't do that back then. Our house was the focal point of our social life, and our friends' social life. We were five kids. We had a rambunctious, playful father who organized all sorts of adventures for us." Ernie Jackson wanted to wait until most of his children had grown up and were out of the house before splitting up with his wife. When he did leave, George, the youngest, was the only one still living at home.

"I tried to talk Ernie out of leaving Barb," says John Cronyn, Jackson's wife's cousin. "Ernie was like a second son to my dad until their divorce."

Norah's life changed a great deal. Not only was she no longer the wife of the prime minister of Ontario, she was not even Mrs. John P. Robarts any more. Some acquaintances who no longer had to put up with her idiosyncrasies, due to her decline in status, dropped her. Things got so bad that she even called up Eleanor Robarts, whom she had never cared for in the past. Norah would invite Eleanor for a visit, and when her sister-in-law arrived, it was clear Norah had been abusing alcohol.

"I'd love to refuse to forgive him for what he did to Norah," adds Judith Grieve about her uncle John. "But she did it to herself."

There was another sad irony in Norah Robarts's life. Not only was she trying to re-establish contact with people whose company she previously had not enjoyed, but she also began to reconnect to a world she previously disliked intensely. Strangely enough, at this time she could often be found in the committee back rooms of the London Progressive Conservative Association. "She sat with a phone book and looked up the names and addresses of known Conservative supporters so we could call them and get out the vote," remembers Ann Rudd.

"She was a lonely woman," adds her husband, Bill Rudd, general secretary of the Ontario PC Association during John Robarts's premiership. "But it was a link to her past."

Ernie Jackson had a new woman in his life. Wilma Mossman, named after her father, Wilmot, worked for the Progressive Conservative Party of Ontario at the party's headquarters at 2 Carlton Street, a few doors from Maple Leaf Gardens. She had an attractive, outgoing personality and two children from her first marriage. She had worked for the party for many years, and ironically, given that she ended up marrying John Robarts's best friend, she had actually worked on the Robert Macaulay campaign at the 1961 leadership convention.

Willie, as everyone called her, became a close friend of John Robarts's as well. He would frequently visit the Jackson home in Toronto's Rosedale neighbourhood. "John was a night owl," Willie Jackson recalls. "Ernie would bring him home and I'd end up talking to John till two or three o'clock in the morning. Ernie would say, 'I'll be right back, just got to get something,' and then he'd be out like a light." So Willie would end up entertaining Robarts solo.

The Jacksons were married for more than twenty years, and John Robarts was best man at the wedding.

One of Toronto's hottest nightspots in those days was a place on Jarvis Street, just a few blocks east of Maple Leaf Gardens, called the Bombay Bicycle Club. It was situated on the second floor of the old Massey mansion, which later became a Keg steakhouse restaurant. Robarts frequented the place. He loved the scene—the music, the booze, the people. One summer night in 1973, he was with his friend Don Early when they encountered two women at the club. One of them would change Robarts's life forever, initially for the better, but ultimately for the worse. Katherine Sickafuse was an American nurse who had divorced her husband five years earlier. She had one child, a daughter. She was twenty-eight years old, twenty-eight years younger than John Robarts, and very sexy.

"You girls look pretty warm in here," said Robarts, wearing sunglasses even though it was nighttime. "Why don't you come over to our table and we'll buy you a drink?"

The woman on the receiving end of that pickup line had grown up in a very modest home in Rome, New York. When she first met John Robarts in Toronto, she was less than impressed. "Who the hell do you think you are with shades on at ten o'clock at night?" she asked him.

"Oh, nobody," Robarts answered, a bit chastened, then removed the glasses and stuck them in his pocket. In all his years in public life, nobody had had the sass to talk to John Robarts that way. Now, here was this young thing charming, teasing, and blazing her way into his consciousness.

The two began to spend time together. One of the reasons the pair may have got off to such a good start was that Katherine had no idea she was dating the former prime minister of Ontario. Actually, she had no idea what a prime minister of Ontario even was. After all, she was an American and not at all plugged in to Canadian political nomenclature. "I really wasn't knowledgeable enough to know what a premier was," she now admits. "If they'd said *governor*, I would have gotten it."

Robarts asked Katherine to accompany him on a fishing trip, and he was thrilled when she said yes. He was even more excited when he discovered she was an avid fisher, who energetically engaged him in debates over which made the better fishing lure: flies or worms. "He said he was doing it the professional way," Katherine remembers. "I told him, 'Okay, you do things the professional way and I'll just catch the fish.'"

He adored her youth, her brazen talk, and her willingness to try new things. For example, Katherine had not yet learned how to hunt but was a quick study and, unlike Norah, happily dove into Robarts's world without cynicism or complaint.

"I thought it was a good thing that he'd had that arrangement with Katherine because he'd had a very unhappy first marriage," says Rendall Dick, Robarts's friend from the Ontario public service.

Even Robarts's daughter noticed a positive change in her father. "Dad finally had a playmate," Robin says. "She would hunt and fish and get involved in all the things that he liked to do. And that was really special for him because he hadn't had that in Mum. He really enjoyed having a partner. It was fun to see him so happy and really enjoying himself."

However, one time on Katherine's birthday, Robarts made a faux pas unworthy of the Prince Charming he had become. He was in Texas on a hunting trip, so he arranged to have his secretary send some flowers to Katherine, whom he was now seriously dating. "I got a big bouquet of roses, and the card said, 'Happy Birthday from the Honourable John P. Robarts,'" Katherine remembers. "He heard from me on that one."

"I was the secretary who sent Katherine the flowers," Margo Carson admits. "I didn't know what to sign. He told me afterwards how mad she was! But she was so good for him," Robarts's former secretary adds. "She really did bring him joy." The two called each other by their own personal pet names. He became Jonathan. She was Katherinesen or, more informally, just Kasia, the Polish diminutive of Katherine—her maiden name was Kwasniewski.

Robarts began to integrate her into his social circles. He wanted his friends to meet his new love and, more important, to approve of her. One day, he called up his old friend Don Matthews and invited him to have lunch in a restaurant in Yorkville. "I'm bringing along a new friend" was Robarts's mysterious advance billing for the lunch.

Shortly after their meeting, Robarts called Matthews to get his friend's opinion. "I didn't want to give him any advice," Matthews now says. "She didn't impress me a helluva lot. But he liked her, so that was fine by me."

If Katherine was bringing joy into his life, Norah certainly was not. She was miserable back in London, buoyed by those who stuck by her who could not figure out what had got into her estranged husband. Despite his entreaties, Norah was refusing to grant Robarts a divorce. Nevertheless, he pressed ahead and eventually the couple was divorced.

Three years after meeting Katherine, Robarts suggested they marry. Curiously enough, while the rest of their lives together appeared to be quite romantic, his proposal was anything but. He was sitting on the sofa in the living room of the couple's home on St. Andrews Gardens in Rosedale when he simply blurted out, "I guess we should get married." And with that, they were engaged.

The wedding took place on August 22, 1976, at Katherine's parents' home in Rome, New York. Both Robin and Tim, Robarts's children, were in attendance, as was their first cousin Andrea. "Tim was having a tough time with John," Andrea remembers. "He was isolated and angry. He spent lots of time in the back of the limousine on his own."

Unlike the first time, because he had been overseas at war, Robarts's brother, Bob, was the best man. However, Bob's presence and apparent support belied his true feelings about the marriage. "The wedding was great, except for the tension with Eleanor and Bob," Katherine says. "They made it clear they were there under duress."

Well before the wedding, John Robarts was most anxious that his brother approve of his choice and lobbied hard to ensure an ideal setting for their first encounter. Bob, in truth, did not want to meet her. He was skeptical of Katherine's motives from the start and thought his brother's normally sound judgment had deserted him. He also was not alone in those views. Nevertheless, John was extremely persuasive, so the brothers agreed to meet for a picnic double-date lunch, halfway between London and Toronto.

What does Bob's wife remember about the picnic? "She made good vichyssoise," Eleanor Robarts says of Katherine's culinary skill.

Later, Bob put all his cards on the table. "Parm, what do you think a woman twenty-eight years younger than you wants with a man with a big stomach?"

Robarts was taken aback: "Mind your own damned business," he told his brother. During another debate over Katherine, Robarts sang her praises by telling his brother what a wonderful cook she was. Bob Robarts's response was "You know, Parm, you could hire a cook."

By not minding his own business, Bob dared to say what so many of Robarts's friends were thinking: that Katherine was too young for him, would never fit in with his older friends, and had dubious motives.

As far as Katherine was concerned, none of that mattered. "The age difference didn't bother either one of us because we enjoyed each other so much," she says. "If you'd seen us together, you wouldn't have thought there was any age difference at all."

"In Toronto, there were no ripples whatever," Richard Rohmer says about the news that Robarts would marry again. "But people in London were extremely upset with his carrying on with Katherine and the divorce and the eventual marriage. They really were unhappy about that."

"I wasn't their choice," Katherine admits. "But I didn't want to fight with them. I just wanted us to live our lives. And it was *our* life, not theirs. They didn't understand that he wanted a new life."

"No one could have talked him out of Katherine," says Richard Dillon.

Nancy Poole, another long-time friend from London, puts it simply: "He was besotted."

Robarts's love letters, which Katherine has kept to this day, confirm both of the previous observations. When Robarts would go fishing, he never failed to write Katherine a letter, which usually began with "My darling Kasia." The notes were filled with sweet phrases from someone obviously in love. One note ended, "Good night, little one." Another concluded, "Thinking of you, my darling Kasia. As always, John." Yet another said, "Kasia, sweetheart, so much I want to say and share with you." Or "I have had enough fishing and now want only my beloved Kasia. Your John."

"There's no question, we personally were disappointed," adds Richard Dillon, who was not a fan of Katherine's. "But we never discussed it, obviously." Dillon's comment provides an interesting insight into the kinds of relationships that Robarts had with other men. There was no friend in the world whom Robarts had known for as many years as Dick Dillon, and yet there is no indication the two men ever talked about Robarts's marriage to Norah as it was failing, or his decision to marry Katherine, which Dillon opposed. There were, apparently, some things one just did not discuss with the former prime minister of Ontario, even if you had known him, as Dillon had at this point, for more than forty years.

"His old friends didn't like to see his marriage to Norah broken up," adds John Cronyn. "But we also didn't think Katherine was the gal for him. I could see right through her. But I never took him aside. It was his decision, his business. My saying something wouldn't have made any difference anyway."

"He definitely had poor taste in women," sums up Barb Prevedello.

Paul Beeston only acknowledges the following: "I knew Katherine. And this is where we stop talking."

Joan Smith remembers the first time there was major indignation in London over Katherine. A picture appeared in *The London Free Press* on the occasion of the couple's first anniversary. The picture was snapped while they were out to dinner. "Those pictures don't just happen," Joan Smith insists. "His wife orchestrated that photo op in the restaurant." London was not amused.

But another Robarts colleague, who wishes to remain nameless, has a different interpretation. "They resented Katherine's influence on him," this observer says. "They made him premier and then they lost influence. He didn't care about that any more. He just wanted a happy life and was apparently having it."

Katherine has another theory about why so many of Robarts's friends of long standing disliked her. She became convinced that they saw her as the main impediment to his seeking higher office. "That's what *they* wanted—John as prime minister of Canada," she says.

She tells of one encounter with a businessman friend of her husband's who put it very bluntly. "It's your fault that John refuses to run federally," the man told her.

"Really?" she responded. "Is that what you think? Well, if this man can be so easily influenced by his wife, would you want him to be prime minister?"

"You're American, divorced, and a Roman Catholic," the business-man shot back, suggesting those three qualities would render Robarts unelectable. It seems an odd comment to make since the Canadian prime minister of the day, Pierre Trudeau, was Catholic, and in the process of seeing his marriage break up, two facts that did not prevent him from winning another election. Katherine says that the only other political job Robarts was interested in was to be Canada's high commissioner to the United Kingdom. He loved Britain, travelled there for business frequently, but the appointment was not to be.

As much as Robarts was smitten with Katherine, he was also still smart enough to know that marrying her represented a giant leap of faith, for all the reasons his friends were secretly thinking. Today they insist that if Robarts did have concerns about the advisability of his marriage to Katherine, he kept them to himself—with one exception. On one occasion, after a few drinks, Robarts told Willie Jackson he had his doubts. But by then, the die was cast.

Why did John Robarts marry Katherine Sickafuse? In some respects, it was a union that on paper seemed to be doomed from the start. Robarts must have known that his older friends would never accept her. And, as his law firm partner Fraser Elliott pointed out, "Katherine didn't come from Toronto society," meaning his colleagues in the big city were not likely to cut her much slack either.

Some of Robarts's friends now offer blunter explanations about why he married her than they were prepared to put on the record at the time. "Katherine was looking, and John was needy," says Judith Grieve.

For her part, Katherine felt she got along with her husband's brother quite nicely. But she describes her sister-in-law Eleanor as "a force to be reckoned with," and she does not mean that as a compliment. Bob and Eleanor had a place in Montserrat, the tiny Caribbean island southeast of Puerto Rico, where Katherine and John would occasionally visit. One time, according to Katherine, she and Eleanor got into such a dust-up that John could not take it any more and announced the couple was leaving. Eventually, Bob played peacemaker and they stayed. "But she intimidated me," Katherine says. "You've never seen Eleanor in full throttle, have you? She hated me. She's out of my league."

Katherine theorizes that Eleanor was jealous of the fact that it was John Robarts who became prime minister of Ontario, despite Bob's being eighteen months older. "She thought her husband should have been premier, not John," Katherine says.

Despite the obstacles, John and Katherine Robarts did get off to a good start in many respects. He was earning an excellent living at Stikeman Elliott and on his corporate boards. His desire to remain a relevant national figure was enhanced through his work on the Pepin-Robarts task force. And he was getting a second chance in the love department with a vivacious, exciting woman. They both immersed themselves in Toronto's social scene. Robarts finally had someone with whom to attend all those political events, gala openings, and dinner parties. And Katherine, dressed to the nines, could not have minded being seen on the arm of one of the most respected national figures in the country. The Ontario Archives are filled with pictures of this dynamic duo, Katherine looking smashing, Robarts in a tuxedo looking elegant but overweight; Katherine in conversation with Pierre

Trudeau or the actor Jack Lemmon at some fancy event; Robarts schmoozing with Premier Bill Davis with the omnipresent drink in hand.

Katherine could be a handful, but at this stage in their relationship, Robarts seemed to find that amusing and take it in stride. One day, she called him out of a board meeting, distraught and in tears, to tell him a dog catcher had captured her pooch, intending to impound the poor creature. Robarts instructed her to put the man on the phone, whereupon he brought to bear his inimitable powers of persuasion. He convinced the man to give the dog back and was happy to pay whatever fine was appropriate to bring the crisis to an amicable conclusion. Robarts then returned to his board meeting and told his colleagues, "While you guys are talking about millions of U.S. dollars, I went and solved the dog catcher problem."

Since she enjoyed the outdoors as much as he did, Robarts also took Katherine to his cottage at Grand Bend. The Oakwood Park gang tolerated her but never befriended her or enjoyed her company as they had Norah's. However, that view was not universal. Many younger boys in the area quite liked Katherine, particularly when she sunbathed nude in the backyard. They would gather and peek through the cedar hedges in hopes of catching a glimpse of this woman whose sex appeal was unrivalled by anyone within several hours' drive.

Robarts also appears to have learned his lesson concerning making this marriage succeed. While he took very seriously the work of his national unity task force, he did not let it consume his life. "Occasionally he missed meetings simply because he felt his first marriage had suffered because of the time away," says Ron Watts, one of the commissioners on the panel. "He said he didn't want to do that to his second wife." Nevertheless, the task force did require Robarts to do more travelling than he perhaps wished, and the more sedentary his life got, the more he drank and the more his weight ballooned. For her part, Katherine says she never resented the time the commission took away from the couple. She was accustomed to her husband's frequent absences.

"He was never a nine-to-five kind of guy," she says. "Even on our honeymoon in New York City, he attended a directors' meeting at Met Life."

The new direction of John Robarts's life had very different effects on his two children. Robin, perhaps because she had been so independent for so long, continued to thrive.

"John was always very busy, and Norah was inattentive, and funnily enough, Robin developed freedom and confidence," observes Joan Smith, the former Ontario Liberal cabinet minister and family friend from London. "Freedom didn't destroy her. I give her 100 percent credit for that."

Tim was a different story. Robin describes her brother, three years her junior, as "the cute one—the one that was stopped in elevators." He was artistic, creative, and imaginative. But Tim was also subject to depression, sickly from the time he was a baby, and experiencing very troubled teenage years. "He had the same upbringing I did, but he just didn't respond the way I did," is how Robin describes her brother. "I was very independent. I think he needed more."

"We both felt intimidated by our fathers' success," admits George Jackson, the youngest of Ernie and Barbara Jackson's five children, who was one of Tim's best friends. "We were expected to follow in their footsteps."

The Robartses and Jacksons spent endless hours together in Grand Bend. Once, while sailing, Robarts, who was prime minister at the time, sat Tim and George down on the poop deck and told them, "I count you young men as my friends."

"That was the kind of moment you don't forget," says George Jackson. "We were fourteen years old and friends of the prime minister." (They may have been friends, but each of the boys still called the other's father "Mr. Robarts" and "Mr. Jackson." After all, the men were the most powerful people in the Ontario government.)

"Tim was a delight," remembers his aunt, Judith Grieve. He was funny and charming. Filled with jokes and laughter." But something changed as Tim progressed through his teenage years.

"Tim was very proud of his father, but he was living in the shadow of a great man," says George Jackson. "He was expected to be great." It soon became apparent that by the yardstick of conventional society, Tim just was not great. He showed little ambition for "getting ahead." Unlike George or his other friends, who took summer or weekend jobs painting fences or picking up garbage at Pinery Park on Lake Huron, Tim did neither.

One thing he did show a passion for was cars. He would spend hours with a compass and protractor, engineering designs for futuristic-looking cars. A few years ago, when Dodge came out with its Viper—a spiffy sports car with a very high-tech, space-age appearance, George Jackson was convinced that he had seen the design before. Then he remembered. His old friend Tim Robarts had drawn something that looked just like it twenty-five years earlier. Tim also loved vintage cars. He got himself a 1950s-era Aston Martin, the same kind of car James Bond drove. He hoped to fix it up and resell it. But most of the time the car just sat in the garage at the Robarts home on the Parkway in London.

At one point, the Robartses thought sending Tim to a private boarding school might ignite something more constructive in him. But it did not. He attended Lakefield College School near Peterborough, but by all accounts it was an unpleasant experience for everyone. Tim tried to run away from the school on several occasions. His mother, now all alone in London, missed him terribly. He came home.

"I wasn't bothered by the long absences of Ernie," says George Jackson, who always refers to his father by his first name. "I found it easier to manoeuvre around Mum, so it was better to have him out of town." The same was not true for Tim. The lack of fatherly influence five days a week hurt.

"Norah leaned on Tim to be her man," says Judith Grieve. "She'd yell at him, then hug him. It was the worst parenting."

Robin completely disagrees with Grieve's recollection. "Never in my life did I see her yell at Tim one minute and hug him the next," she insists. "Mum adored Tim. She was a kind, generous, and loving person to Tim. Her descent into hell hurt her far more than it hurt anyone else."

Tim graduated from high school but had no plans at all. The son of the man who approved the redesign for the entire post-secondary education system in Ontario declined to attend either a community college or a university. As well, he refused to get a job. Essentially, Tim Robarts was home a lot, with an unhappy mother, too much time on his hands, and too many opportunities to get into endless trouble. Which he did.

"We were concerned because he was drinking quite a lot," recalls George Jackson. "It was a full bottle of Jack Daniel's every day. He wasn't even getting high, just swilling." Then, when the booze failed to do the trick, Tim graduated to harder stuff. The London of the late 1970s became a kind of way station for the drug trade between Toronto, Buffalo, and Detroit. As a result, without much ingenuity, Tim was able to get his hands on LSD, THC, and PCP, and experimented a great deal with all of them. With his father essentially an absentee parent and his mother descending into her own hell, Tim Robarts became increasingly depressed.

"Norah wasn't cut out for motherhood," Judith Grieve says. "It might have been quite different if John had taken a different path. As time went on, it was just a horror story."

The horror reached its zenith just a month after Robarts was appointed to co-chair the national unity task force, and a matter of days before his and Katherine's first wedding anniversary, in August

1977. In the town of Bright, Ontario, under a bridge on the banks of the Thames River, Timothy Parmenter Robarts died of a self-inflicted shotgun blast. He was twenty-one.

"Robarts left the office without telling anyone what had happened," recalls Richard Rohmer. "He was shattered. He'd been called to go and identify the body of his son. This was really a tremendous blow for him in every way."

Robarts and Katherine drove to the morgue in nearby Woodstock, Ontario, to identify Tim. What John Robarts may not have known was that Tim's suicide did not come as a complete surprise to Robin. A few years earlier, Tim had let slip in a conversation with his sister and mother that he intended to take his own life when he reached the age of twenty-one. Neither woman believed the comment, or perhaps refused to believe it. But it had come to pass.

Tim left a suicide note of almost a dozen pages, and it is a good thing he did. Not that it assuaged the guilt or remorse of his parents at all. But it did clarify his state of mind before he took his life, and it was not as utterly bleak as one might have suspected. Robin read, and remembers the contents of the note. "He just said that he'd had a great life," she says. "This was no one's fault. He didn't see a future for himself in this big world, and he just thought it was time to go. And it was really funny. Now I don't mean that meanly. It was just that his sense of humour was incredible. So every time he started to get a little bit serious, he would turn it and make it humorous.

"I just remember thinking what a wonderful legacy to leave," Robin continues. "He didn't make anyone feel bad that he'd done it. It was nobody's fault. It was almost like it was meant to be. He was meant to be on earth for twenty-one years."

"I'm amazed it didn't happen sooner," Judith Grieve says sombrely. "But Tim was faced with an increasingly irrational mother, a largely absent father, too much money, no responsibility, drugs, and access to firearms. What a lethal combination."

Because Tim Robarts's parents were divorced, the post-funeral activities were even more awkward than usual. Andrea, Tim's cousin, goes further: "The whole thing was a nightmare."

Robarts took Katherine to the funeral, which many observers found to be in poor taste and a further insult to Norah. "Norah was in her own hometown, in a funeral home, with her son in a coffin, and she had to publicly deal with an ex-husband and a new woman on his arm, and they were late," Andrea says. "Katherine was always late. She needed to have the spotlight on her. It was an incredibly inappropriate time for her to do it, and for John to tolerate it. She was dressed to the nines, incredibly coiffed. I was so angry with him."

But Norah showed tremendous dignity in the face of it all. She walked up to her former husband and his new wife, extended her hand to Katherine, and said, "How do you do. I'm Norah Robarts. I don't believe we've met yet."

London, which never accepted Katherine to begin with, got even angrier with her after the funeral. Some of Norah's friends were appalled that she visited the house after the funeral. Others thought she ostentatiously tried to take front and centre at the proceedings.

Based on conversations with nearly one hundred friends and family members, a wholly different portrait of John Robarts emerges after Tim's death. To say he was never the same person again is obvious and trite. His son's suicide sucked much of the life out of him. His accomplishments in the worlds of politics, business, and even love simply had less meaning.

Robin Robarts had thought her father could meet any challenge or adversity in life, but the tragedy affected his sense of certainty. Mixed with the agony of the loss were deep feelings of guilt due to his frequent absences from home over the years.

Given that Robarts almost never discussed his private life, even with his closest friends, it is interesting to note that he did significantly come out of his shell to try to understand why his son took his own life. He had conversations with his former political advisers Hugh Hanson and Don Martyn, men from a younger generation who might have had a greater insight into Tim's distress. He also felt he could unburden himself more with them without losing face. And Robarts would often spend time in his Rosedale living room, just sitting by himself, thinking.

Once, while they were sailing, Tim Robarts had asked his father what he thought about the concept of suicide. "The word is not even in my vocabulary," Robarts answered firmly. But over time, his thinking on the issue evolved. Eventually, he even told Robin how extraordinarily courageous he thought Tim had been to take his life.

Over time, many Canadians reached out to Robarts. He received numerous letters from complete strangers, or people he barely knew, each letter describing the writer's own loss. "Everybody seemed to give him a little glimpse of how they got through it," says Robin Robarts. "And I know that helped him."

In an appalling coincidence, the Jacksons and Robartses would share another of life's journeys together. Not only had John Robarts and Ernie Jackson entered politics together, run for the leadership of the Tory Party together, won two elections together, and divorced their wives and remarried, but they also shared this final sorrow: the death of a child. One of Jackson's daughters, Kathleen, died many years later, in 1989, of alcohol-related problems at age forty-four. She entered hospital and never regained consciousness.

John Robarts did have another child in his life. Tim was deceased and Robin was off on her own. But still living with him was Kimberly Sickafuse, Katherine's daughter from her first marriage. At the time of Tim's death, Kimberly was finishing elementary school at Our Lady of Perpetual Help, a school in the Roman Catholic system near Mount Pleasant Road and St. Clair Avenue East in Toronto. Her home-room teacher was Cathy White, whose father, coincidentally, had been an assistant deputy minister of education when both Robarts and Bill

Davis were education ministers. Cathy White had already been a teacher at the school for a few years before Kimberly became her pupil. She remembers Robarts being a dutiful father, attending parent-teacher meetings, and showing considerable interest in Kim. "He was the perfect gentleman," she says. "He accepted everything I said. He was a super-classy guy. To his credit, he didn't even mention who he was. He didn't come swaggering in as an ex-premier. Just as this girl's concerned father."

Kimberly started at the school using Sickafuse as her last name but changed it to Robarts after John announced his intention to formally adopt her. Considering Kimberly came into the picture relatively late in his life, Robarts had a warm, close relationship with her. On one occasion, he walked in the door of their home at seven o'clock in the morning, having stayed out all night long playing poker. Kimberly was already awake and saw him come in. The two made a deal. Robarts gave the girl a share of his poker winnings, on the condition that she not tell her mother about his all-nighter. (Kimberly kept the secret for ten years after Robarts's death.)

As the 1970s came to a close, something else was happening in John Robarts's life. His friends thought Katherine was exercising an increasingly tight grip on almost every aspect of his life, the most obvious manifestation being the plans to adopt Kimberly. But it went beyond that. Robarts's old friends simply did not enjoy being in Katherine's company. They found her domineering, rude, and unpleasant. As a result, there were fewer dinner invitations offered by the Robarts household to the former prime minister's friends, and fewer still from his friends to him and Katherine. Robarts became more isolated, even from his best friend, Ernie Jackson, despite their living just minutes from each other in Rosedale.

"Ernie's feelings were hurt by not being able to see John," says Willie Jackson. "John didn't stick up for himself against Katherine. He was putty in her hands."

"Katherine was different," adds J.J. Barnicke. "She was not an asset. But he made his bed and he slept in it."

A good example of Robarts's increasing isolation came one Thanksgiving. Every year on that holiday, a couple of dozen of Robarts's pals would hire a bus and go north of the city for a picnic dinner. One year, the bus collected everyone at Ernie and Willie Jackson's place. When it came time to go, there was no John Robarts. The bus eventually left and drove past the Robarts home. There he was in the front yard, the most gregarious fellow you could ever meet, but for some reason unable to continue the tradition that year. "We waved to John," remembers Willie Jackson. "He looked so sad." The bus just kept going.

"We tried being 'couple friends' but couldn't," Willie says. "She was too difficult and crass to be with. I haven't laid eyes on that woman in fifteen years."

"They both made a bad deal," another long-time friend says of John and Katherine. "He wanted sex and she wanted his power and position. Both ended up disappointed."

Life was no better for Norah Robarts. Once, John, Katherine, and Norah Robarts all ended up at the same wedding reception. Before long, Norah was in tears. "She and I sat and chatted," recalls Bev Shrives, who had known both John and Norah since their teenage years. "She was shaking, she was so mad."

Her pain would not last much longer. In May 1981, alone at home, Norah Robarts got drunk while eating a steak dinner. She accidentally choked to death on her supper. "It was a sad ending to a sad life," Judith Grieve, her niece, says matter-of-factly.

John Robarts attended the funeral of his ex-wife at St. John the Evangelist Anglican Church in London—the same church where he and Norah had married almost thirty-seven years earlier. "I remember seeing John outside the church. He was in agony," says Nancy Poole. "He felt very bad about what happened to Norah. It was tragic. She was difficult but quite a woman."

"Right until the bitter end, he loved Norah," insists John Cronyn, "even though she was sometimes hard to take. Then he met this damned Katherine and got swept away by her."

Joan Smith often thinks back to those times, and the sequence of events that led to Norah's demise. "I don't know if she could have been helped," Smith says. "Being the premier's wife meant they'd all try to bury that situation [Norah's alcoholism]. It was a vicious circle. Did she originally have a drinking problem, or did her isolation prompt it?"

A final, biting observation comes from someone who once worshipped John Robarts. "I told you that Robarts was my hero as a premier," says David Peterson. "But he's also been the antithesis of where I want to be in my personal life."

That personal life was about to become, if it can be imagined, immeasurably worse.

12

THE FLIGHT TO HOUSTON

IN MANY RESPECTS, the 1980s were an exciting decade for Canada. The leader of Her Majesty's Loyal Opposition, Pierre Trudeau, came out of retirement and shocked Joe Clark's Progressive Conservatives by storming back into power. On election night, he welcomed Canadians to the 1980s in his own inimitable fashion, from the Château Laurier Hotel.

The great Montreal Canadiens had just won the last of their six Stanley Cups of the 1970s, with a roster of household names such as Lafleur, Dryden, Lemaire, Shutt, Robinson, and Savard.

In Canada's biggest province, the Ontario PCs had successfully negotiated their way through the choppy waters of two consecutive minority governments. The technocratic, awkward William Davis of the early 1970s was replaced by the avuncular, trustworthy, comfortable (and, yes, bland) William Davis of the 1980s. On March 19, 1981, Davis brought the Tories all the way back to where they had been on election night a decade earlier, by reclaiming majority government status for his party.

There were also big changes for the other two parties in Ontario. Within a few weeks of each other in February 1982, David Peterson and Bob Rae became leaders of the Liberals and New Democrats, respectively. Even though he had been out of provincial politics for more than a decade, Robarts kept his political antennae up and followed the careers of both men. Of course, David Peterson he knew well as a fellow Londoner, and the son of Clarence Peterson, whom Robarts had bested for MPP in the 1955 election. And Bob Rae's reputation as a whiz kid from the national scene preceded him to the Ontario NDP leader's job.

On the surface, the 1980s also seemed a pretty fine time for the Honourable John P. Robarts. "He was a man in demand," says J.J. Barnicke. "Corporations were going after him for directorships. He was turning 'em down."

Robarts was still a major player and rainmaker at Stikeman Elliott Robarts and Bowman. One day at the law firm, he encountered a young lawyer working at his first job after graduating from law school. That was Greg Sorbara, who today is the minister of finance for the Liberal government of Ontario. Their meeting happened in an awkward place: the men's bathroom, side by side, urinal by urinal. "They let articling students pee once a day," Sorbara jokes as he remembers the encounter. During the less than a minute it took each man to do his business, Sorbara asked Robarts about the new NDP leader who had just won a seat in a by-election in York South. "What do you think of Bob Rae?"

"Bright young man," Robarts answered. "Could be premier someday." Talk about prescient.

(Speaking of prescience and possible future first ministers, Robarts had also had a conversation by this time with a rising star in the federal Liberal Party; the story was reported on television last year by the CBC Newsworld anchor Don Newman. Robarts bumped into Jean Chrétien at some political event and urged him to run for the leadership after Trudeau departed the scene. "They might need a compromise candidate," Robarts told him. "That's how I won, and maybe you will too." Again, Robarts's powers of prognostication were spot on, even thought it would take Chrétien two kicks at the can before winning the leadership in 1990.)

When Robarts left politics in 1971, having just turned fifty-four years old, he was in reasonably good shape for a man who had abused his body with alcohol and not got much exercise. But ten years later Robarts was quite a different physical specimen. The years of hard living began to manifest themselves. What used to be a pronounced paunch over his belt was now unmistakably just a big fat gut. He looked tired and old.

On August 12, 1981, just three months after Norah Robarts had died, John Robarts experienced an alarming health episode of his own, which put his life in jeopardy. During the course of the previous week, he had complained to Katherine during a fishing trip that for some reason his balance was off. "My leg keeps giving out on me," he told his wife. Neither thought it was anything to get overly concerned about. From time to time, the big man's old football injuries would flare up. He had even undergone surgery on one knee to fix the problem, but the surgery was not successful. The knee continued to bother him.

After the fishing trip, Robarts attended an executive committee meeting of the board of governors at York University, where he was now the chancellor. His old friend and former chief economic adviser Ian Macdonald was now running the university. After the meeting broke up, Robarts made for the airport to take a flight to New York, to attend a board of directors meeting at Metropolitan Life. Later in the day, Ian Macdonald mentioned to his wife how concerned he was, because, quite candidly, the chancellor had looked awful.

Robarts made it through his meeting at Met Life, then caught another plane to Houston for yet another meeting. He was chairman of the board of Reed Shaw Stenhouse, an insurance brokerage and consulting company, one of whose vice-presidents was Ernie Jackson. On the flight to Houston, John Robarts had a stroke. Somehow, on that August day, Robarts managed to get himself to his hotel, whereupon he called Katherine back in Toronto.

"What's wrong with you?" she asked him. "Why are you stammering like that?"

"I don't know," Robarts replied. "I got off the plane and I started staggering and having trouble talking." He could barely get the words out. Later he told her that onlookers at the airport had been convinced he was drunk.

Katherine said to call the front desk immediately and get a doctor up to his room. After an hour she called the hotel back and was told Robarts had been taken to the hospital. He had lost control of his left arm and leg. Then, while in hospital, he suffered a second stroke. He was in critical condition.

At this point, Ernie Jackson took charge of Robarts's care and had him transferred to another hospital, which specialized in the treatment he would now need. Thereafter, Katherine and Robin Robarts, who was working at the Bay in Montreal when she got the call about her father's condition, flew down to Houston. To say both were shocked when they saw Robarts does not begin to describe their despair. They found a man in intensive care, unable to speak, and crying, although able to recognize them both.

"He was grey. He looked old," says Robin in a hushed voice, recalling that occasion. "It was the first time I ever thought of my father as being old. I was petrified."

Making matters worse for Katherine were her own health problems. She had been experiencing severe abdominal pain and was scheduled to go to the Mayo Clinic in Rochester, Minnesota, for an examination, when her husband's stroke hit. She began taking Demerol, prescribed by Robarts's doctor.

When Bob Robarts got the news, he too made for Houston. Thus began another chapter of "Katherine versus the rest of John Robarts's friends and family," as to who was going to be in control of the sick man's care. When Bob arrived at his brother's room, he was greeted by a very young, very armed guard. Katherine had arranged it because the place was crawling with media. Earlier, she had called Premier Davis's office in Toronto, asking for security, but she says she was turned down.

Bob went to see his brother. Later, he and Katherine had a very frosty exchange when Bob told her he had made the visit. Katherine was not pleased. She felt singularly responsible for her husband's care and wanted to strictly monitor who visited Robarts and how often. She admonished Bob for visiting without her permission. Bob reminded her that as the brother he did not need or intend to ask for Katherine's permission.

Ernie Jackson also wanted to see his best friend but had no stomach for a confrontation with Katherine. So he accompanied Bob to the hospital but did not plan to go into Robarts's room to see him. When they arrived at the hospital, Katherine was actually not there, so Jackson did go up to visit. Finding out later, she froze Jackson out of any further role in Robarts's recovery efforts.

Richard Rohmer called Katherine around this time, and she was happy to hear from him. He told her he was coming to Texas and asked if there was anything she needed. She asked him to bring some of her favourite perfume, which her husband also liked, Bal à Versailles. With Robarts as disoriented as he was, she thought a familiar scent in the room would remind him that she was there.

On September 12, one month after suffering his first stroke, Robarts was considered stable enough to fly back to Toronto. He was admitted to Toronto General Hospital for further observation and an intensive physiotherapy regimen. His left foot dragged when he walked. His left hand was alternately extremely weak or making involuntary spastic motions. "He'd keep trying to hold it down because it kept doing things he had no intention of it doing," recalls Katherine Robarts. "He couldn't control it."

She had been a nurse, but nothing in that career had prepared her to be a full-time nursemaid, in her late thirties, to a much older, incapacitated husband. John Robarts's life was now truly terrible, and so by extension was hers. "They get very frustrated and angry and depressed, so it's not easy to live with," Katherine says of stroke victims in general. "There were times I felt I was talking to a stranger, because the stroke alters a personality in so many ways that I can't even describe it to you."

During his worst moments, Robarts was in a state of total confusion. Sometimes the old tender man would be present. Other times, he would get loud, angry, and irrational. Katherine's frustration frequently boiled over. She had to get out of the house for her own sanity. Whenever any of Robarts's friends heard stories of her out socializing, it gave them added ammunition to further dislike a woman they already detested. "It certainly became apparent that she wasn't a good wife," Richard Dillon says. "She could have been a lot more caring."

For people who loved Robarts, it was so difficult seeing him in his condition. Three weeks after his return to Toronto, Bill Davis visited. More than twenty years after that encounter, Davis is still visibly disturbed and unable to describe it. "I found it very depressing," he says. "I'd rather not talk about those things."

"I thought for sure he was going to recover," says Robin with an enthusiasm suggesting she almost still believes it. "That was my dad. He did these things. He'd get past this. But, of course," she adds, "he didn't."

Robarts did work his way back somewhat, at least to the point that he could minimally function. One of the boards he sat on gave him a car and a driver so he could get around more easily. But he looked so different. Although no one knows for sure, pictures of Robarts after his stroke suggest he had lost about eighty pounds. He now walked with a permanent limp. He was no longer the Chairman of the Board.

"He couldn't do much after the stroke," admits Fraser Elliott, his law partner. "He had to be the rainmaker, but he was too handicapped after that. He couldn't be the leader he used to be, with the troops around him."

Robarts's old political nemesis, Robert Nixon, recalls driving on King Street in downtown Toronto, when he saw a limousine temporarily double park. "They were helping someone out and it was John Robarts," Nixon says. "They were assisting him to go to his office. His mobility was seriously impaired. It shocked me."

"He just didn't emit confidence any more," his niece Andrea Robarts says. "His energy and his speech changed. He had to lift his leg to get out of a car and he used a cane."

Robarts's stroke also interrupted his plans to adopt Kimberly. He actually had the forms and was in the process of filling them out but never completed the endeavour. Kimberly continued to use Robarts's surname.

It was at this point that Ernie Jackson now felt Katherine's sting most severely. She forbade him to visit the couple's home, imposing her sanction on him for daring to visit Robarts in the hospital in Houston. Eventually, mutual friends conspired to arrange visits on neutral territory, without her knowledge.

But Jackson was not the only one. Judith Grieve was also persona non grata at the Rosedale home. She pleaded with Katherine, who always claimed her husband was too sick to see visitors. Grieve is still bothered by the possibility that her uncle thought his family had abandoned him.

John Robarts virtually disappeared from Toronto's social scene, in part because many of his old friends did not make the effort to see someone who was no longer the powerful, dynamic former prime minister of Ontario. "After the stroke, I noticed a lot of people just didn't care about him any more," says Douglas Bassett, the Toronto businessman who sat on the board of the Canadian Imperial Bank of Commerce with Robarts.

"You can't blame it all on Katherine," says another of his friends, who did stay in touch. Others did urge Robarts to reintegrate himself into their activities, but he often seemed too ashamed. Once, Ian Macdonald asked him to come to convocation at York University to try to resume some of his duties as chancellor. "You don't have to stand. Just sit there. Be with us," Macdonald told him. "I'll do the handshaking and everything I can to help."

Robarts refused. "I really wouldn't want to be on display if I wasn't at my best," he said.

Another time, on a Canadian Pacific flight from Vancouver to Toronto, Robarts found himself one of only two people in the first-class section of the airplane. The other was Alan Eagleson, the former PC Party president whom Robarts had not seen since those days at Queen's Park. "It was heart-rending," Eagleson says of his first glance at Robarts in more than ten years. "But in that four hours, even with slurred words, it was wonderful to talk to him. I never saw him again. He probably got off the plane thinking, I'm not pleasant company any more. But that four hours with John was one of the great joys of my life."

One day, while out for a walk in his Rosedale neighbourhood, Robarts bumped into Eric Dowd, the Queen's Park journalist who lived not far from the former prime minister. "Eric," he began, "if I had my life to live over again, the one thing I'd definitely do is be in politics."

Dowd remembered the conversation for what it said and, more important, for what it did not say. "It was obvious he had regretted some of the other things," Dowd says.

Andrea Robarts was discussing politics with her uncle at this time, when she mentioned one politician in rather disparaging tones. She found her uncle's response both moving and revealing. "Andrea, a man is lucky to have the talent for his time," he said. "He's even luckier when he's chosen and given an opportunity to use his talent." It taught Andrea not to be so quick to criticize.

Most of the things that made life worth living for Robarts—fishing, sailing, schmoozing, and, quite frankly, sexual relations with his beautiful, young wife—were over. He once told Katherine he dreamed of taking a year off from all his responsibilities, getting a cabin in the woods, and reading all the great books he never had time for. "When he had a stroke, he could only read a few pages at a time," Katherine recalls. "Books would be piled up and marked two or three pages in, because he couldn't even concentrate to read."

Robarts's friends pestered him to get out of the house and not waste away. John Cronyn, for instance, persuaded him to go for a sail from Wiarton up the Bruce Peninsula to Tobermory. "He loved being at the wheel of the boat," Cronyn says. "We rigged up the boswain's chair and lowered him into a dinghy so he could fish."

On another occasion, Hugh Hanson and Don Martyn, the smart young kids from Robarts's second term as prime minister, took him to Barbados. While Robarts and Hanson were walking on the beach, a big wave came in, causing Robarts to lose his balance and fall down. Another man was walking by and asked if Robarts needed a hand getting up. "Christ, no!" he bellowed, leaving it to the slight and diminutive Hanson to pick up a man who weighed considerably more than he did.

Another evening in Barbados, Robarts and his colleagues were walking to a restaurant. Halfway there, Robarts was dragging his left foot so badly that he wanted to quit and go back to the hotel. "I can't stand it," he told them.

Don Martyn got tough. "You can keep going and get something to eat or take the same amount of time to walk back to the room and get nothing." They all continued to the restaurant.

There were flashes of the old competitive Robarts on that trip. The three men faced off in a three-day Scrabble tournament. Hanson won the first night, Martyn the second, and Robarts the third. And he won fair and square, with no concessions from the other two.

Back in the city, Hanson and Martyn became part of Robarts's routine. The trio would regularly have lunch at the Market Grill downtown. Or they would all go for a sail, which became increasingly frustrating. Robarts liked to take the helm, until one time he lost his balance and his leg got stuck on the tiller, causing the boat to head straight for a wall.

Heading straight for a wall might have been an appropriate metaphor for Robarts's life, because before long he suffered two more strokes—making four in total. His depression now completely absorbed him. He started seeing a psychiatrist but found the experience a waste of time. He even made things up during his sessions, then came home and bragged to Katherine about how he had put one over on the doctor.

"People were embarrassed to see him sick, weak, and with a woman they hated," one friend said. "It was tough."

"The two more strokes affected his body drastically," says Richard Rohmer. "It shrank. He was paralyzed on one side. His speech was slurred. He was a different person intellectually and emotionally. He was ashamed of the body he had grown into."

"It was obvious he was depressed and discouraged," explains William Davis. "We went to the odd dinner where he was at the head table, and he found it very difficult. I knew he was suffering mentally from not being able to portray the kind of robust person he once was."

Remarkably, Robarts actually did attempt something different after his third stroke. He gave a public speech. "I arranged it," says Peter Hunter, the advertising guru from Robarts's days as prime minister. It was at the Four Seasons Hotel in Toronto in front of three hundred people. The Canadian Diabetes Association was honouring him as its man of the year. It was harder than hell for him to get through it, but he did it, and the evening was unforgettable. "He was a little hesitant, but he did a remarkable job," recalls Hunter.

"I just thought that took amazing courage," adds Robin, "because he did mix up his words and he didn't get sentences exactly right and his face didn't look the same. And he knew all that."

In August 1982 Robin experienced a terrible déjà vu. Her father invited her over to his home for a one-on-one dinner. She was expressly told to come alone. At the dining room table, Robarts told his daughter the same thing she had heard several years earlier from her brother, Tim: that life was intolerable and suicide was the only option. "It made me very angry," Robin remembers of that extraordinary conversation. "He said he had done a lot with his life and that everyone was taken care of."

"Wait a minute," she said. "There's more I need from you." Robin told her father that with her mother and brother already dead, he was the only family she had left and it simply was not fair to take that away from her.

Robarts was firm. She told him better days would come, that she would help him experience new things worth living for, but he was unmoved.

Robarts continued to put his affairs in order. In September 1982 he sold his beloved boat, *Trillium,* to a Brighton, Ontario, man named Vernon Cavanaugh, who got the distinct impression that Robarts was liquidating all his assets when he sold the boat.

"It must have been difficult for Katherine," says Richard Rohmer. "It was difficult for him. It was a whole new ball game for both of them." Indeed it was. The marriage started to deteriorate. Then Robarts asked his two lawyer friends Richard Rohmer and Fraser Elliott to be his executors.

"In fairness to Katherine, it's very difficult living with a stroke victim, especially one that has decided they don't want to go on,"

Robin says. "I know he did try some rehabilitation but not as much as was available to him. She's young and it didn't look like much of a life ahead. So I can see why that fell apart."

Life for this once joyously happy couple was becoming increasingly intolerable. One day, Robarts phoned his friend Don Matthews in London. "What are you doing for lunch today?" Robarts asked.

"I guess I'm having it with you," Matthews answered.

Matthews drove to Robarts's law office at Commerce Court, where the two had lunch.

"I have a terrible story to tell you," Robarts began. The previous day, Robarts told Matthews, he had descended the staircase of his Rosedale home. His wife was downstairs. He asked her if she would make him some breakfast.

"You're not going to eat breakfast here today," she told him. Robarts retreated back up the stairs. The same scene was repeated a few hours later, around lunchtime, and again Robarts retreated upstairs. But as the afternoon wore on, Robarts's hunger began to get the better of him.

"I'm too damned hungry for this," he told Katherine, as he tried to make his way into the kitchen. Matthews says the former prime minister then told him Katherine shoved him. Because Robarts was so unsteady on his feet, he fell on his backside.

"No, you can't have anything to eat," she repeated.

Matthews says Robarts then told him that Katherine grabbed a knife and began to threaten him.

"What the hell should I do?" Robarts asked his friend.

"Well, the first thing is, divorce her," Matthews responded unequivocally.

Robarts agreed. Matthews urged him to move out of his home and gave him the keys to an apartment he had at the Manulife Centre at the corner of Bay and Bloor Streets. He also instructed Robarts to share the story with someone else, for his own protection. Robarts said he would tell Richard Rohmer, but apparently he did not do so.

"I've never heard that story," Rohmer insists. "But you should know that Don Matthews is a very credible source."

When I told Katherine Robarts the story, she denied it had ever taken place. In fact, she says her husband was becoming so depressed and violent that she sought a meeting with G. Emmett Cardinal Carter, the highest-ranking Catholic official in the country, to seek his advice.

"I didn't know how to deal with a stroke victim," Katherine says. "He'd start yelling and screaming that he was going to kill me. Then he'd sit and weep and say, 'I don't know why I did that.'" Katherine tells the story not at all defensively but rather through tears and sorrow, as she recalls some of the worst moments of her life.

In the summer of 1982—almost a year after his first stroke at the age of sixty-four, Robarts went sailing with John Cronyn and Dick Dillon. After a nightcap, he was in a particularly blue mood, so he put all his cards on the table, in what might have been the most intimate conversation he had ever had with either man. "He wanted to divorce her," Cronyn insists. "He said, 'I've had a very satisfactory public life, but I've made a godawful mess of my personal life.'"

Robert Macaulay, Robarts's former roommate and cabinet colleague, tells a similar story. Macaulay also had a boat and went sailing with Robarts several times during that summer. "We'd talk about whether things were going well with Katherine," he says, confirming they were not. "What made me sad was he was such an honourable guy. I felt it was a shame."

The problem was, Robarts really could not afford to get a divorce. Yes, he was on several boards and had a nice home in Rosedale. But he certainly did not have the kind of big money he thought he would need to end his marriage. Don Matthews was a sharp businessman and, at Robarts's request a year earlier, had gone through his friend's financial situation. He discovered Robarts was worth about $800,000, which included his house.

"We both want to get a divorce," Robarts told John Cronyn, "but neither of us can afford to live separately."

Robarts did add one other thing to Cronyn and Dillon that at the time seemed odd. "If things get worse, I'll know what to do," Robarts said mysteriously. "I do know one way I can get out of it." The reference was left up in the air, not pursued by either man.

"I knew what he meant," Cronyn says today. "I didn't comment because it was his business."

Katherine's meeting with Cardinal Carter produced some unusual advice. He recommended that she "rattle his cage," and go away for a while to let Robarts think about life without her. So Katherine did. She went to Rome, New York, for a few weeks, lived in a motel, and spent time with her family. While there, she got a call from her husband, who confessed he had gone to a lawyer inquiring about a divorce. That concerned Katherine enough to get her back in her car to return to Toronto.

Apparently, calmer heads prevailed at this point. The next time Don Matthews and John Robarts got together, Robarts confirmed to his friend that "we've decided to try to make a go of this."

When Al Hurley, Robarts's old football teammate from their UWO days, visited Robarts at his home in October 1982, he was alarmed at how depressed Robarts had become. Robarts descended the staircase with the aid of a cane and began to complain that Katherine wanted to take his shotgun away. Hurley tried to buoy his spirits. He talked about Charlie Hay, the oilman from British-American, who had served on the former prime minister's Committee on Government Productivity and had suffered a stroke similar to Robarts's. "He made a marvellous recovery, John," Hurley told him. "You know Charlie Hay. Call him up and talk to him." There is no indication Robarts made the call.

The final indignity came midway through October 1982. He and Katherine took their annual trip to Griffiths Island to do some hunting. By the time the weekend was over, Robarts was even more chagrined. "Katherine," he told her, "I can't shoot any more." The webbing between his thumb and forefinger had got caught in the trigger, cutting him badly. Furthermore, he could no longer handle the gun's recoil and sustained bad bruising on his arm.

"So he realized he couldn't do *any* of the things he liked," Katherine now says.

On Sunday night, October 17, 1982, Katherine and John Robarts went to bed separately. She says that was typical at this stage of their marriage. Often Robarts could not sleep, so he would use the guest room in order not to disturb his wife. She went into that room to say she was going to bed.

"Good night, sweet princess," Robarts said to her. "I love you." Those would be the last words John Robarts said to anyone.

13

OCTOBER 18, 1982

FOR MORE THAN TWO DECADES, the official version of John Parmenter Robarts's last night on earth has always included that memorable quote: "Good night, sweet princess. I love you." Two decades later, other commentators' new information has come forward, which for the first time, casts at least some doubt on that account.

"'Good night, sweet princess'? I would question that very much," says J.J. Barnicke.

"I wouldn't give an ounce of credence to that," agrees Alan Eagleson.

Of course, it is possible that Robarts, knowing what he intended to do after Katherine turned in for the night, did utter those words. If he did not say them, there is only one witness who knows it, and his widow is certainly sticking by the official version of events that night.

However, several sources are now prepared to go on the record and confirm details that previously were not included in the official version of Robarts's last days. Why this information has stayed secret for more than twenty years may have something to do with the confidentiality of lawyer-client privilege. Or perhaps enough time has finally passed that people now feel more comfortable discussing matters they never would because of the way John Robarts died.

Whatever the case, what is now known is that on Sunday morning, October 17, John Robarts had a private meeting with one of Toronto's most prominent divorce lawyers, Phil Isbister from the firm Lash Johnson. Isbister was considered the dean of the family law bar. He made it a point to mentor young lawyers, one of whom was Richard Devinney. Devinney's credentials were impressive. He had served as a clerk to the Ontario Supreme Court chief justice William Howland, and then got a job working at Lash Johnson.

Several days after the meeting took place, Isbister and Devinney had a lawyers' chat after business hours one evening. Isbister was in what Devinney describes as an expansive mood, leaning back in his chair and sharing his thoughts on a wide range of subjects, one of which was the Sunday morning meeting with Robarts. Isbister said he was rather shocked to see Robarts so physically hindered by his four separate strokes. He also confirmed that he spoke with Robarts for about an hour, offering his professional advice on how simple or difficult it would be to divorce Katherine. "I thought this information would die with me," Devinney says.

Unfortunately, Devinney does not know what specific advice Isbister gave to Robarts. Isbister himself died in 1995, and his widow has no knowledge of the meeting with Robarts, nor the location of any files that might shed light on the matter.

However, Robarts's law firm partner Fraser Elliott also confirms the Sunday meeting took place and that despite the couple's determination to try to "make a go" of their marriage, consideration of divorce proceedings against Katherine was the subject of the meeting. Elliott thought he could be helpful advising Robarts on this issue: his first wife, with whom he'd had six children, had died. But Elliott married again and, like Robarts, soon came to realize it was a mistake. The couple separated and ultimately divorced. But unlike Robarts, Elliott was able to handle the difficulties surrounding the end of his marriage.

"John just couldn't," Elliott says. "Mentally, he was just not prepared for it. He was *désolé*," he adds, using the French word to suggest Robarts was desperately alone. More than twenty years later, Elliott genuinely looks wistful, even fighting back feelings of guilt, that he did not intervene more directly at this moment in his former rain-maker's life. "I still feel bad that I didn't go over to his house and say, 'John, come and live with me until this is all over.' I might have got him to go. Some of us should have rescued him."

We cannot know for certain what advice Isbister gave Robarts that Sunday morning. However, Don Matthews and Richard Rohmer did have a prior meeting with Isbister, where the three speculated how much it would cost Robarts to get out of the marriage. Matthews suggested Robarts pay Katherine $300,000. Rohmer figured $400,000 would get the job done. Matthews disagreed and suggested Robarts's lawyer start at $200,000 and negotiate from there. When Matthews gave Robarts that advice, Robarts was incredulous. "I don't even want to give her $200,000," he told Matthews.

Given what Robarts chose to do early Monday morning, it is probably safe to speculate that none of the options put forward during the Sunday meeting with Isbister was very appetizing. A divorce from Katherine would almost certainly have been protracted, expensive, and embarrassing, none of which could have appealed to Robarts.

The night before the Isbister meeting, at about nine-thirty or ten o'clock, Robarts called the Jackson residence to talk to his best friend. Ernie, however, was not there. He had gone up to Griffiths Island for the day to do some hunting. But Willie expected him home soon. "I'll have him call you," she said to Robarts.

"No, no," Robarts said. "Just tell him I called."

Then there was silence on the line for a few seconds, so Willie moved to fill it.

"John, it's really nice to talk to you," she said, not perfunctorily but with heartfelt emotion.

Again, silence, this time broken by Robarts. "I can't tell you how nice it is to talk to you too," he said, matching her sincerity and depth of feeling.

After the Sunday morning meeting with Isbister, Robarts met up with Hugh Hanson and Don Martyn. Both had made it a point to stay in Robarts's life with regular visits. Apparently, neither one had run afoul of Katherine, even though neither liked her very much. In fairness, Hanson says, "I never felt any animus from her toward me." Hanson says Robarts referred to the Isbister meeting, but only "obliquely." The three went for lunch at the Market Grill, where Robarts unhappily showed them his hunting injury from the day before. Since the weather was lovely, the friends went for a walk in a nearby park after lunch. They then took him back home.

Later that day, Sunday, October 17, Hanson returned to the Robarts home for a private dinner—John and Katherine Robarts, Hugh Hanson, and his then girlfriend. It was a relatively uneventful dinner, and after it was over, Hanson recalls, "There was nothing unusual about our goodbye that night."

Early the next morning—October 18, 1982—John Robarts took the one-of-a-kind gun, specially fitted for him in London, England, and given to him by the London PC Association. He went into the bathroom of his home on St. Andrews Gardens in Rosedale and shot himself through the roof of his mouth.

Katherine heard the gun blast. But at first, she says, she was not sure of what actually happened. She was asleep at the time, and her first thought was that perhaps John had gone to the bathroom and accidentally slammed the toilet seat down. "Then I listened for a while and didn't hear anything," she explains. So she got out of bed to find her husband. She checked inside the bathroom and in the shower stall but saw nothing. But she was looking at eye level, so she left to search elsewhere. Unable to find him anywhere else, she returned to the bathroom, glanced down into the shower, and saw his body.

A flood of thoughts entered her head. Robarts had casually mentioned suicide in the past, but she had always presumed it was an idle threat. Nevertheless, she had endeavoured to remove as many of her husband's shotguns as possible, just as a precaution. She gave one to his driver. She made sure several others were left at Griffiths Island. But Robarts had recently told her he wanted to try to hunt again the following weekend, and could he please have one shotgun back. According to Katherine, he'd tricked her with that ruse and she'd given him the gun. "He obviously had it planned," she says.

The phone at Don Martyn's place rang at seven forty-five in the morning. "Donald, can you get over here," he heard Katherine's voice say. "Something dreadful has happened."

Hugh Hanson's phone rang next. Again, it was Katherine asking him to come over quickly. "She didn't say what had happened, but I suspected what the truth was," Hanson says. When he arrived, Kimberly Robarts and Don Martyn were already on the scene, as was police superintendent William J. McCormack.

"I got a call from the chief, who said, 'Get there and get there fast,'" McCormack remembers.

Hugh Hanson immediately got on the phone and made two calls. The first was to Robin. "It's Dad, isn't it?" Robin asked.

"Yes," Hanson answered.

"Goddamn him," she replied.

Hanson's second call was to Robarts's brother, Bob. When he got the news, his first question was, "Did *she* do it?"

More calls were made and other Robarts associates began showing up, such as Richard Rohmer and J. Keith Reynolds, Robarts's secretary to the cabinet. The scene was a proverbial beehive of activity. Robin remembers very few details of the day, saying she was in a complete daze most of the time. "I can't honestly say that it was my favourite time, going up and seeing Katherine there sad," Robin says, "because I knew they'd been having a great deal of trouble. And I didn't think she had a right to be sad at that point, quite frankly."

Robin was not shocked. After all, her father had given her fair warning this day was coming. In fact, Robarts had told a few people in the autumn of 1981 that he intended to give himself a year to recover. If he did not make satisfactory progress, he warned he would take other measures. No one specifically asked what that meant, but given how Tim departed the world, it did not take Sherlock Holmes to fill in the blanks.

So, no, Robin was not shocked. But she was experiencing other emotions. "I was just furious," she says. "My instinctive reaction was fury."

When Robin arrived, many members of the media were already camping out in front of the house, preparing to write the first draft of this terrible part of Canadian history.

"It was a bit of a zoo after a while," Hugh Hanson says. "But I don't remember much more. I was in a pretty shook-up state."

Robarts's body was wheeled out on a gurney. Representatives from the Humphrey Funeral Home, whom Don Martyn had called (it was the same funeral home that had handled his own father's death) placed the body in their station wagon. Television crews dutifully recorded the entire scene.

"I looked high and low, but there was no [suicide] note," Katherine says. "I wish there had been, but there wasn't."

There are moments when it becomes the responsibility of someone to explain to the world what, in fact, is going on. In John Robarts's case, it was Don Martyn who stepped up to the plate. He saw the media recording it all and decided they deserved to know what had happened.

Martyn walked out of the house, announced he had something to say, and confirmed that Ontario's seventeenth prime minister was dead at the age of sixty-five. He did not mention that the death was caused by suicide, nor did he take questions from the reporters.

Immediately the media began disseminating the story. Since these were the days before twenty-four-hour television news, it was the responsibility of radio to break the story first. Ernie Jackson got the news from his wife, who heard it on the radio. Jackson quickly got into his car. He started driving and driving and driving, north up Highway 400, past Barrie. "That's how he dealt with it," recalls Willie Jackson. "He was really angry." Later, when he came home, he and Willie "shed a tear or two," according to her. Then he asked her, "Why would he do that?"

Darcy and Joyce McKeough were in Bermuda when they received a phone call. They were stunned and both began to cry. "He was a father figure to me," says McKeough, who got his first big political promotion to cabinet from Prime Minister Robarts. "But the more you thought about it, you could understand the reasons."

Ian Macdonald gets misty-eyed when describing his reaction. "It was like a knife slicing through my chest as I heard that," he says. "It's one of those things where you feel this couldn't be. It's incomprehensible. We were enjoying this relationship at York University, and then it was suddenly all over," he says. "But the more I thought about it, it was the final shot, so to speak, in his proposition that he only wanted to be at his best."

"Knowing him," offers David Peterson, "you'd think he would be the last person prone to that kind of depression and would commit suicide. So obviously something went terribly amiss. His sunny optimism was an essential side of his character."

Don Matthews was in France when his secretary called him with the news. He immediately came home and sought a meeting with Toronto's police chief, Jack Ackroyd. Matthews feared foul play was involved, and he told the chief of the threats Robarts had said he'd received from his wife.

One of the reasons Chief Ackroyd wanted Bill McCormack on the scene immediately was not only McCormack's experience in public affairs dealing with the media but also his many years of investigating homicides. And before long, it was not just Don Matthews who had serious questions about the nature of Robarts's death.

"There was a lot of speculation about that," confirms Bill McCormack. "A lot of people had some very strange ideas. I was right there at the scene. There was no doubt in my mind it was a suicide. There was no question in my mind, as a former homicide man, that he had reached a point of no return." McCormack directed more resources to investigate the possibilities of foul play, but there was never any evidence to proceed.

McCormack and two other homicide officers went to the Robarts home to question Katherine, who was totally mystified by their presence. Years later, she found out why the police returned to interrogate her. "Don Matthews wanted me arrested for murder," she says bluntly today. "It's an indication of how much they hated me."

Robarts's niece had gone back to school to become a palliative care nurse. She was to begin her new job at Riverdale Hospital in Toronto on October 18. At nine in the morning she was wakened by a knock at her door in the nurses' residence and advised that there was an emergency phone call for her. Her long trek to the phone included an elevator ride with a man who was incessantly talking to another person. As the man exited the elevator, he looked back at his colleague and said, "Oh, did you hear the news on the radio this morning? Former premier John Robarts shot himself." The elevator doors then closed. That's how Andrea Robarts learned of her uncle's death.

Andrea left the hospital and made for St. Andrews Gardens. On the way, she saw some linemen effecting repairs on hydro lines. She wanted to shout at them, What are you doing working? Don't you know my uncle is dead? She began to cry.

Barb Prevedello visited the home of her father, Ernie Jackson, on Cluny Drive in Rosedale the night of Robarts's death. "It was as if his life was over as well," she recalls. "It was as if he'd lost his right arm."

"By the end," Ernie Jackson once told his son, George, "he couldn't raise a glass of Scotch without having it dribble down his chin."

Gordon Walker replaced Robarts as the Tory MPP for London North. He regarded his predecessor as a mentor. He saw himself as an apostle. "I don't think John Robarts would have fared well in a nursing home," Walker says, "and the last place any of us would like to have seen him is in an unfortunate situation, even more debilitated than what he was."

Naturally, once the manner of Robarts's death sank in, his colleagues began to replay conversations for clues. George Jackson says at one point that a depressed Robarts had told his father, "I think Tim had the right idea."

Hugh Hanson thought back to their last meal together. Robarts had not mentioned suicide on that occasion. But come to think of it, Hanson recalled, he had discussed it several times before, both in relation to Tim and as a possible option for himself. "He once was talking about someone else who'd had a stroke and he got his health back after a year," Hanson says. "We were on the boat and he said, 'I'm going to give myself a year.'" Hanson never tried to talk Robarts out of a possible suicide attempt because he *did* understand what drives people to that despair. Hanson had three close friends who had committed suicide. "If he couldn't do the things that made life meaningful for him, it was a sensible course of action," he says.

Robarts had once had a conversation about suicide with his son, Tim. He told him each day was a gift. Ultimately, Tim disregarded his father's advice. Now, five years after Tim's suicide, it was Robarts who no longer saw each day as a gift.

Richard Rohmer had an answer for those who wondered, How could he have done it? "I always say John Robarts [at the end] was *not* the John Robarts we all knew," he says. "He'd been changed by the strokes, dramatically, enormously, in every way. The person who took his own life was *not* the person who would have done that had he been well."

Robin has another explanation. "I often think that maybe if Tim hadn't killed himself, he might have found some more resources to go forward and try and beat it," she says. "But so much was taken out of him when Tim died that I just don't think he had enough left."

Inevitably, her anger subsided. She came to understand why her father took his own life, even the method by which he did so. "What could be tidier, quite frankly?" she asks. "Now, his method of committing suicide—a shotgun—is not generally tidy, but if you're going to use that, I suppose the shower is the best place." That may sound cold, but Robin says it in a sympathetic way. She believes her father deliberately chose the location he did to be as little bother as possible to those who would have to deal with the aftermath. She is a plainspoken person who does not shy away from discussing difficult topics straight on.

Why a shotgun, rather than something much less violent, say, pills and alcohol?

The answer, of course, is unknowable. But Robin points out correctly that her father loved and knew guns well. John Robarts hunted with both his father and his children. When Robin turned twenty-one, her father gave her her own shotgun, made to measure. The two hunted together on Griffiths Island. Robin also speculates that her father may have been thinking of his son in choosing to kill himself the way he did. "I do remember him making a comment about how extraordinarily courageous he thought Tim was to do that," she says.

The more Fraser Elliott thought about how Robarts departed the world, the angrier he got. Elliott was convinced that if Robarts had

had a different wife, he would not have taken the ultimate decision he did. "You have no idea how she treated him," Elliott insists. "He couldn't get rid of her."

If the funeral arrangements around Tim's death were complicated, they were nothing in comparison to what needed to be done for his father. Katherine was adamant that the funeral be for immediate family only. The intergovernmental affairs department at Queen's Park, which houses the protocol office, was equally adamant that something beyond that was necessary.

Tom Wells was the intergovernmental affairs minister at the time, and as it happens, he was the right man for the job in so many ways. He was a member of the legislature, having been elected for the first time in 1963, Robarts's first election as prime minister. Just three years later, he was one of five up-and-coming Tory MPPs to be appointed to cabinet in anticipation of Canada's Centennial and a provincial election. And he was now a much-respected member of William Davis's cabinet.

Wells had more than his hands full negotiating funeral arrangements with Katherine Robarts. According to someone close to the negotiations, she wanted no part of any public service or public viewing. "She was so protective, to the point of an ego trip," the observer says. "Wells spent hours in her living room negotiating with her. She gave us an unbelievable difficult time."

Whenever Katherine would demand less rather than more involvement for the protocol office, Wells would say, "You can't ignore the fact he was the premier." At one point, Wells actually went to Bill Davis, urging Robarts's successor to get directly involved. Davis declined. "You can handle this, Tom," he said. "Just keep meeting with her."

On another occasion, Katherine met with Keith Reynolds and Richard Rohmer and felt they were coming on too strong. "They were rambling on and on about something," she says, "so I just got up and said, 'Let me go ask John what he'd like to do.' I'm sure they thought

I was crazy, but I'd just had enough." Eventually, she and Wells came to an agreement. She essentially gave in on almost everything. "It was all taken out of my hands," Katherine says. "I wasn't involved in the funeral arrangements. I was told what to do."

John Robarts's body would lie in state at the Ontario legislature. There would be a guest book for the public to sign. There would be a full public service at St. Paul's Church on Bloor Street East in Toronto. However, the burial would be for family members only. Protocol could live with that.

Negotiations were not over. Because Robarts's death was a suicide, Cardinal Carter refused to attend the service. Even the Anglican archbishop, Lewis Garnsworthy, refused to preside over a *funeral* service. He said he would do it only if organizers would call it a *memorial* service, which they did.

Hugh Hanson began to think about the elements that he felt the service should contain. Then he wrote the eulogy that Canada's former governor general Roland Michener would deliver.

Before the service took place, the politicians of the day had their say via tributes in the Ontario legislature. Premier Davis spoke generously, if not accurately, when he said, "Some of us saw him a few nights ago, making such great progress." There was no progress, and Davis knew it, but he tried to put the best face on what was a horrible day for him and his province.

The funeral was, in a word, impressive. The church was packed to the rafters with leaders from the business and political communities. Of course Davis was there, but so was Prime Minister Pierre Trudeau. As the hearse containing Robarts's body proceeded down Church Street, just north of Bloor, construction workers took off their hard hats as a sign of respect. "That impressed me," Hugh Hanson now says. It was a moving sight.

Once again, there was some last-minute diplomacy necessary between Katherine and, this time, the men who were charged with carrying Robarts's casket in and out of the church. The list of pall-bearers was to include Ernie Jackson, Richard Dillon, Keith Reynolds, Don Martyn, Hugh Hanson, and Richard Rohmer. Don Matthews was also supposed to be on the list, but Katherine vetoed him. She also wanted Jackson gone, but when she mentioned that, she triggered a near revolt led by Dick Dillon. Matthews would go, but Jackson stayed. Pat Gillick and Paul Beeston from the Blue Jays were honorary pallbearers, along with several dozen others.

At one point before the service began, a man in a wheelchair rolled himself down the aisle and touched the casket. He was not a premier or prime minister, just one of hundreds of anonymous people John Robarts had apparently touched. "Those are the moments that fill your heart," recalls Andrea Robarts.

For a man who had serious doubts about participating in the service to begin with, Archbishop Garnsworthy set, by all accounts, a wonderful tone. In a memorable sermon, he did not dwell on how Robarts died, but to his credit he did not duck it either: "The manner of his passing saddens all of us," he said. "But I am not the judge of that, and you are not the judges. The issues of life and death are in the hands of a loving and forgiving God. And I am content that it should be so. I am content to pray for him this day, rest after pain and peace after struggle. I am content to pray for his family, God's strength, God's comfort."

"There was an enormous outpouring of respect and affection," recalls Ron Watts, Robarts's fellow commissioner on the Pepin-Robarts national unity task force. All the commissioners sat together and shared the experience in solemnity. In fact, Jean-Luc Pepin and Solange Chaput-Rolland both told Andrea Robarts how important her uncle had been to their commission. "There were times we were so frustrated that we wanted to throw in the towel," Pepin told her. "It was at those times that John buoyed them up again and regained their hope." What a wonderful legacy, Andrea thought. "Canada has lost its greatest listener," Pepin added, referring to a quality in short supply in political life these days.

Margo Carson, Robarts's first secretary at Stikeman Elliott, was there. "I was very, very sad—a lot of people were," she says. "Sad that he was gone, but also because his life had been such misery after the stroke. It was almost a relief."

"His funeral was a clear indication of the respect and, just as important, the affection people had for John," Davis says. "He passed on really shortly after he had made his contribution to Ontario and Canada, and people had not forgotten."

There were a few items in the ceremony that struck a sour note with some. Hugh Hanson wrote for the governor general what he thought was a lovely eulogy. But he thought Michener did not exactly rise to the occasion. "He was one of the worst speakers," Hanson now says. "He really fucked it up. Wonderful man, but no orator."

But that did not compare with what many regarded as a major faux pas committed by Pierre Trudeau. According to officials from the Humphrey Funeral Home, protocol dictated that Robarts's brother, Bob, should walk Katherine out of the church. Frankly, neither party was thrilled at that prospect, but being the dutiful brother, Bob agreed to do it. But Katherine turned him down and Bob's wife, Eleanor, got into a verbal sparring match with her sister-in-law over the slight.

Why Katherine turned down Bob Robarts became evident at the service's conclusion. She had already made other plans to leave the church, and in style—on the arm of the prime minister of Canada. She had asked the funeral home organizers to pass on a message to Trudeau, requesting that the prime minister walk her out of the church. The Humphrey's people disagreed with the request but would pass it on to Trudeau. When Humphrey's officials told the prime minister it really was not protocol for him to do so, Trudeau responded: "Fuck protocol. If she wants me there, I'll be there." That Humphrey's official, quite red-faced, then quoted the prime minister verbatim to Katherine, in confirming Trudeau's participation. (Although, when she told this story, she replaced the actual *f* word with Trudeau's other favourite, *fuddle-duddle*.)

"Her parade up the aisle after her husband's funeral on the arm of Trudeau turned not a few stomachs," says Judith Grieve. "We thought John would be rolling."

"I thought it told the whole story," Don Matthews says. "She was more interested in promoting herself than mourning John."

The Trudeau escort was not the last opportunity that mourners would have to raise their eyebrows. After the funeral, interment took place at the St. James Cemetery and Crematorium, just a few minutes' drive from the church, at the corner of Bloor and Parliament Streets. There were suggestions that Katherine tried to keep this an immediate-family-only event. But some, such as the Grieves, refused to play along. "There was no bloody way she was going to keep us away," says Judith Grieve, Norah Robarts's niece. "We hired a limo and got right behind the hearse. I told the driver, 'Your payment depends on your getting us in.' He did, and she stared daggers at us."

Considering he was one of the most significant political leaders in Canadian history, John Robarts's final resting place is surprisingly modest. The gravesite is not featured in any way. There are no signs indicating a former Ontario prime minister is buried there. In fact, there are numerous headstones surrounding Robarts's that are much more prominent. The headstone is grey and simply designed with two straight vertical sides and a horizontal top, which starts high in the middle, then slopes to the sides. It features two trilliums, Ontario's official flower, in the top left and top right corners, and the following inscription:

ROBARTS
The Honourable
John Parmenter Robarts
PC, CC, QC, BA, LLD, DCL
Jan. 11, 1917–Oct. 18, 1982
Prime Minister of Ontario
1961–1971

There are two more phrases, in quotation marks, across the bottom of the headstone. Katherine wrote them herself:

Rest in peace my darling Jonathan
Beloved husband and dearest friend

When Hugh Hanson saw the inscription Katherine had chosen, he had one reaction: "Yuck."

Andrea Robarts was also peeved. "I felt angry about Katherine's words at the time because they were so false."

Other colleagues reacted similarly. John Cronyn thought, "She had a big shovel." Dick Dillon simply shook his head in disgust. "Isn't that amazing?" he said. Ernie Jackson did not go to the burial service. When he saw the headstone on a later occasion, he came home and said to his wife, "You're not going to believe this …"

For nearly ten years, John Robarts's friends had thought Katherine was a gold digger and not in his league. Some future actions confirmed their suspicions. Katherine had a houseful of Robarts's memorabilia and intended to sell whatever she could through an auction house. When Darcy McKeough got wind of the plan, he put together a group of Robarts's friends to raise some money so his Order of Canada and other important mementos could be more appropriately saved and showcased.

The last year of John and Katherine Robarts's marriage was, as we have seen, quite rocky. However, more than two decades after her second husband's death, Robarts's widow seems to be a very different person from the woman in her thirties all those years ago. She is still tall and slim and very attractive. She is also almost sixty years old and a grandmother of two, thanks to her daughter, Kimberly. Katherine Robarts still lives in the same house in Rosedale, where her husband took his life on October 18, 1982.

Two years after John Robarts's death, she married a third time. Her husband, Edward Bodner, owned a cosmetics trade magazine. He was a widower, his wife having died from cancer a year earlier. The marriage lasted only four years. "It happened too quickly for both of us," Katherine says. "We were looking to replace what we'd lost."

Did she ever feel uncomfortable continuing to live in the house John Robarts died in? "I never think of it that way," she says. "It's the house my husband *lived* in."

She still has the Mercedes-Benz her husband used to drive, complete with one of the first personalized licence plates ever sold in Ontario: JPR 111. If things ended badly between her and John Robarts, the passage of time has made her yearn for the couple's early years, which were happy ones. "He was my best friend. He was my buddy," she says. "He has a presence that doesn't go away. He was able to go into a room and people would know he was there without even seeing him. He has a presence still." In fact, a large portrait of John Robarts still graces the dining room of his former home on St. Andrews Gardens.

IN THE SPRING OF 1992, even though he had not smoked for twenty years, Ernie Jackson developed lung cancer. Amazingly, he had two-thirds of his lung removed and then was back golfing six weeks later.

In the autumn of 1994, his family convinced him to return to a place he said he would never set foot in again: Italy, where he saw so much violent action during the Second World War. The plan was to visit the family of his son-in-law, Franco Prevedello. Jackson had a medical before leaving for Italy, and mostly checked out fine, with one exception. He was experiencing dizzy spells. He would feel unsteady on his feet after standing up. Nevertheless, he did go to Italy and seemed to enjoy it.

Later that year, Ernie and Willie Jackson drove to their place in Sarasota, Florida, which was their tradition. But the dizzy spells got worse. Jackson got himself checked out by a doctor in Florida, who confirmed through an MRI that he had a brain tumour. Within twenty-four hours, he was back in Toronto, having an operation on his brain at Wellesley Hospital. He made it through the operation, came home for Christmas, underwent radiation therapy, and met his first great-grandchild, Jackson Bieman.

But in January 1995, he was back in hospital, Princess Margaret this time.

"He didn't want to eat," says Barb Prevedello, who was constantly by his side. "He wouldn't talk, but I would. He had no pain. No tubes. No hookups. He decided he didn't want to be an invalid."

On January 21, 1995, Ernie Jackson simply shut his eyes. Just like his best friend, John Robarts, although much less violently, he decided he had had enough. He was one week away from his seventy-third birthday.

"They were too much a part of life to be comfortable in half death," says Barb.

With Jackson's death, the John Robarts era in Ontario had truly come to an end.

Conclusion

Every president, prime minister, governor, or premier is different from the rest of us. They must be to get to the top of whatever political mountain they're trying to climb. Some are particularly ruthless. Some possess an outstanding knowledge of key issues. Some have extraordinary "people skills" but not much grasp of the intricacies of policy. Others still are able to demonstrate superior judgment when it comes to evaluating the direction a country or province needs to take, then balancing all the appropriate concerns to lead the way.

John Robarts was not a ruthless, brass-knuckles politician like Jean Chrétien. He was interested in policy but hardly an academic, obsessed with every detail and nuance of policy development, the likes of Preston Manning or Stephen Harper. His people skills with his friends were legendary, but with ordinary voters he had no particularly special gifts, à la Bill Clinton or Ralph Klein.

No, Robarts's greatest talent as a political leader was having a reliable internal compass. Instinctively, he seemed to know where his province ought to go, and how it ought to get there. He was masterful at synthesizing information from many different sources, evaluating their merit, and successfully arbitrating competing interests. He found the appropriate consensus to keep Ontario prosperous, relatively harmonious, and moving in the right direction. His was an extremely steady hand on the tiller.

"He laid the foundations in many areas for the development of Ontario for the next thirty to forty years," says Richard Rohmer.

"When you put it all together, it's a formidable group of achievements by one guy leading a team as Chairman of the Board."

"I think Chairman of the Board was a good title for him because he was always very good at weighing things and coming up with a really good decision," adds Robarts's daughter.. "He thought things through, and because of that, to me he seemed very wise. I trusted his decisions and his viewpoints. And hopefully that will be part of his legacy."

John Robarts's vision went beyond his province. When ministers in his cabinet tried to impress a more parochial prescription on some issue—something that might play better in Ontario's heartland but perhaps at the expense of national unity—the prime minister would have none of it. "The very idea of a go-it-alone policy for Ontario has always been anathema to me," he would say in a typical stump speech. "As I've said on many occasions, I'm a Canadian first." The line would always bring the house down.

Robarts's life did end tragically, but perhaps not as prematurely as one might think. He once told his friend Don Matthews he had done everything there is to do in life. "I even slept one night in Buckingham Palace," he said, smiling.

For all the strength and brilliance he showed in his political career, his personal choices were often misguided. He was a balanced decision maker, but that balance did not extend after hours. He lived hard, and as time passed, the effects of overindulgence began to show. And his hopes for a romantic, simpler, post-political life with his second wife proved to be short-lived and ultimately destructive. Many men have shown how effective they can be in the outside world while at the same time struggling with the personal aspects of life like family and marriage. John Kennedy and Bill Clinton are no doubt the best examples of those characteristics. John Robarts belongs on the same list.

The only surviving member of Robarts's original nuclear family is Robin. She has endured a lot: a father and brother who both committed suicide and a mother whose final years were spent fighting a sad solitude, culminating in a premature death. Despite it all, Robin Robarts has an unusually positive outlook on her life, which she has described as unbelievably great, punctuated by moments of tragedy. The passage of time has also given Robin added insight into her father's death. She now says, "I think he probably did the right thing for him."

The accomplishments and innovations of the Robarts government are still evident throughout Ontario, more than thirty years after his departure from public life: the Ontario Science Centre, GO Transit, Ontario Place, numerous colleges and universities, the Niagara Escarpment Commission, improvements in civil rights, the Ontario Arts Council, and the list goes on. His trials were less public: the suicide of his son, two marriages that ended badly, and considerable health and sobriety struggles.

His public triumphs were the stuff of political legend. His private tragedies were worthy of a Shakespearean drama. Such was the double life of John P. Robarts.

Epilogue

ALMOST FOUR YEARS after John Robarts's death, many of his disciples convened in his hometown to officially open the John P. Robarts Research Institute. David Peterson, the only other Londoner to reach the pinnacle of Ontario provincial politics, was there in his capacity as the new premier of Ontario, a job he had held at that time for only a year. William Davis, Robarts's successor as premier, was there as honorary chairman of the new institute. William Stewart came bearing gifts. The former agriculture minister and MPP from nearby Middlesex North formally offered a decorative fountain for the institute's lobby—a gift from onetime Robarts cabinet ministers. The Oakville PC Association commissioned a bas-relief bronze sculpture of Robarts, which was unveiled by his brother, Bob, and his daughter, Robin. Darcy McKeough, Matt Dymond, and, of course, Ernie Jackson were all there.

There were speeches galore to mark the occasion. Perhaps the most amusing moment came when the emcee introduced the premier of Ontario to say a few words, and Bill Davis automatically took half a step forward before catching himself. He had been out of the job for almost two years, but old habits presumably die hard.

"I felt there should be something in London that recognized his contribution to the health system," Bill Davis told me. "We did insist ... not insist ... you couldn't insist ... *suggested* that it be named after John." A *suggestion* from Bill Davis was apparently enough for the stakeholders to commemorate Robarts's memory by naming the institute after him.

The $12 million John P. Robarts Research Institute actually came in $800,000 under budget, thanks in large measure to Robarts's old friend Don Smith, whose company, EllisDon, built the facility. "We gave them 50 percent more building for less money," Smith says of the project. The institute is affiliated with the University of Western Ontario and London Health Sciences Centre and focuses on tackling several health care challenges: heart disease, diabetes, multiple sclerosis, Lou Gehrig's and Alzheimer's diseases, and perhaps most appropriately, given whose name is on the building, stroke and aging. Since the institute's inception, it has tripled the size of its research staff to the current complement of six hundred and doubled its physical space. Its motto, carved into the building's cornerstone, is "To strive, to seek, to find," the immortal words from Tennyson's "Ulysses."

Fortunately, the building does more than just bear Robarts's name. Displayed in the lobby are his miniature medals from the Second World War (which his daughter donated), his Order of Canada, and other memorabilia that Darcy McKeough raised the money to purchase from Robarts's widow, Katherine.

"We had a great luncheon of about thirty or so people who had contributed to make all this possible," McKeough says, "including port and cigars, which may not be the most appropriate thing to do in a medical research institute, but John would have appreciated it."

There was one unusual event that transpired on that September day in 1986 when dignitaries opened the research institute. Eleanor Robarts, the late prime minister's sister-in-law, was approached by a woman she did not recognize. "I'm Timmy's biological mother," the woman said. Until then, no one had known the identity of the birth mother of John Robarts's only son.

"She drove me home," Eleanor Robarts says. "She was a university student [in the 1950s]. She wanted her baby to have a better life." It was the only contact Tim's birth mother and Eleanor would ever have.

Considering the influence John Robarts had on his home province and country, there are actually very few public commemorations of his contributions. The research institute and the library at the University of Toronto are the most prominent. In addition, there is the Robarts School for the Deaf, established in London in 1973.

In May 1984, York University established the Robarts Centre for Canadian Studies. Some of its better-known directors and/or chairs include Thomas Courchene, Kenneth McRoberts, Ramsay Cook, Susan Swan, and Seth Feldman. The annual Robarts Lecture is the culmination of the chair's research each year.

To find the best example of a significant effort to keep the former prime minister's memory alive, it is best not to look on the front of any building in particular, but rather behind some very large closed doors. The Toronto Club is one of those venues that evoke a different time and place. Its massive wooden doors with big brass handles have greeted members and guests on the south side of Wellington Street since 1935. On entering, one is welcomed by a steward, very formally dressed, and invited to hang up one's coat in an adjacent room. All briefcases, notebooks, magazines, and other belongings must be left there as well. And, of course, if you are a man, don't even think about going beyond the front door unless you are appropriately attired in a jacket and tie.

On the second floor of the Toronto Club, a couple of dozen men, almost all of them from a bygone political era, gather every December to schmooze over old times. Most of them are in their sixties and seventies, some in their eighties. There are enough Order of Canada pins attached to the lapels of blue pinstriped suits here to sink a small freighter. Decades ago, these men were the captains of government and industry. Today, for most of them, their schedules and responsibilities are considerably lighter.

They have many things in common. They are all men. They are all Tories. They are almost all white Anglo-Saxon Protestants. But the most important thing they share is a love for the seventeenth prime minister of Ontario.

This is the annual John P. Robarts Luncheon that, in spite of the honouree's absence for more than two decades, has been going strong for thirty-three years. The lunch has survived Robarts's death because these men delight in an opportunity, just once a year, to get together and remember their former prime minister and friend. They start with drinks at a pre-lunch reception, then move to an ornate yet cozy dining room for a fabulously prepared, multicourse meal, which will last for two and a half hours. Political correctness has not invaded this space, so the odd cigar and pipe are present.

This luncheon has survived throughout the years in large part because of the efforts of John Cronyn and Darcy McKeough. Robarts gave McKeough his first big political break by making him a cabinet minister, and McKeough seems all too happy to reciprocate by keeping the Robarts flame lit. "John was my hero," McKeough explains. "He personified what was good about public service. And to me personally, he was such a civil person." Robarts was godfather to McKeough's son James, born in 1968.

Every year, McKeough books the Toronto Club, sends out the invitations, and gets the lunch off to a humorous start. "I'm going to read a long grace," he begins. "You can all doze off."

On this occasion, there is something different about the gathering. There is a woman present. It is Robarts's daughter, making a guest appearance. McKeough acknowledges her presence. "This is a grace your father would have liked," he says, before reading a traditional sixth-century Celtic prayer:

I should like a great lake of finest ale
For the King of kings.
I should like a table of the choicest food
For the family of heaven.
Let the ale be made from the fruits of faith,
And the food be forgiving love.

I should welcome the poor to my feast,
For they are God's children.
I should welcome the sick to my feast,
For they are God's joy.
Let the poor sit with Jesus at the highest place,
and the sick dance with the angels.

God bless the poor,
God bless the sick,
And bless our human race.
God bless our food.

With grace out of the way, McKeough continues in his unofficial capacity as chairman of the gathering. He updates everyone on some developments of the past year and begins a series of toasts. Quickly, it becomes apparent that this is what comedians might call a rough room.

"Darcy, are you going to do all the talking?" interrupts J.J. Barnicke, to plenty of laughter.

"God, it was so nice that you came late," McKeough fires back, and again, more chuckles fill the room.

One by one, several of Robarts's cronies get up to propose a toast, or tell a story from days gone by.

"I represent the poor here," jokes Eddie Goodman, the guy who got Robarts into Progressive Conservative politics in the first place. "We've lost our memories, but we're not dead yet!" In Goodman's case, he is not kidding. "Fast Eddie," whose prominent Toronto law firm, Goodmans, employs two former premiers of Ontario (Bob Rae and Mike Harris), is starting to show signs of slowing down. He has some bad days, forgetting things he should not be forgetting. But thankfully on this day he is very much on his game. After Goodman finishes speaking, I ask him where his old friend Richard Rohmer is.

"Not here yet," he says, then adds, "Thank God." Even after forty years, some of the old rivalries persist.

Richard Dillon then rises to perform his annual duty. "It is my great honour to propose a toast to the person I've known longer than anyone else," he begins, in reference to a friendship dating from 1935. Dillon completes his toast and the program continues.

Don Early gets up to tell a story. Goodman, in full rhetorical flight, interrupts.

"What the hell did you ever do for the Conservative Party?" he asks.

Tom Kierans, former president and CEO of the C.D. Howe Institute, supplies the answer: "He gave, he gave, and he gave."

As the first course is served, the former media magnate Douglas Bassett begins to explain to others at his table why he and his father, the legendary John W. Bassett (owner of three Toronto institutions, the *Telegram,* the Maple Leafs and the Argonauts), actually backed Robarts's rival, Kelso Roberts, for the leadership in 1961. "Kelso lived kitty-corner from us, so we supported him," he explains. "He got to know father very well. The *Telegram* supported Kelso for leader."

"That's why it went under," chimes in Robin Robarts, with a brilliantly timed heckle.

And just to prove Eddie Goodman still has what it takes to break up a table, he offers the following observation: "You know, when you look around this room, you wonder how Robarts did so well," he says, we think, in jest.

Next, John Cronyn offers a toast to Ernie Jackson, then tells an amusing tale from the same leadership campaign. "Ernie told John, 'No drinking during the campaign. There's rumours around that you drink too much.'" Cronyn says. "Robarts answered, 'This isn't fair. I haven't had a drink in a week and you guys are all out having fun.'"

Cronyn, who loved participating in John White's yellow-jacketed volunteer brigade at that leadership convention, stands as a stark contrast to Robarts. Now eighty-three years old, Cronyn has needed thrice-weekly kidney dialysis for four years. His health has markedly deteriorated, but he continues to hang in. "You can live with anything as long as you live," he tells me. Clearly, that philosophy was rejected by his friend the former prime minister of Ontario.

Bill Rudd approaches me to confirm he and Robarts went a long way back—to their days together at the Delta Upsilon fraternity house at UWO. The Robartses also lived just up the street. "I went in 1951 to the Ontario election campaign headquarters in London and simply asked, 'Can I help?'" Rudd says. "They gave me a canvass kit and sent me into the night."

Beyond the jokes and reminiscences, this thirty-second annual Robarts Luncheon will be more memorable than most, because one of the participants is about to reveal some important news. During the course of the past year, Robin, the first adopted child of John and Norah Robarts, and now approaching age fifty, has finally learned the identity of her birth mother.

After her father's death, Robin Robarts discovered that her original name had been Laura Jean Sonmor. Then, in December 2001 at Robin's annual office Christmas party at Bosley Real Estate in Toronto, where she'd been working since March 1998, she was approached by a fellow agent named Regan Devine. He introduced his wife, who was a reporter with *The Toronto Sun*. Her name was Jean Sonmor. Robin's eyebrows went up. The three then spent the entire evening together, comparing notes and trying to determine whether they were related.

The evening ended inconclusively. Then, at four o'clock in the morning, something in Jean Sonmor went *eureka*. She called Robin the next morning and told her she thought she knew something but wanted to investigate further. Three days later, the pair had lunch together. When Robin arrived, Jean was already crying.

"I've talked to my sister," Jean Sonmor said. "You're my niece."

The pieces of the Robin Robarts puzzle started to fall into place.

Back in 1953, Robin's birth mother, Katherine Sonmor, was a twenty-one-year-old living in Hamilton. She got pregnant, moved to London, ostensibly to look for a new job, or so the story went. Several months later, she returned to Hamilton, skinnier, claiming that the job search simply had not worked out. In fact, Katherine Sonmor had her baby and had given her up for adoption. She had actually stayed with Laura Jean/Robin long enough to breast-feed her. Leaving her baby behind was excruciatingly difficult, but in 1953, single motherhood simply was not an option.

Interestingly enough, after Robin's adoption went through, her birth mother "snuck a peek" at who her daughter's new family would be. "So she's always known," Robin says.

Soon after her lunch with her aunt, Robin connected with her birth mother, Katherine Sonmor Duncan. She also discovered Katherine had two daughters in their late thirties—new sisters for Robin. And in a final irony, she learned her birth mother had lived only ten minutes away from her for the past twenty-five years. When they finally did meet in 1992, Katherine Duncan was well aware of the tragedies that had befallen Robin Robarts's family. "I thought you would never want to meet me after I left you with that family," Katherine joked at their first encounter in almost half a century.

Besides her now-frequent get-togethers with her aunt Jean and her two new sisters, Robin has also connected with her birth mother's brother, Glen Sonmor, whose name may ring a bell. Born in Moose Jaw, Saskatchewan, Glen Sonmor played twenty-eight games over two seasons in the National Hockey League for the New York Rangers, from 1953 to 1955. His playing career ended when he lost an eye while playing for the Cleveland Barons in the American Hockey League. However, he had some success as a coach in Minnesota, first at the University of Minnesota, then with the Fighting Saints of the old World Hockey Association from 1976 to 1977, and finally with the NHL's North-Stars from 1978 to 1982, and for a month in 1987.

He led the North-Stars to a Stanley Cup final berth in 1981 but lost to the New York Islanders.

For Robin Robarts, they are all now family—the Sonmors, the Robartses, and the men who gather at the annual John P. Robarts Luncheon to keep her father's memory alive. "We've all stayed with John to the bitter end," says Bill Rudd.

Yes, they have.

Where Are They Now?

(All information is as of October 2004)

Jack Ackroyd. The chief of the Metropolitan Toronto Police Force from 1980 to 1984. Died in 1990 of leukemia. He was also chair of the Liquor Control Board of Ontario from 1984 to 1990.

Joseph J. Barnicke, 81. Chairman and CEO of J.J. Barnicke Ltd., the commercial real estate company he founded forty-five years ago. Sits on board of directors of the Viking-Rideau Corp.

Douglas Bassett, 64. Sits on the boards of the Canadian Imperial Bank of Commerce, Rothmans Inc., Retirement Residences REIT, and Mercedes-Benz Canada. Chairman of Windward Investments, a private holding company.

Gérald Beaudoin, 75. Retired from the Senate of Canada in April 2004.

Charles Beer, 62. Recently retired as executive assistant to the Ontario minister of health, George Smitherman. Lives in Newmarket, Ontario.

Paul Beeston, 59. The Toronto Blue Jays' first employee retired from his job as president and chief operating officer of Major League Baseball in 2002. Lives in Toronto where he is "giving back to the community" by doing volunteer work.

Henry Best. The former president of Laurentian University. Died in Sudbury, Ontario, in April 2004 at age 69.

Edward Bodner. Katherine Robarts's third husband is retired, and now lives in Winnipeg.

Ab Campion, 71. For the past five years, has been spokesman for the Alcohol and Gaming Commission of Ontario.

Margo Carson, 54. Manager in the learning solutions group of the shared services bureau of the management board secretariat. The bureau delivers training through the Ontario public service to more than forty-five thousand people.

Solange Chaput-Rolland. Quebec commentator, writer, and Canadian senator. Died in November 2001 at age 82.

John B. Cronyn. The former executive at Labatt's Breweries and chair of the province's Committee on Government Productivity. Died in London on February 23, 2004, after too many years of thrice-weekly dialysis treatments. He was predeceased by his wife, Barbara, who died three months after John Robarts's brother, Bob, passed away. As a result, Cronyn and Bob's widow, Eleanor, established a family friendship that lasted till his death. On Valentine's Day, nine days before his death, he sent Eleanor flowers. Cronyn was 83, and a gentleman to the end.

William G. Davis, 75. Robarts's successor as premier of Ontario has been a counsel with the law firm Torys in Toronto since he left politics in 1985. He is director of a number of companies but is also very active in the non-profit sector. He is a member of: the University of Toronto's governing council, the Toronto City Summit Alliance Steering Committee, the OISE/U of T Advisory Board, the Council for Canadian Unity, the honorary advisory board of the Canadian Association for Community Living, the patrons' council of the Alzheimer Society of Toronto, the business advisory council of French for the Future, the advisory board of the Peel Children's Aid Foundation, and the Toronto Zoo Advisory Committee. He is also a trustee on the Trudeau Foundation, honorary trustee on the Royal Ontario Museum and member of the ROM Foundation, and an honorary patron of the

Habitat for Humanity, Brampton affiliate. He describes his hobbies as watching *Studio 2* on TVO (he is a board member of the TVO Foundation), keeping track of the Toronto Argonauts and Miami Dolphins, and supervising five children, their five spouses, and twelve grandchildren. And yes, he still lives on Main Street in Brampton with his wife, Kathleen.

A. Rendall Dick, 78. The former deputy attorney general lives in Thornhill, Ontario, with Helen, his wife of fifty-three years. Spends his days "smelling the roses," and summers at his cottage on Georgian Bay, opposite Griffiths Island.

Richard M. Dillon, 83. Robarts's oldest friend lives in Toronto with his wife, Elizabeth.

Eric Dowd, 73. Has covered Queen's Park since John Robarts's first election as prime minister in 1963, first with *The Globe and Mail* and currently as a freelance columnist.

Alan Eagleson, 71. Lives with his wife, Nancy, in Collingwood, Ontario, and London, England.

Don Early. Lives in Toronto, Florida, and the south of France.

Fraser Elliott, 82. One of the founding partners of the Stikeman Elliott law firm still goes to the office every day and practises law ("At least that's what I call it," he says). He is on the board of CAE, a provider of integrated training solutions and advanced simulation and controls technologies to civil aviation, military, and marine customers. He is also on the board of the Toronto General and Western Hospital Foundation. He lives in Toronto.

John R. Evans, 75. Chairman of the Board of Torstar Corporation. Vice-chairman of NPS/Allelix Biopharmaceuticals Inc. Chairman of the Canadian Foundation for Innovation, an independent corporation trying to strengthen the capability of Canadian universities, colleges, research hospitals, and other not-for-profit institutions to carry out world-class research and technology development. Also chairs the Medical and Related Sciences (MaRS) Discovery District, a research and development centre that will bring researchers and life sciences companies under one roof, combining the scientific and the business communities.

Robert Fisher, 56. News anchor for CBC-Radio and regular contributor to *Fourth Reading* on TVO. He also teaches law and ethics at Centennial College in Toronto.

Eddie Goodman, 85. The man who introduced Robarts to Conservative Party politics still visits his Goodmans law offices in downtown Toronto daily. He is on the campaign cabinet of Renaissance ROM (Royal Ontario Museum). He has been married to Joan Thompson for ten years and has one daughter.

Judith Grieve, 67. Norah Robarts's niece and her husband, Jim Grieve, have been married since 1958. She takes weekly bridge lessons, plays tennis, and spends much of her time at her cottage on Long Point, Balsam Lake, in the Kawarthas.

Bea Hamilton, 67. Was married to John White, London South MPP from 1959 to 1975, until his death from a heart attack in September 1996. Married retired radiologist Gavin Hamilton, a widower, in August 2000. Has two daughters, three grandchildren, and enjoys bicycling, canoeing, and skating. The couple lives in London.

Hugh Hanson, 69. Just retired after fifteen years on the board of directors of Central Toronto Youth Services. Still does some consulting for a small stock brokerage company. Moved to Newmarket, Ontario, in 2004.

Jerry Heffernan, 85. President of G.R. Heffernan & Associates in Toronto. Chairman of Texas Industries, the Dallas-based construction materials company, which had $1.3 billion in revenues in 2003. Director and shareholder of Clairvest Group Inc., a merchant bank in Toronto. He is also a prime fundraiser for the Canadian Opera Company's new home in Toronto.

Tom Hockin, 65. The former federal cabinet minister is now president of the Investment Funds Institute of Canada, sits on half a dozen boards, and is active with the new Conservative Party of Canada.

Peter Hunter, 74. Retired two years ago from Ontario's Advertising Review Board. Working now to restructure the reserve forces in the Canadian army. Lives on a farm near Schomberg, Ontario.

Al Hurley, 87. Retired in 1978 after thirty-two years at General Electric. Lives in Toronto, where he does watercolour painting and lobbies his MP, Jim Peterson, to reduce the employment insurance premiums.

George Hutchison, 64. The former newspaper reporter and adviser to ex-premier David Peterson is a writer living in Toronto.

Phil Isbister. Robarts's lawyer, formerly with Lash Johnson, died in 1995 at the age of 77.

Barbara Jackson, 82. Ernie Jackson's first wife moved to a seniors' residence in Toronto earlier this year. Suffering from the early stages of Alzheimer's disease.

Ernie Jackson. Died in Toronto in 1995 of a brain tumour, one week shy of his 73rd birthday.

George Jackson, 49. Sales coordinator for the Replay Clothing line and the wine-importing wing of Prevedello Holdings.

Wilma Jackson, 76. Ernie Jackson's second wife lives in Toronto.

Fraser Kelly, 69. The former journalist is the founder and now a senior associate with the CorpWorld Group, a communications skills training and crisis management firm. He also teaches at the Joseph L. Rotman School of Management at the University of Toronto.

Tom Kierans, 63. Chairman of the Canadian Institute for Advanced Research. Corporate director on many boards and chair of several other not-for-profit companies.

Allan Lawrence, 78. Robarts's former minister of mines lives on Bay Street in Cobourg, Ontario ("I'm still a Bay Street lawyer"), with Moira, his wife of fifty-three years. Lawrence is on the board of the local art gallery and active in local church matters. He is a lifetime bencher on the Law Society of Upper Canada ("so I can say what I want to, and they can't get rid of me"). He chairs the society's corporate governance committee.

Stephen Lewis, 66. Was appointed by United Nations Secretary-General Kofi Annan in June 2001 as his special envoy for HIV/AIDS in Africa. Recently created the Stephen Lewis Foundation (www.stephenlewis foundation.org) to help ease the pain of HIV/AIDS in Africa.

Robert Macaulay, 84. Lives in a condominium in downtown Toronto. Retired from the practice of law a few years ago when he suffered the first of two strokes. His wife, Joy, from whom he was separated but never divorced, died two years ago.

Donald C. MacDonald, 90. The former CCF/NDP leader is still going strong as a community activist in Toronto. He is past-president of York Community Services, the country's only institution that provides health, social, legal, and dental services under one roof. He is also president of the Learning Enrichment Foundation in Toronto. He and his wife, Simone, have been married for sixty-two years.

H. Ian Macdonald, 75. Teaches an MBA course in public policy at York University. Chairman of the board of McGraw-Hill Ryerson. Director of AGF Funds. Lives in Toronto with Dorothy, his wife of forty-five years. Has five children and five grandchildren. Plays hockey twice a week with friends at Forest Hill Arena and on the York University faculty team, with players forty years his junior.

Don Martyn, 66. Has his own government relations consulting firm, Martyn & Associates. Operates a farm in Sutton, Ontario. Is vice-chair of the Ontario Environmental Review Tribunal. Lives in Toronto.

Don Matthews, 78. Runs Matthews China Inc., a joint venture with the University of Beijing. Lives in Toronto. Spends some of the year in Stuart, Florida, thirty miles north of West Palm Beach.

William J. McCormack, 71. The thirty-six-year veteran of the Metropolitan Toronto Police Force retired after six years as chief in 1995. He has written two books about his life in policing, has eleven grandchildren, and lives in Queensville, Ontario.

Joyce McKeough, 66, and **W. Darcy McKeough,** 71. Joyce just finished a five-year project with Branksome Hall School in Toronto. She chaired the committee responsible for publishing a book on Branksome's centennial. She is also a member of the Garden Club of Toronto, forging links through that club with the deaf/blind communities. Darcy is chairman of McKeough Supply in Chatham-Kent, Ontario. His sense of humour remains intact, as evidenced by his saying that he is "a director of a diminishing number of Canadian corporations, due to age." The McKeoughs have two adult children and one grandchild, and will celebrate their fortieth anniversary this year. They live in Chatham-Kent and Toronto.

James C. McRuer. The former Ontario chief justice and head of the royal commission on civil rights. Died in October 1985 at the age of 95.

Roland Michener. The former Conservative MP for St. Paul's and governor general of Canada from 1967 to 1972 died in 1991 at the age of 91.

Robert Nixon, 76. The Ontario Liberal leader during Robarts's time retired as chairman of Atomic Energy of Canada Ltd. in September 2001. Lives in St. George with his wife, Dorothy. Frequently found discussing the issues of the day at Dave's Auto Centre in St. George or taking art lessons, the byproducts of which used to hang in the office of his daughter Jane Stewart, the former MP for Brant.

Jean-Luc Pepin. The former federal Liberal cabinet minister and co-chair of the Pepin-Roberts National Unity Task Force died in September 1995 at age 70.

Clarence Peterson, 91. Robarts's Liberal Party challenger in the 1955 election has been married to his wife, Marie, for sixty years. The couple has three children, all of whom went into Liberal Party politics: Jim (Willowdale MP 1980–84, 1988–), David (London Centre MPP 1975–90 and premier of Ontario 1985–90), and Tim (Mississauga South MPP 2003–). Clarence and Marie have five grandchildren and still live in London.

David Peterson, 60. The former Ontario premier is senior partner and chairman of Cassels Brock and Blackwell LLP in Toronto. He is a director of Rogers Communications Ltd., Rogers Wireless, Ivanhoe Cambridge Shopping Centres Ltd., and is international adviser to GPC International. He is also chairman of the Ontario March of Dimes, and a governor on the University of Toronto's governing council.

Shelley Peterson, 51. The best-selling author and actress just finished acting in the play *Steel Magnolias,* in which she played the lead with her daughter Chloe. She and her husband, David, have been married for thirty years and have three children.

Nancy Poole, 74, and **William Poole,** 86. Live in London. Nancy is writing her own book with the University of Western Ontario history professor A.M. "Jack" Hyatt on Canadian doctors and nurses in both world wars and the families they left behind. William still works as legal counsel to Menear & Associates.

Barbara Prevedello, 57. Daughter of Ernie Jackson. Co-owner of Prevedello Holdings in Toronto with her husband, Franco Prevedello. Importer of Italian fashion and wine. Has two daughters.

William Rathbun, 71. Retired as vice-president of the Ontario International Corporation in 1992. Lives in Gravenhurst, Ontario.

J. Keith Reynolds. Suffering from Alzheimer's disease. Moved out of his home in Scarborough a couple of years ago. Now lives in a nursing home.

Andrea Robarts. John's niece is an occupational health nurse, specializing in psychiatric nursing, with the Toronto Police Service.

Eleanor Robarts, 83. John's sister-in-law lives in London, where she plays bridge every week at the London Hunt and Country Club.

John Parmenter Robarts. Born January 11, 1917, in Banff, Alberta. Died October 18, 1982, of a self-inflicted gunshot wound at his home in Rosedale at age 65. Prime minister of Ontario from 1961 to 1971. Buried in St. James Cemetery and Crematorium in Toronto.

Catherine "Kay" Robarts, John's older half sister, moved to California and married Oliver Eaton. She died in Corona Del Mar, just south of Newport Beach, in 1986. The couple had one son, Robert.

Katherine Robarts, 59. Robarts's second wife sells antiques on eBay. Grandmother of two. Still resides in the same Rosedale home where she and John lived.

Kimberly Robarts, 39. John's stepdaughter is married to Neil Coville-Reeves, an insurance lawyer. The couple has two children and lives in Toronto, close to the Robarts Rosedale home.

Marion Robarts. John's younger half sister died in the 1980s near Lindsay, Ontario.

Norah Robarts. John's first wife and mother of his two adopted children died in May 1981 in London, Ontario, one month after her 64th birthday.

Robert Robarts. John's brother died in 2000, one month shy of his 85th birthday.

Robin Robarts, 51. John's daughter has been an agent for Bosley Real Estate in Toronto for the past six years.

Tim Robarts. John's son died near Bright, Ontario, of a self-inflicted gunshot wound in August 1977. He was 21.

Duff Roblin, 87. Owns Aeroguard Group, specializing in passenger and baggage pre-board screening. Company operates in twenty-six airports across Canada. Still goes to his Winnipeg office every day.

Richard Rohmer, 80. Practises aviation insurance law at Rohmer and Fenn in Richmond Hill. Does a television show with his daughter, Ann Rohmer, on The New VR. Is chairman of the Collingwood Police Services Board. Sits on the board of Hollinger Canadian Newspapers. Lives in Collingwood with Mary-O. Rohmer, his wife of fifty-five years.

Ann Rudd, 70, and **Bill Rudd,** 74. Live in London. Bill is a retired pension consultant. They have two adult children living in New York and Vancouver, and six grandchildren.

Beverley Shrives, 85, and **Walter Shrives.** Beverley lives in a retirement residence in Oakville. Was married to Walter Shrives for fifty-six years. Has five children, ten grandchildren, and three great-grandchildren. Walter, former vice-chairman of the Ontario Municipal Board, died of a heart attack in 1997 at age 79.

Don Smith, 80, and **Joan Smith,** 76. Both are still active in Liberal Party politics. In 1996 Don turned over voting control of EllisDon, which he co-founded, to his children. He is still a director. He is currently raising money for a teenage women's group home and sits on the advisory board of the Boys' and Girls' Club of London. Don is also honorary patron at Fanshawe College in London. The couple celebrated their fifty-fifth wedding anniversary last year. They have seven children, twenty-two grandchildren, and one great-grandchild.

John Smith, 67. The former Hamilton MPP has been the rector of St. George's Church in Hamilton for the past two years. He has been married to his wife, Judy, since 1967. The couple has three children.

Glen Sonmor, 75, scouts amateur hockey players for the National Hockey League's Minnesota Wild.

Katherine Sonmor Duncan. Robin Robarts's birth mother; died in November 2002 at age 71.

Jean Sonmor, 60. Writer and teacher, living in Toronto.

Greg Sorbara, 58. Minister of finance for the province of Ontario, MPP for Vaughan-King-Aurora.

Don Stevenson, 70. The former deputy minister of intergovernmental affairs retired in March 1989 after almost thirty years in the Ontario public service. He co-founded the Canadian Urban Institute and now volunteers for several non-governmental organizations. He lives in Toronto.

Tom Symons, 75. The founding president of Trent University continues to teach at several universities. He is chair of the National Statistics Council of Canada and the Association for Commonwealth Studies.

Stan Tkaczyk, 67. The three-decade veteran of Stelco is now retired and lives in Hamilton with Shirley, his wife of forty-three years. He has two children and five grandchildren.

Trillium. Robarts's boat, a gift of the PC Party, is currently owned by Robert Mazza of Hamilton and moored in Jacksonville, Florida.

Gordon Walker, 63. Robarts's successor as the MPP for London North co-owns First Canadian Property Investments Ltd., a brokerage business. Recently appointed to the board of Hollinger Inc. Lives in Toronto.

Ron Watts, 75. Fellow at Queen's University's Institute of Intergovernmental Relations.

Robert Welch. MPP for Lincoln and Brock ridings for twenty-two years. A cabinet minister in the Robarts, Davis, and Miller governments. Was chancellor of Brock University from 1985 to 2000, and on the International Joint Commission from 1986 to 1992. Died in 2000 at age 72.

Tom Wells. The former Scarborough North MPP and Robarts and Davis cabinet minister. Died in October 2000 at the age of 70.

Peter Widdrington, 74. Retired from Labatt's Breweries in 1992. Currently chairman of Brick Brewing, Waterloo. Lives in London.

Cathy White. Kimberly Robarts's teacher now works at St. Timothy Catholic School in Toronto. Celebrated her thirtieth year of teaching in 2004.

George Willis. Robarts's friend from his UWO days; died in 2003 at age 90.

Results of Ontario Elections During John Robarts's Time in Politics

1951 ONTARIO GENERAL ELECTION
John Robarts's first as an MPP for London
(seat count)

Progressive Conservatives	78
Liberal	7
Cooperative Commonwealth Federation	2
Labour-Progressive	1
Liberal-Labour	1

1955 ONTARIO GENERAL ELECTION
John Robarts's second as an MPP for London North
(seat count)

Progressive Conservatives	83
Liberal	10
Cooperative Commonwealth Federation	3
Liberal-Labour	1
Progressive Conservative Independent	1

1959 ONTARIO GENERAL ELECTION
John Robarts's first as a cabinet minister
(seat count)

Progressive Conservatives	71
Liberal	21
Cooperative Commonwealth Federation	5
Liberal-Labour	1

1963 ONTARIO GENERAL ELECTION
John Robarts's first as prime minister of Ontario
(seat count)

Progressive Conservatives	77
Liberal	23
New Democratic Party	7
Liberal-Labour	1

1967 ONTARIO GENERAL ELECTION
John Robarts's second as prime minister of Ontario
(seat count)

Progressive Conservatives	69
Liberal	27
New Democratic Party	20
Liberal-Labour	1

1971 ONTARIO GENERAL ELECTION

William Davis's first as premier of Ontario
(seat count)

Progressive Conservatives	78
Liberal	20
New Democratic Party	19

1961 ONTARIO PROGRESSIVE CONSERVATIVE LEADERSHIP CONVENTION

First Ballot

Kelso Roberts	352
John Robarts	345
Robert Macaulay	339
James Allan	332
Alfred Downer	149
Matthew Dymond	138
George Wardrope	45

Second Ballot

John Robarts	423
Kelso Roberts	385
Robert Macaulay	363
James Allan	324
Alfred Downer	104
Matthew Dymond	93

Third Ballot

John Robarts	498
Kelso Roberts	380
Robert Macaulay	372
James Allan	344
Alfred Downer	93

Fourth Ballot

John Robarts		533
Kelso Roberts		419
Robert Macaulay		377
James Allan		336

Fifth Ballot

John Robarts		746
Kelso Roberts		479
Robert Macaulay		438

Sixth Ballot

John Robarts	61%	976
Kelso Roberts	39%	633
Difference		343

1971 ONTARIO PROGRESSIVE CONSERVATIVE LEADERSHIP CONVENTION

Fourth Ballot

William Davis	51.4%	812
Allan Lawrence	48.6%	768
Difference		44

Speech by John P. Robarts

August 21, 1961

IT IS MY INTENTION to seek the leadership of the Progressive Conservative Party of Ontario at the convention, which has been called for October 23, 24, and 25, as a result of Mr. Frost's announcement of his retirement as leader of the party in Ontario.

I have not reached this decision without giving the matter great thought and consideration. I have consulted with people from all parts of the province, and as a result of these consultations I have decided to let my name go before the delegates to the convention.

If I should be so fortunate as to be chosen to lead the party, it will be my endeavour to continue building with a strong governmental team from the talented men who represent the Progressive Conservative Party in the present legislature. I will devote myself wholeheartedly to the service of the people of Ontario, and it is with great enthusiasm that I look forward to the coming convention.

As has been proven in the past, the government of the province of Ontario will require active, vigorous leadership to deal with the many problems of expansion and development which lie ahead. During my ten years' experience under the outstanding leadership of the present prime minister, the Honourable Leslie Frost, I feel that I have acquired the knowledge, qualifications and training to carry on the great tradition of our party in serving the many and diverse needs of the people of our province.

Tribute to John P. Robarts
at the London Club

By John Cronyn
January 26, 1971

I DON'T KNOW how it was decided that I should have the honour of making this presentation to our good friend John Robarts, but let me assure you that it is a labour of love, and I do it on your behalf with great humility.

It has been a long, eventful and exciting road that John has taken since those days back in 1950, when he was elected an alderman in the city of London—since 1951 when he was elected the MPP for London North [*sic*].

As I look around the room tonight, I can see many of the people who worked for him by knocking on doors, driving cars, and who helped in less obvious ways. I see a few members of ADSEPA, who were his original active supporters, and I can think of a number of them and others who can't be with us tonight—Bill Shortreed's and Gordon Gilbride's names obviously spring to mind.

Then there are those who worked for and with John through four provincial elections. I see a lot of the old "yellow-jacket gang, " who participated in what had to be the most exciting point in John's career—the winning of the leadership campaign in 1961! Ernie Jackson, his closest associate through all those years, is with us and we will hear more of him shortly.

The "London Mafia," as Conservatives in the rest of the province fondly refer to us, are out in force! But no matter what part each one has played in supporting John along his chosen road during the past twenty years, each of us has said again and again, "Thank God that a man of John Robarts' stature, character and integrity has stood for election. Thank God that we have John Robarts as prime minister of this province."

Tonight we are saying thank you directly and personally to John Robarts himself.

In my travels across the country, I have on many occasions run across people who have told me they have just had the opportunity of meeting our prime minister and what a great person he is—easy to talk to, down to earth, understanding, and a real human being. Yes, these are some of the attributes for which we are saying thank-you. There are many, many more which most of us have had the good fortune to observe at first hand:

His ability to get a consensus out of chaos, to listen to all sides and then make a superb decision.

Political astuteness of the highest order.

Secretly a swinger.

Great sense of timing—even from down to the smallest details of such things as when to get out of a chorus line at a Grey Cup celebration or when to leave some of us behind at the Bombay Bicycle Club and head for home, to the very big decision of when to retire.

Completely genuine.

Absolutely unflappable—never loses his cool or his control.

Never stumped for an answer for something to say—except once. I recall one night in a bar when he turned to the person next to him, as he is wont to do, put out his hand and said in his most disarming manner, "I'm John Robarts." The person to whom he spoke was carrying a fair load, looked him right in the eye and said, "So am I." When someone writes John's biography, the title should be "I'm John Robarts."

He is a man of great courage, and a leader. The respect and high regard in which he is held by his cabinet ministers and deputy ministers bears witness to this boss—"the boss," as he is fondly referred to by everyone.

He is a man's man, with an undying love for the outdoors and nature, as anyone who has fished or shot with him well knows.

He is a family man who reserved what weekends he could for his wife and children. And although I know the old rule about not mentioning women in a men's club, I hope that you will forgive me if I break it tonight to pay a small tribute to Norah Robarts for the part that she has played in his life. As well as being a good mother to their children, she has had that great knack of never letting the PM forget that he was human just like the rest of us.

His accomplishments while in office were many, and he will go down in history not only for what he did for Ontario but for what he did for Canada. From the day he decided to stay as head of Canada's most prosperous and populous province rather than head for Ottawa to his firm stand on the FLQ kidnapping, he has done more than any other Canadian to hold the country together! Your trip to Quebec City just before announcing your resignation was symbolic of your stand, and we hope that no matter what you do after retirement, you will continue to play a leading role in the fight for Canadian unity.

This present, John, is but a small token of our huge respect—no, I will use one of your favourite words—a small token of our enormous respect for you, not only for what you have done for the people of London, for the people of Ontario, for the people of Canada, but as a person, a very human person.

The gun in this case represents the one which is waiting for you in England to be fitted exactly to your taste. When the gunsmith comes out from England next month, this envelope contains a ticket to get you to England (and back, which is certain proof of our high regard for you) and a ticket for Norah to accompany you. There can be just no excuses for missing any ducks next fall. And finally, a gift for Norah to remind her that we have recognized her part along that eventful road that has been your life to date.

Good luck, John, and may your second career be as great as your first.

Luncheon for Friends of John Robarts at the John P. Robarts Research Institute

By Richard M. Dillon
November 25, 1995

JOHN PARMENTER ROBARTS touched the lives of literally millions of Canadians. But the wonder surrounding the man was, I think, that so many who came to know him even casually carry with them to this day warm and deeply personal recollections.

I remember him first here at Western, Big Man on Campus, strong, confident, a good-looking guy, immaculately turned out in sports jacket and tie, flannels pressed to a razor's edge. There was an aura about the man which seemed to set him apart somehow above the crowd.

I remember him best and with greatest affection after he left politics. Unburdened by affairs of state, a principal passion was his thirty-two-foot sailboat, *Trillium,* so aptly named for, some of you may remember, it was he who chose that flower to be Ontario's emblem. And he presided over *Trillium* with the same good humour and bewildering detachment that previously he had applied to his leadership in government.

I will always remember our first overnight race, from Grand Bend to Goderich, '71 or '72 I think it was, when, undeterred by inexperience or the obvious onset of a violent electrical storm, our skipper insisted on a full load of canvas, including a very large balloon spinnaker.

As any experienced sailor will tell you, this was quite simply a recipe for real disaster!

In the pitch black, we were sailing blind when suddenly the storm hit.

Immediately, John gave the order, "Down spinnaker!" and in a few seconds, the foredeck, together with its crew, was completely enshrouded in a billowing cloud of nylon. Just then, thanks to the frantic screams of an incredulous bystander on the Goderich pier and a fortuitous flash of lightning, John saw that he was heading straight for the breakwater; he reacted at once, and with tremendous strength, he veered sharply to starboard and roared into the harbour, missing the end of the pier by a fraction of an inch. And after all this incredible performance, his only comment was a cheerful "Well done, chaps."

Shortly afterwards the youngest member of the crew confided in the navigator, "I just can't get over how cool and clear-headed Mr. Robarts was tonight. He sure as hell is a great man in an emergency," to which his older and badly shaken companion replied, "And a damn good thing too, since he steers us into so bloody many of them."

Seriously, though, he truly was a wonderful sailor, strong and reliable, and I would have sailed anywhere with him. And obviously, the British Navy thought so too, when in 1943 they mentioned him in dispatches for cool and courageous action during the Allied landings at Salerno.

After the war, in 1951, having established a law practice here in London, he informed a group of friends that he had decided to become a politician and that he needed help to get himself elected. Somehow, he conveyed such a subliminal sense of purpose and excitement and a quiet determination to get deeply involved in running the country that immediately we all agreed to follow.

Thus was born the London Mafia.

A unique band of Grits and Tories alike, the Mafia began by electing Robarts to the provincial legislature, and from there they never looked back. Four separate London ridings, two provincial and two federal, were organized and run by a single executive with JPR as Chairman of the Board. For nearly two decades, this group left an indelible mark on the political map of Ontario. Finally in 1970, when John, an old warhorse by then, announced his retirement from active politics. Its work was done, and quite properly, it ceased to be.

Nothing like the London Mafia could have transpired were it not for the deep affection and respect there was for John, from everyone, regardless of political stripe, or station in life, who espoused his cause. No question, Robarts was our man, quite literally, the man for his time.

At Queen's Park, he quickly proved himself an extremely capable and prescient political leader.

As chairman of the royal commission on toll roads, and later as minister of education, he opted for freeways, reorganized secondary education, and created a province-wide network of community colleges and universities. Later, he recruited administrators from business and academe to expand and modernize Ontario's civil service, and having done that, he set up the Committee on Government Productivity under John Cronyn, an old friend and charter member of the London Mafia, to re-engineer the machinery of government at Queen's Park.

All this was a marvellous contribution to the social and economic infrastructure of burgeoning, modern Ontario. But Robarts went far beyond this.

His vision of Canada was crystal clear. Absolutely on the mark, well ahead of his time. It was, for instance, Robarts who first sensed a need to modify the federal system in the interest of national unity. He forged closer personal ties with Quebec premier Jean Lesage and established the Ontario Advisory Committee on Confederation to conduct an exhaustive study of Ontario's role in Confederation. This culminated in the first-ever convention of provincial premiers.

Held in Toronto during Canada's Centennial year, this bold initiative signalled profound changes in the nature and conduct of Canadian federalism. Small wonder we thought of him as our father of re-confederation.

Stories about the man abound, and he loved them all. For he had a tremendous sense of fun. John Cronyn recently reminded me of one I simply must retell. The two of them walked into a Toronto tavern after working very late. They sat at the bar, waiting for a nightcap. John put his hand out to the man sitting next to him. "Good evening, I'm John Robarts." To which the bleary-eyed character, very slowly, raised his head and said, "So am I."

The Chinese philosopher Lao-tzu counselled, "To lead the people, walk behind." He also said when the best leader's work is done, the people say, "We did it ourselves." Robarts believed implicitly in this approach to leadership and practised it with consummate skill.

One obvious advantage, of course, was happy, effective government for a well-run, prosperous province. Less obvious, perhaps, but just as important, was that the leader found time occasionally to slip away from the office, to indulge in a little fly fishing somewhere in Quebec or pheasant shooting at Griffiths Island.

Now, I'm no fisherman, but I've heard a story which goes like this. A glorious long weekend in the mid-sixties, Robarts, Keith Reynolds, and an old friend on the shores of Hudson Bay, trout fishing superb, strict instructions from the leader not to be disturbed by anyone for any reason. Except that Reynolds, impeccable secretary of the cabinet, had the prudence to insist that the Lands and Forests Beaver, which had dropped the party there in the beginning, should appear overhead precisely at noon each day, prepared to relay radio incoming messages, from Queen's Park through Moosonee and, in the event of emergency, to land and take them home.

On the dot, the pilot appeared and radioed from above. There was a crisis in Sudbury. McKeough had been dispatched to the scene. The acting premier advised the leader's immediate return. Through the static, Robarts heard every word, then growled at Reynolds, "Tell him to go back, Darcy can handle it."

And thus, in those more tolerant and trusting times, the Ontario ship of state sailed on!

But toward the end, John's life was beset by sadness. A son lost, and a crippling stroke, which effectively denied him access to the outdoor recreation he loved so much. And yet no one I know ever heard him complain. A sparkling, resolute sense of humour and restless energy seemed to sustain him as long as he chose to live.

At his funeral, Bishop Garnsworthy intoned, "He held up a candle in the darkness to give us a vision of a land of rich mosaic."

Stephen Lewis, hardly a political admirer, called him "a supremely good man." And so very many thousands of people there at St. Paul's Church and all over the country from every station and walk of life loved him and called him John.

It's time now to drink a toast, and since John was a sailor, and since we are told that due to limited headroom aboard Nelson's *Victory*, sailors drink toasts sitting down. I ask you to remain seated and to join in a toast to the memory of John.

His Final Resting Place

JOHN PARMENTER ROBARTS is buried at the St. James Cemetery and Crematorium on the southeast corner of Parliament and Bloor Streets in Toronto. He was laid to rest in Section D, two rows in, on the east side of the pathway. There are no plaques or signs indicating the location of the gravesite. However, visitors should look for Robarts's headstone behind the St. George's Society of Toronto marker, which is very tall and plainly visible from the pathway.

John Robarts is buried in a family plot along with
- Thomas Parminter (*sic*) Robarts, born in Plymouth, England, formerly of Barbados, West Indies, died in Toronto in 1963
- Henrietta Robarts, wife of Thomas P. Robarts, died in 1934
- John Williams Robarts, fifth son of Thomas and Henrietta Robarts, died in 1867 at age 30
- Henrietta Robarts, daughter of Thomas and Henrietta Robarts, died in 1909
- Frank C. Robarts, died in October 1944
- Victoria Learmonth, wife of the late Frank C. Robarts, died in 1967
- Vera Robarts, 1909–1979

Acknowledgments

FIRST AND FOREMOST, I owe a debt of gratitude to the nearly one hundred of John Robarts's family, friends, and colleagues, who agreed to speak to me for this book. I am from a generation that has no first-hand memory of Robarts's time in politics. I was only a year old when the Chairman of the Board became prime minister of Ontario, so this project has required me to talk to as many people as possible from the different avenues of Robarts's life, to understand a man I had never even seen, let alone met. Like too many people my age, I knew almost nothing of Robarts's life, other than the fact that I spent a good deal of time as a University of Toronto student in a library with his name on it. I wrote this book, in large part, because I don't want others of my generation to be as ignorant of this great Canadian as I was.

This book would not have been written without the persistence of one of Robarts's former cabinet ministers, Darcy McKeough. Despite the fact I was in the midst of writing a second book and had grave doubts about being able to manage a third in just four years, I agreed and am so glad I did. Thank you, Darcy, for convincing me (perhaps strong-arming is a better description!) to write this book. I hope your generation finds this to be a nostalgic trip through a better time in our province's history. And I hope younger people will pluck it off a library shelf and gain an understanding of the greatest generation, as I did when I checked *John P. Robarts: His Life and Government* out of my local public library in the summer of 2001.

Eddie Goodman warned me not to make the book a hero-worship puff piece, and I have taken his words to heart. This book describes the great accomplishments of a public man, plus the tragic failures of his private life. That combination made him an endlessly interesting person to write about.

My thanks to Fraser Kelly, who gave me the single most important piece of advice, at a crucial time, in the midst of this effort. That advice will remain between the two of us. It reminded me (not that I needed it) why I considered it a privilege to work for Fraser at CBLT-TV in the 1980s, and why he was always my prime role model in journalism.

A small but hardy band of Robarts associates offered to read successive drafts of this manuscript to ensure that I did accurately capture the essence of Ontario's seventeenth prime minister. Thanks to Joyce McKeough, for her always helpful and exquisitely phrased advice via email, and to Darcy McKeough, who did so much more than launch me on this journey. His assistance was so helpful and constant that I am tempted to give him a research assistant's credit. He kept me on track and frequently reminded me that it was "Prime Minister" Robarts, not "Premier." To Ian Macdonald, whose sharp eye caught more mistakes than I care to remember, and his wife, Dorothy, who found even a few more. And to John Cronyn, who was such a great source of knowledge for the London years, and who passed away just a week before the manuscript made it to the publisher. He, as much as anyone, deserved to see the finished product in bookstores, and I am sad that he will not. Their assistance made this book much better than it otherwise would have been. Of course, any mistakes that remain are mine.

I need to say a few words about Cynthia Good. The former president and publisher of Penguin Group (Canada) green-lighted this project two years ago. It was a considerable leap of faith for her, particularly since almost no one under the age of fifty knows much about its subject. But since the outset of our collaboration more than four years ago, Cynthia has shown remarkable faith in this never-before-published author and his unorthodox choice of subject material. She served as editor on this book, as she did for my other two efforts. I hope I have repaid her judgment with three reasonably interesting works of non-fiction. I know that the books would not be as good as I hope that they are without the thousands of Post-it suggestion notes she has left in the margins of my manuscripts.

Thanks also to my literary agent, Denise Bukowski.

I owe a major debt of thanks to Julian Lebourdais, the former United Press Canada photographer, who has so graciously allowed me to use the fruits of his labour from more than three decades ago. Those who want to see more of his work are advised to peruse the Julian Lebourdais Collection at the Ontario Archives in Toronto.

In my world of public broadcasting, I need once again to thank Roberta Garcia and Joanne Souaid in TVO's membership department for getting my books into the hands of our members. And to Susanna Kelley, producer extraordinaire of *Fourth Reading*. Frankly, she had nothing to do with this book but deserves a mention for two reasons. First, she and I have worked together every week for twelve seasons to make provincial politics come alive for TVO viewers—my longest and happiest association with a producer in my broadcasting career. Second, she assured me the fun would be over if I failed to mention her. Susanna, may the fun continue.

Of course, nothing is possible in life without the love and support of family. Lucky for me, I struck gold on that front. To my parents, Marnie and Larry, and my brother, Jeff, all of whom almost single-handedly have turned my previous books into bestsellers; to my children Zachary, Henry, Teddy, and Giulia, the most fascinating people I know, and helpful too—Zachary recommended the title of one chapter, Henry and Teddy offered advice on the cover design, and Teddy helped with marketing all three books by drawing terrific pictures for me to display on sales tables; and finally, to my wife, Francesca Grosso, who has been a remarkably patient literary widow for the past few years, as her husband has pursued a lifelong dream to write books. *Mille grazie,* Fra.

In my first two books, I used the last paragraph of this chapter to thank Frank Sinatra and Ted Williams, who obviously had nothing to do with either book but for different reasons brought enrichment to my life. I'd like to continue that tradition by mentioning someone I have known and admired since I was six years old. It is rare indeed when a childhood idol turns out to be everything you hoped he would be and more. Such is the case with Ron Ellis. Number 6 for the Toronto Maple Leafs recently wrote his autobiography, in which (if you can imagine) *he thanked me* for choosing him as my favourite player. He autographed my copy, adding, "It helps give my career meaning and purpose." Imagine that. No wonder I still carry my Ron Ellis autographed hockey card in my wallet and would love nothing more than for my four children to possess the qualities he so brilliantly exemplifies.

THE AUTHOR AND PUBLISHER gratefully acknowledge the assistance of the John P. Robarts Research Institute, a world-class medical research centre in London, Ontario, in making this book possible. In turn, the Robarts Research Institute acknowledges with thanks the contributions of Ralph Barford, J.J. Barnicke, Douglas Bassett, Paul Beeston, Lord Black of Crossharbour, the late Douglas Crashley, the late John B. Cronyn, Paul Desmarais, Rendall Dick, Richard M. and M. Elizabeth Dillon, Alan Eagleson, Fredrik and Catherine Eaton, John Craig and Sally Horsfall Eaton, Fraser Elliott, John T. Evans, James and Florence Gibson, Eddie Goodman, Hugh Hanson, Jerry Heffernan, Richard and Beryl Ivey, H.N.R. Jackman, Tom Kierans, John Laschinger, John D. Leitch, Philip B. Lind, Ronald and

Annabelle Logan, H. Ian and Dorothy Macdonald, Don Matthews, W.F. McCormick, Don and Marion McDougall, Don and Joan McGeachy, the late William McKenzie, Darcy and Joyce McKeough, Arthur Mingay, William and Nancy Poole, Charles Rathgeb, the Honourable Duff Roblin, Richard and Mary-O. Rohmer, Bill and Ann Rudd, Richard Schmeelk, Hugh Segal, Richard Sharpe, Don Stevenson, Janet Stewart, Cal and Angie Stiller, the late William Watson, David Weldon, W. Galen Weston, William P. Wilder, the late George Willis, L.R. "Red" Wilson, and Michael Wilson.

Name Index